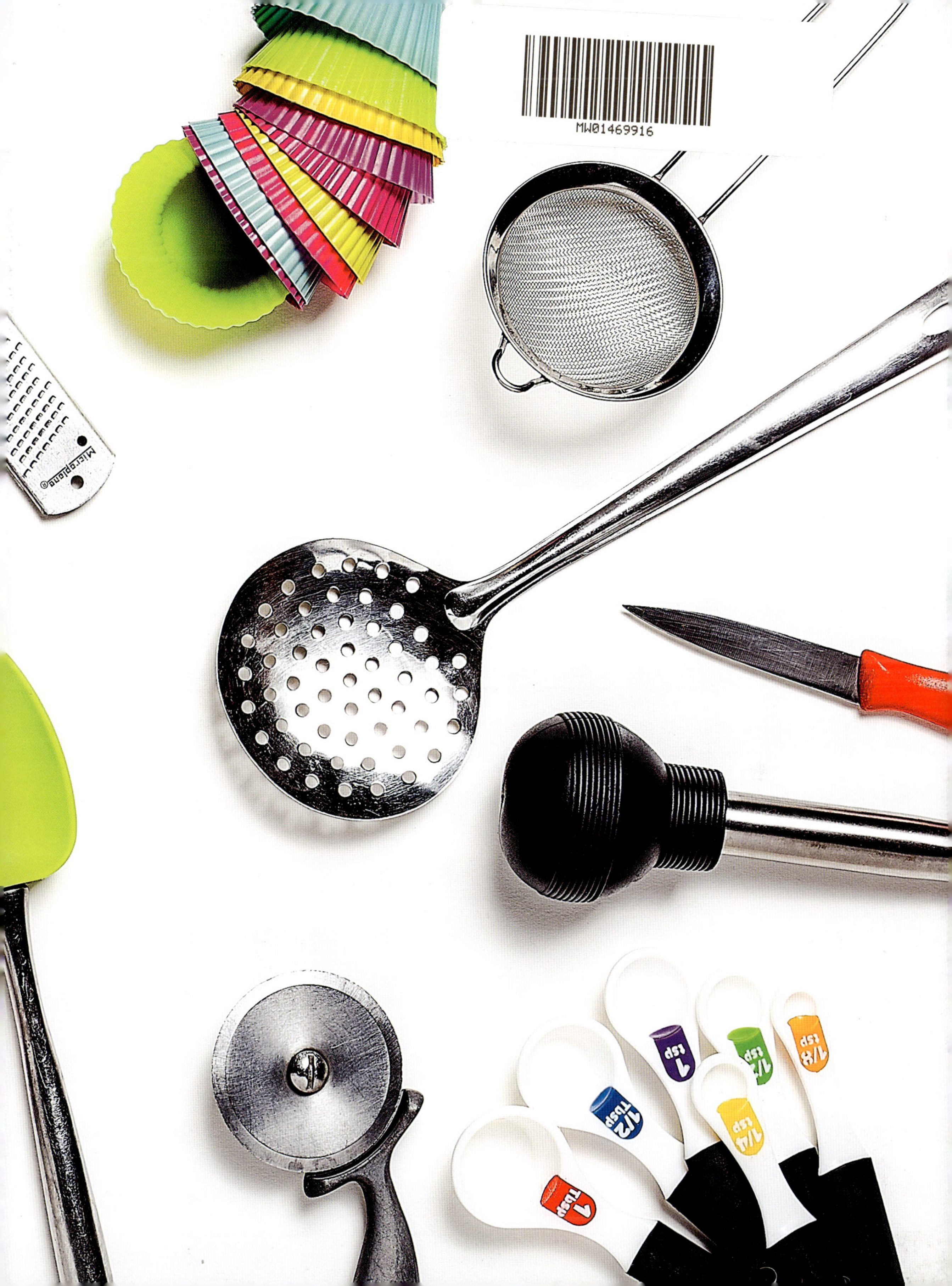

Microplane®
1 Tbsp
1/2 Tbsp
1 tsp
1/4 tsp
1/8 tsp

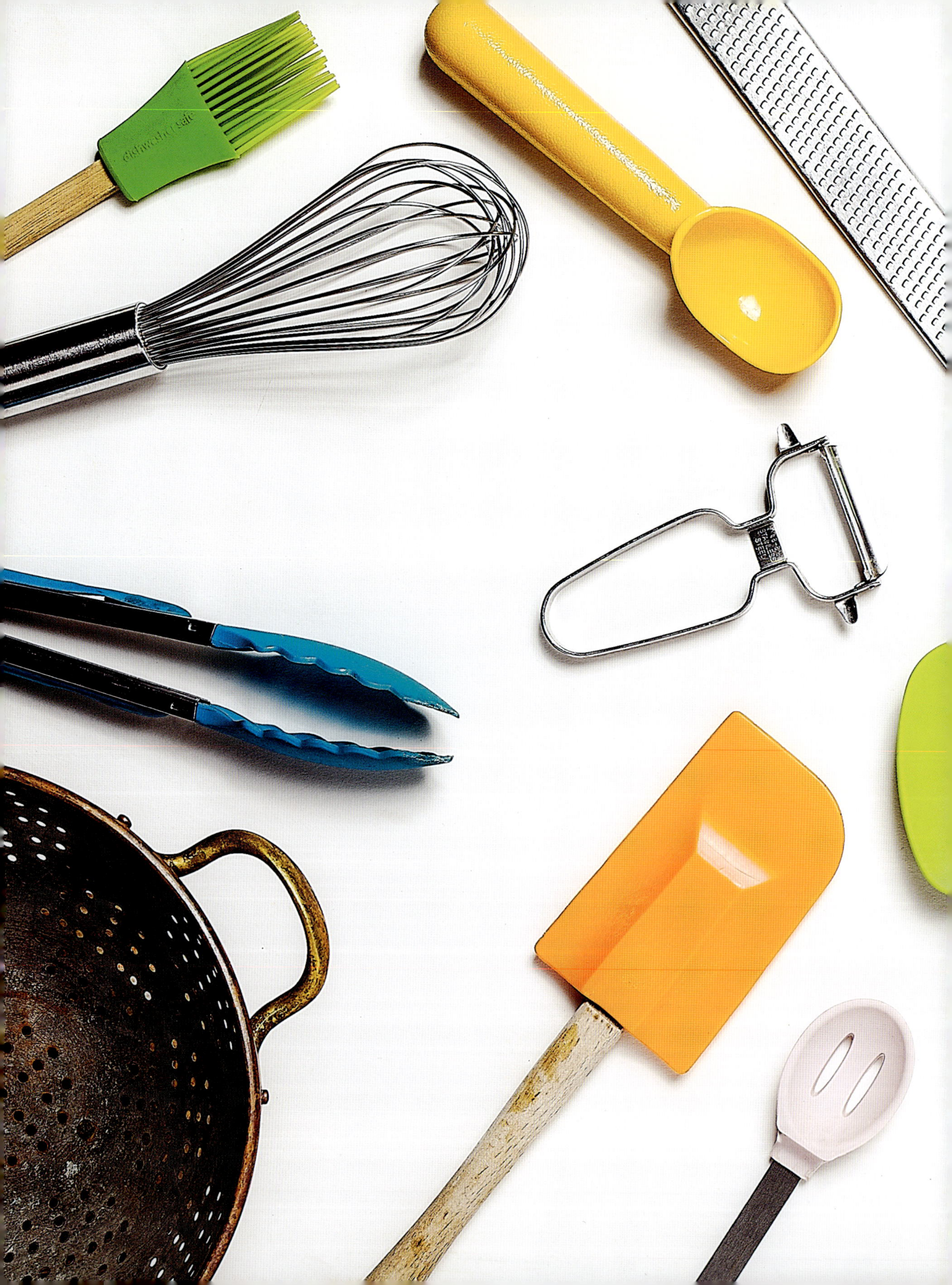

LET'S EAT

LET'S EAT

Recipes for Kids Who Cook

DL ACKEN AND AURELIA LOUVET

Copyright © 2023 by DL Acken and Aurelia Louvet
Photographs copyright © 2023 by DL Acken

All rights reserved. No part of this publication may be reproduced, stored in a retrieval system, or transmitted in any form or by any means, electronic, mechanical, photocopying, recording, or otherwise, without the prior written permission of the publisher. For more information, contact the publisher at:

TouchWood Editions
touchwoodeditions.com

The information in this book is true and complete to the best of the authors' knowledge. All recommendations are made without guarantee on the part of the authors or the publisher.

Edited by Lesley Cameron
Cover and interior design by Jazmin Welch

CATALOGUING INFORMATION AVAILABLE FROM LIBRARY AND ARCHIVES CANADA
ISBN 9781771514132 (hardcover)
ISBN 9781771514149 (electronic)

TouchWood Editions acknowledges that the land on which we live and work is within the traditional territories of the Lkwungen (Esquimalt and Songhees), Malahat, Pacheedaht, Scia'new, T'Sou-ke, and WSÁNEĆ (Pauquachin, Tsartlip, Tsawout, and Tseycum) peoples.

We acknowledge the financial support of the Government of Canada through the Canada Book Fund, and the province of British Columbia through the Book Publishing Tax Credit.

Canada   BRITISH COLUMBIA

This book was produced using FSC®-certified, acid-free papers, processed chlorine free, and printed with soya-based inks.

Printed in China

27 26 25 24 23   1 2 3 4 5

For Caitlin, William, Georgia, Charlie, and Alice—it's because of you that every dish I make is made with love!
LOVE YOU ALL, MUM

To my dearest Chloë and Félix—watching you grow and discover cooking has been my greatest joy!
LOVE, MUMMY

CONTENTS

READ BEFORE YOU COOK! • 8

LEARN THESE FIRST! • 28

RISE & SHINE! • 54

KEEP IT FRESH! • 94

MAKE IT THE MAIN EVENT! • 120

POP IT IN A POT . . . OR PAN! • 148

DON'T FORGET DESSERT! • 184

With Thanks! • 227

Index • 229

ns

READ BEFORE YOU COOK!

Good Kitchen Practices • 13
Tools • 14
Techniques • 20
Other Useful Terms • 22
Ingredients • 23
Allergens • 25

If you've picked up this book, you're probably excited to get in the kitchen and learn to cook some of your favorite foods. Before you jump in, have a read through this introduction to find out how we wrote the book and what the icons mean, and to become familiar with the terms, tools, and techniques mentioned in the recipes. With the help of William (17), Georgia (15), Charlie (13), Chloë (11), Félix (10), and Alice (7)—who tested, critiqued, tested again, and devoured everything in sight—we've put together a collection of recipes that will give you a solid knowledge base to get you started. These are the building blocks that offer multiple variations for you to experiment with . . . sort of like a choose-your-own-adventure book!

The first chapter, Learn These First!, gives you a group of recipes that you'll refer back to as you go. They're the foundation for a bunch of recipes scattered throughout the book. Rise & Shine! features some of our favorite breakfast recipes—and we're sure they'll quickly become yours as well. The Keep It Fresh! chapter is filled with fruits and veggies recipes and covers everything from salads to sides, while Make It the Main Event! is packed with familiar family favorite main courses. Pop It in a Pot . . . or Pan! is a chapter full of one-dish meals. Some are baked or braised in the oven, some simmered in a slow cooker, but all are easy and require fewer dishes in the end—a bonus if you're on cleanup duty! And of course there's Don't Forget Dessert!—as if you could!

Before you cook be sure to:

Read through the introductory material. We've given you a list of tips, terms, tools, and techniques to help you on your culinary journey.

Read through each recipe completely before you start to cook and be sure you understand the tools and terms used. If you don't know what something is or means, check the lists on pages 14–22.

Look for the WARNING ICONS. If you see one, ask an adult or a more experienced cook to stay close at hand to help you.

means that you'll need knives or other sharp tools	means that you'll use hot cooking methods	means that you'll need to handle raw meats	means that one of the top allergens is included in the base recipe (see pages 25–27 for alternatives to allergens)	means that the recipe includes a long prep or cook time that you should note before diving in

If a recipe seems like it may be too difficult, ask an adult or a more experienced cook to help you through the first time you try it. After you've made each of these recipes once, you'll be able to fly through easily the next time.

Now let's get cooking!

LET'S EAT

GOOD KITCHEN PRACTICES

- Wash your hands: This is the golden rule! Always wash your hands before you start cooking to ensure you don't add germs to whatever you're preparing. If you're working with raw meats, be sure to wash your hands before AND after handling them.
- Wear an apron: This will protect your clothes.
- Read the recipe: Before you start to cook, read the entire recipe to make sure you understand what is required and that you have the time, tools, and ingredients you need. There's nothing worse than jumping into a recipe for dinner only to see that it needs to "rest overnight."
- Do your *mise en place*: This is a French cooking term that translates roughly as "everything in its place." It means having all of the items in your ingredient list measured, peeled, chopped, etc. BEFORE you begin to cook. It may seem like an extra step, but it will make cooking so much easier and efficient.
- Clean as you go! This is one of the best habits you can adopt in the kitchen. Half of cooking is cleaning, and if you tidy up, wipe counters, return pantry items, etc. while you cook, you'll save yourself from facing a huge mess at the end.
- Be sure to use a timer for foods cooked in the oven or breads that need to rise. A few minutes too long and your dinner may be burnt or your bread may be flat.
- Turn off all burners and ovens: Double-check that you have turned off all heat sources and appliances once you've finished using them. Now check again.
- Check best-before and use-by dates: It's a good habit to check the dates on your dairy, condiments, opened sauces, etc., especially if they have been in the fridge for a while. Best-before and use-by dates have different purposes. A best-before date tells you when a product will still be at its optimum quality. Most products are still good for a few days after their best-before dates. Use-by dates are for safety. Don't consume anything after its use-by date has passed. You run the risk of getting sick.

There are a few rules that make working in the kitchen safer, easier, and more efficient. Follow these and you can't really go wrong.

READ BEFORE YOU COOK!   13

TOOLS

Most recipes require some kind of tools, whether that's **pots and pans, baking sheets, or mixers**, etc. Here is a list of tools used in this book. You'll find the tools highlighted in ORANGE. If you don't know what they are, refer back to this list.

Air fryer: This is a fun gadget that is versatile and easy to use and can be cleaned quickly. So much can be cooked in its baskets.

Aluminum foil: Good for wrapping foods in the oven so that items steam and roast evenly without the outer layers burning.

Blender: Useful for making smoothies, milkshakes, soups, and more.

Bowls: Stainless steel **mixing bowls** are good for mixing or to hold ingredients as you prepare your food. Glass bowls are heatproof and microwave-safe. Never heat or microwave plastic! Both glass and stainless steel can be used if a recipe tells you to use a non-reactive bowl.

Box grater: Useful for grating soft cheeses (like mozzarella or cheddar), carrots, apples, lettuce, onion, zucchini, etc.

Cookie sheet: This is a specialized **baking sheet** that has no sides at all and is usually double thick with an insulating layer to make sure cookies bake evenly throughout. A regular baking sheet will work if you don't have one of these. Just keep a close eye on the time so that the bottoms of your cookies don't burn. Most full-size cookie sheets come in 18 × 26 inches (45 × 66 cm) but you can also get half sheets that are 13 × 18 inches (33 × 45 cm).

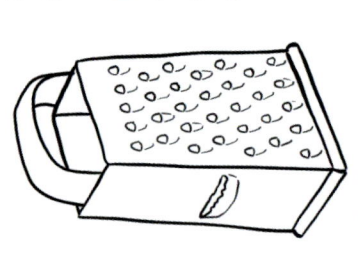

14 LET'S EAT

Baking dish: These usually have sides at least 1 inch (2.5 cm) high, and up to 2–3 inches (5–7.5 cm) high. They're good for cooking casseroles, cakes, bars, and anything that needs to be cooked in liquid or produces a lot of liquid while cooking. Ceramic, glass, and Pyrex baking dishes are the most common types. Useful sizes to have on hand are 9 × 9 inches (23 × 23 cm) and 9 × 13 inches (23 × 33 cm).

Baking sheet: These sheets usually have relatively low sides, ¼–½ inch (0.6–1.25 cm) high. They're great for roasting veggies and cooking one-pan dinners. Most full-size pans come in 18 × 26 inches (45 × 66 cm), but you can also get half-sheet pans that are 13 × 18 inches (33 × 45 cm).

Basting brush: This is a kitchen tool that looks a bit like a paint brush and comes in traditional bristles or heat-proof silicone. It's used for brushing sauces over meat, or butter or egg wash onto pastry. Anywhere you need to brush something, reach for this.

Cake pans and tins: Cake pans come in many shapes and sizes—some even have springform sides that can pop open to reveal the cake inside. Check your recipe to see what kind and what size of pan is needed for the quantity of batter you'll be making. Fully greasing the pans with butter and dusting them with flour will help ensure that cakes and breads come out easily. Bread tins or loaf pans are good for bread but also for pound cakes, banana bread, and meatloaf.

Colander/strainer/sieve: Used for draining the liquid from something while holding the solids (for example, pasta or potatoes).

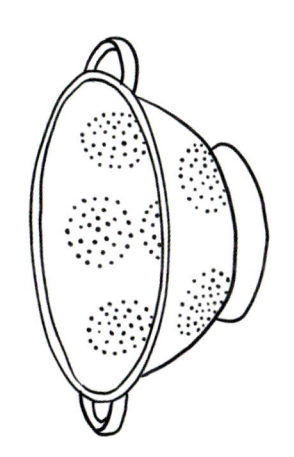

Cooling racks: These are wire racks that allow air to reach all parts of cakes, pastries, cookies, etc. so that they can cool from underneath as well as on top. You can place your cookies and cakes directly onto cooling racks or slide them still on the **parchment paper** from the hot cookie sheets to the cooling rack.

Cupcake/muffin pans (also called tins): Used for making muffins and cupcakes. Metal pans/tins may need to be lined with paper or silicone liners while silicone pans are generally nonstick.

Cutting boards: Plastic cutting boards are great for raw meats as they clean up well with hot, soapy water. Bamboo or composite boards are a great choice for cutting vegetables.

READ BEFORE YOU COOK! 15

Mallet: A wooden kitchen tool that looks a bit like a large hammer. Used for pounding out meat when you need to make the meat thinner for a quick fry.

Measuring cups: Use dry measuring cups to measure ingredients like flour and sugar. They usually come in ¼, ⅓, ½, and 1 cup, although you'll also find ⅛ cup and ¾ cup. Dry ingredients are measured by gently scooping the ingredient and leveling off the excess with the back of a butter **knife** (some cups even come with a matching leveler!). Liquid measuring cups are normally clear with a spout. We love a 2-cup (500 mL) heatproof glass cup. Fun fact: 1 cup of liquid measure is NOT the same as 1 cup of dry measure, so be sure to use the correct measuring cup when cooking.

Measuring spoons: Use these to measure small amounts of dry ingredients. They come in ⅛ tsp, ¼ tsp, ½ tsp, ¾ tsp, 1 tsp, and 1 Tbsp.

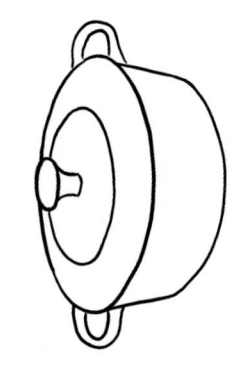

Garlic press: This handy tool is used to press individual cloves of garlic into a chunky paste. You can also use a **rasp** to do this and it's a good tool to use anytime you are asked to mince garlic.

Heatproof oven mitts: An essential item for any chef. Wear them when you're removing hot items from the oven or stirring splattery items on the stove top. Long, thick mitts are a good idea.

Dutch oven: These dishes look like **pots** that come with fitted lids and are usually made of cast iron or enamel. They can be used in the oven at high temperatures as well as on the stove top.

Electric griddle: This cheap and portable piece of equipment is a great alternative to the stove top that makes it super easy to cook French toast—or even quesadillas—for a crowd.

Electric hand mixer: Also known as a **hand mixer**, this is a practical tool for making cakes, cookies, and frostings if you don't have a **stand mixer**. They are lightweight and affordable, and don't take up much kitchen space.

LET'S EAT

Food processors: Good for sauces, pastries, etc. Most food processors come with blade attachments for slicing and grater attachments that make grating large amounts of things like carrots or cheese quick and easy.

Food storage containers: Used to store leftovers. While plastic containers are cheap and easily available, glass containers are heatproof, so they are microwave-safe and oven-safe.

Frying pans: These come in many forms, and some are better for certain tasks. Nonstick frying pans are great for frying eggs, making omelets, making pancakes, and anywhere that you really want things to NOT STICK. Stainless steel frying pans offer even heat and are great for sautéing vegetables, simmering sauces, and cooking meats. Cast iron frying pans are wonderful for searing meats and giving French toast a nice super-crispy crunch, and can move from stove top to oven easily.

Ice-cream scoop: An ice-cream scoop not only ensures perfect scoops of ice cream but also can be used to dish up even portions of cookie dough, muffins, etc.

Icing bag: Triangular bags with room for an icing tip at the end. Used for applying icing to cakes and cookies. Plastic icing bags usually come uncut so that you can cut the tip yourself and don't require a special tip to apply icing to gingerbread, etc.

Knives: A small paring knife, a larger chopping knife, and a bread knife should cover most of your cutting and slicing needs. It's important to keep your knives sharp, sharp, sharp. Be sure to have a grown-up help you while you practice your knife skills.

Meat thermometer: Used to ensure that meat is fully cooked. Beef is fully cooked at 145–160°F (63–71°C), chicken and salmon should reach 165°F (74°C), and pork is done at 170°F (77°C).

Mixing bowls: Having different sizes on hand is always useful. You'll see these referred to as small, medium, and large mixing bowls as well as nonreactive.

Paper towels/tea towels: Useful to help clean up messes as they happen. Keeping your workstation clean is a good cooking practice.

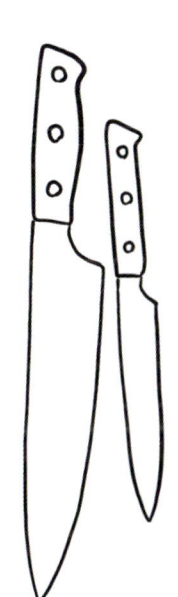

READ BEFORE YOU COOK! 17

Parchment paper: Used to line baking and cookie sheets for a nonstick surface.

Pastry brush: This tool looks a bit like a paint brush and is used for brushing egg washes, BBQ sauce, etc. over the surface of foods. Pastry brushes come in traditional bristle and silicone versions.

Pizza cutter: This tool has a sharp, round wheel-shaped blade that can cut through pizza crust easily. Be careful when using one of these. A large **knife** can be used if you don't have one.

Rice cooker: Much like an **air fryer**, a rice cooker is a set-and-forget item. Not only does it allow you to cook any rice to fluffy perfection, but you can also add vegetables to the rice as it cooks or use the rice cooker to make other dishes like soups and stews.

Rolling pin: Used for rolling out dough but also for pounding out meat if you don't have a **mallet** on hand.

Silicone mats: A sustainable alternative to **parchment paper**. These mats provide a nonstick surface and can be washed and reused.

Slow cooker: Great for a set-and-forget recipe (making something the morning or night before you plan to eat it) or for recipes where slow, tender cooking is needed.

Stock pot: This extra-large **pot** is great for making soup or large amounts of pasta.

Timer: A kitchen timer is handy when you need to keep track of how long something has been cooking, baking, proofing, or chilling. You can use the one on your stove or a small countertop one as well.

Tongs: Treat these as an extension of your hands for turning over or moving hot items.

Vegetable peeler: These items are sharp and used to remove the skins from carrots, potatoes, apples, etc. Always be careful of your fingers and peel away from your hands.

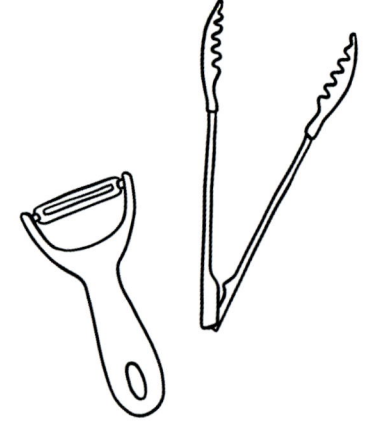

LET'S EAT

Potato masher: Used to—you guessed it—mash potatoes, but it's also good for mashing any fruit or vegetable.

Potato ricer: A specialty tool used to make perfectly smooth mashed potatoes. You put boiled potatoes in and squeeze so that a smooth potato purée comes out the other side. Be sure not to overmix your potatoes after using a ricer so they don't get gluey.

Pots and pans: These come in small, medium, and large sizes. Tight-fitting lids ensure proper cooking when steaming, simmering, or braising.

Rasp: Useful for removing the zest from citrus but also for grating hard cheeses like Parmesan as well as garlic, ginger, nutmeg, etc.

Waffle iron: This handy tool gives waffles their crispy exterior and familiar pattern—you can't make waffles without one!

Whisk: This is a handheld mixing tool made of tin metal or threadlike silicone pieces. Use it to mix air into items like whipped cream, meringue, etc.

Wooden spoons: These are invaluable in the kitchen for mixing dry ingredients together, mixing or folding heavy batters, stirring hot soups or chili, browning meats, etc.

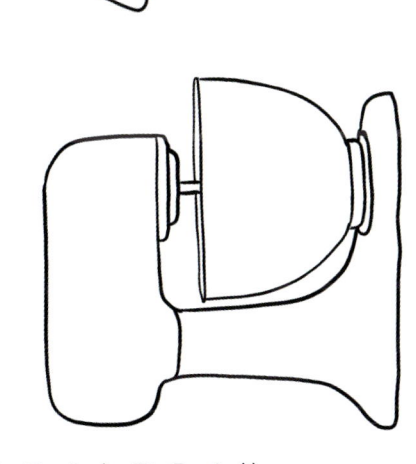

Spatulas: These are handy tools for mixing, folding, and scraping down **bowls**. You'll find wooden spatulas, rubber spatulas, and offset spatulas readily available in stores. Offset spatulas are perfect for spreading frostings onto cakes.

Stand mixer: This item is useful for pretty much everything and makes whipping up cakes, doughs, cookies, and frostings super easy. The paddle attachment is used for things like creaming butter and sugar, mixing cookie and muffin dough or frostings, etc. The **whisk** attachment is for whipping eggs or cream and makes making meringues a breeze. Use the dough hook to mix bread or pizza dough. If you don't have one, another great option is a **hand mixer**.

READ BEFORE YOU COOK!

TECHNIQUES

You may come across some terms and techniques that you don't recognize in the recipes. We've highlighted these in GREEN for an easy reference. If you can't remember what a particular technique is, just flip back to this page. (And for fun, we've included a couple of terms that we don't use in this book but that are useful to know.)

Boil: Heat your liquid until large, rolling bubbles appear.

Braise: Sear brown food in a pan at high heat and then add a liquid such as stock, reduce heat, cover the pot, and simmer for a long time at a low temperature.

Cream: Beat butter and sugar together until the sugar is completely mixed in and the mixture becomes light and fluffy, usually about 3 minutes.

Infuse: Meld the flavor of a spice, herb, or other aromatic into a cooking liquid. You can infuse milk by heating it with herbs, vanilla beans, or other spices. When you remove the items, you will have flavored, or infused, milk.

Line: This refers to lining a cookie sheet or baking pan with parchment paper or aluminum foil.

Shred: Tear your ingredient apart. Soft cheese, lettuce, carrots, cabbage, apples, etc. can be shredded on a box grater, while meats like chicken, pulled pork, etc. can be shredded by pulling them apart with two forks.

Simmer: Keep a pot of liquid on a low heat so that small bubbles are released slowly and constantly.

Toss: Loosely mix your items together.

LET'S EAT

Whisk: Mix your items together while adding lots of air. You normally use a handheld whisk or the whisk attachment on a stand mixer to do this. You whisk liquid whipping cream to get that lovely fluffy whipped cream that tastes so good on hot chocolate.

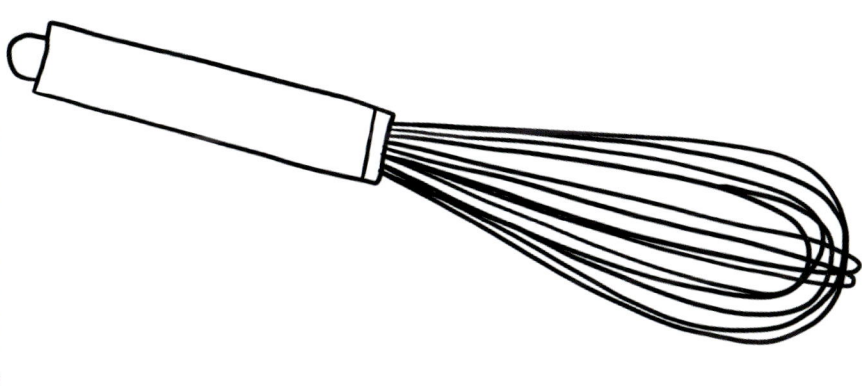

Matchstick: To cut vegetables into matchstick shape—usually 2 inches (5 cm) long and ½ inch (1.25 cm) wide.

Mince: Cut an ingredient into very small pieces, as tiny as you can. A rasp works well for mincing things like ginger, garlic, onions, etc.

Score: Cut into an ingredient without going all the way to the bottom. You're just drawing shallow lines with your knife.

Sear: Place your food item on a hot frying pan so that it forms a crust. When you sear something, you seal in all the juices but don't cook the item all the way through. You normally finish the dish in the oven or a slow cooker.

Set: When a liquid sets, it takes on a more solid form. For example, when you make Jell-O, you add hot water to your gelatin mix, giving you a liquid. Once it has set, it's in its jiggly, Jell-O-y form and won't become any more solid than that.

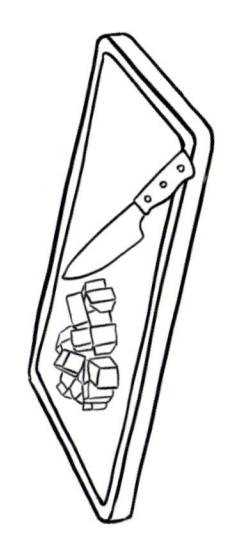

Dice: Cut your items into small cube-shaped chunks that are evenly sized all around, like game playing dice. Dice can be large (¾ inch/2 cm), medium (½ inch/1.25 cm), or small (¼ inch/ 0.6 cm).

Fold: Lift the ingredients with your spoon or hands from the bottom outside edge of the bowl and turn the mixture upside down and onto the middle as opposed to stirring round and round.

Grate: Turn something, usually hard cheese, zest, garlic, etc., into small shreds. Items can be grated on a box grater or rasp.

READ BEFORE YOU COOK!

OTHER USEFUL TERMS

Divided: When a recipe calls for an ingredient to be divided, it means you use part of it at one point in the recipe and the rest at another. For example, the bread recipe (page 51) calls for a total of 1¾ cups (435 mL) of water. You use 1 cup (250 mL) of the water at the beginning of the recipe and the remainder a little later.

g: Abbreviation for gram.

kg: Abbreviation for kilogram.

L: Abbreviation for liter.

lb: Abbreviation for pound, a standard weight measure.

mL: Abbreviation for milliliter.

Nonreactive: This usually describes a mixing bowl needed for items that contain acid, like lemon juice or vinegar. If you use copper or iron with an acid, you get a chemical reaction that changes the taste of your food. Glass and stainless steel are both nonreactive.

oz: Abbreviation for ounce.

Roux: A combination of butter and flour lightly cooked together to thicken liquid.

Soft peaks: When you're whisking whipping cream and you lift your whisk up to check it's thick enough, the "peaks" that fall over are called soft peaks.

Stiff peaks: When you're whisking whipping cream and you lift your whisk up to check it's thick enough, the "peaks" that stand straight up are called stiff peaks. This state comes after **soft peaks**.

Tbsp: Abbreviation of tablespoon measure.

To taste: This means to add as much of an ingredient as you like for yourself. For example, do you prefer things spicy? If so, your "to taste" may be lots of hot sauce. You don't like things too salty? Your "to taste" may be barely any salt at all. The measurement here is not precise but instead is up to you according to how much you like.

tsp: Abbreviation of teaspoon measure.

LET'S EAT

INGREDIENTS

When shopping for recipes, try to choose organic fruits and vegetables that are at their ripest and freshest. For meats and dairy, always try to get happy options that are organic and come from ethical farmers. But what about the other stuff? All the dried and canned ingredients that go into recipes? Those are called your pantry items. They are the things that live in your cupboards and are shelf-stable—that means they are packaged in such a way that they don't go bad quickly. Other ingredients that are considered essential items to have on hand may need to be stored in the fridge or freezer once they are open.

Here is a list of some items that are the building blocks for many recipes. Having these on hand makes whipping up just about any dish whenever you feel like it super easy. Shop once for all of these to stock up and then replace them as needed.

PANTRY

- Baking powder
- Baking soda
- Black pepper
- Canned beans: kidney beans, black beans, chickpeas (also known as garbanzo beans)
- Canned pineapple bits
- Canned pumpkin purée
- Canned tomatoes: diced and puréed
- Chili flakes
- Chocolate chips: these come in dark, semisweet, milk, and white. Dark chocolate is quite bitter and then it gets sweeter and sweeter as you move toward milk chocolate. White chocolate is just the cocoa butter extracted from the cocoa (chocolate) beans and is very sweet.
- Cocoa powder
- Condensed milk
- Cornstarch
- Dried fruits: blueberries, cherries, raisins, cranberries
- Dried herbs: herbes de Provence, thyme, rosemary, oregano, sage
- Dried pastas: whatever shapes you like best
- Flour: all-purpose, self-rising, or all-purpose 1-for-1

One of the golden rules to follow for delicious food is: *the fresher the ingredients, the better the taste!*

READ BEFORE YOU COOK!   23

- Food coloring: go for natural varieties
- Garlic powder
- Honey
- Meringue powder
- Milks: shelf-stable, unopened almond and oat milks
- Nutritional yeast
- Oils: extra virgin olive oil and a neutral oil like grape-seed or canola
- Onion powder
- Panko bread crumbs
- Rice: white, brown, and sushi-style sticky rice
- Rolled oats
- Sea salt: coarse for garnishing; fine for baking and blending into recipes
- Sesame seeds
- Spices: ground cinnamon, ground ginger, ground cloves, ground allspice, smoked paprika, cumin, bagel spice, pumpkin spice
- Stock: a flavored soup base that usually comes in chicken, beef, fish, or vegetable. It's made from slow cooking roasted bones (or not, for veggie) with vegetables, and is the foundation for soups, gravies, curry, etc.
- Sugars: granulated white sugar, brown or demerara sugar, icing sugar, coarse golden sugar, or alternatives
- Taco seasoning
- Tea bags: black, green, and herbal
- Vanilla extract: get the real stuff; it's much more expensive but the imitation or artificial versions don't taste nearly as good and are filled with extra chemicals

FRIDGE

- Butter: always use unsalted, because you can always add salt, but you can't take it away!
- Dijon mustard
- Fish sauce
- Ketchup
- Maple syrup
- Mayonnaise
- Peanut butter or alternative: crunchy and smooth
- Sambal oelek or other chili paste
- Sesame oil
- Vinegars: apple cider, red wine, white wine, balsamic, rice wine, and basic white
- Worcestershire sauce

FREEZER

- Active bread yeast
- Frozen berries
- Frozen veggie mix
- Nuts and seeds: almonds, pecans, walnuts, sesame seeds, and pumpkin seeds can all be kept in freezer bags in the freezer so that they last longer. They are oily ingredients and can go rancid (yuck!) if left on the shelf for too long.

ALLERGENS

Food allergies are quite common nowadays, but thankfully there are lots of substitutions for the most common allergens. If you know that you or someone you will cook for has a food allergy, be sure to read the recipe carefully. Look for the peanut icon and refer back to this section for substitution options. When you're buying packaged food or food from a bakery, always read the ingredients carefully or ask someone to make sure there are no allergens.

Here is some helpful information about common allergens.

GLUTEN

This is the protein found in wheat. It helps keep wheat products together, like glue. (Think fluffy bread.) There are many gluten-free flours available on the market today that can be used in a "cup-for-cup" or "1-for-1" ratio, meaning you can simply use 1 cup (250 mL) of gluten-free flour where the recipe calls for regular flour. These flour mixes contain all the ingredients you need for baking and cooking. People can be gluten-free for several reasons. The main one is if they have celiac disease: that means their body triggers an immune reaction in response to gluten, creating intestinal problems. If you're cooking for someone who has celiac disease, make sure to clean all of your utensils and work surfaces well and avoid having gluten nearby. Use a 1-for-1 gluten-free flour. If you're using oats, make sure that the packaging is labeled gluten-free. Always advise people that the food you've prepared does not come from a certified gluten-free kitchen. Some people prefer to avoid products and food items that contain gluten for personal reasons, even though they don't have celiac disease. If someone is avoiding gluten as a personal dietary choice, you can easily substitute a 1-for-1 gluten-free mix in place of flour. There is no risk of an allergic reaction, so you don't need to take the same precautions as you would for someone who has celiac disease.

In place of gluten flour, use:

- Baking: 1-for-1 gluten-free mix or almond flour
- Thickening (soups, sauces, etc.): chickpea flour, almond flour, oat flour
- Bread/pizza: 1-for-1 gluten-free mix

READ BEFORE YOU COOK!

DAIRY

Cow's milk and milk products like cheese and yogurt are a common allergen but there are a lot of alternatives available. Oat milk, almond milk, cashew milk, and soy milk are the most common nondairy milks. We find that oat milk and cashew milk (if you can eat nuts) produce the best results in baking and cooking. Nondairy milks come in sweetened and unsweetened varieties, as well as flavored like vanilla and chocolate.

In place of dairy, use:

- Milk: oat milk, soy milk, cashew milk, almond milk
- Yogurt: coconut yogurt
- Butter: coconut oil and olive oil–based margarine
- Cheese: cashew cheese, soy cheese

PEANUTS AND TREE NUTS

Peanuts are a serious allergen. Nowadays, most packaging will advise if a product was made in a peanut-free facility. Allergies to tree nuts like almonds, cashews, and pistachios are also becoming quite common.

In recipes that call for nuts, a great substitute is seeds such as pumpkin or sunflower, or beans such as roasted chickpeas. A great nut butter alternative is sun-butter, made from sunflower seeds.

In place of nuts, use:

- Butters: sunflower seed butter or pumpkin seed butter in place of peanut butter
- Seeds: use pumpkin or sunflower seeds instead of nuts in cookies and cakes

EGGS

Many people have allergies to eggs. Be sure to carefully read the ingredients lists on packaging. When you're baking, substituting eggs is a little tricky as they function as a binder, stabilizer, and volume maker. However, for most baking recipes, you can replace the eggs with ¼ cup (60 mL) of applesauce, mashed bananas, or a commercial egg replacer. The results will be more dense but still delicious.

In place of eggs, use:

- Baking: applesauce, mashed banana, commercial egg replacement

SOY

Soy has an almost identical protein composition to dairy milk, so many people who are allergic to dairy are also allergic to soy. Soybeans, soy sauce, soy milk, tofu, miso, soybean oil, and edamame beans are all soy products. Coconut amino sauce is an excellent allergen-friendly substitute for soy sauce (it's soy-free, gluten-free, and vegan). Maggi sauce or Worcestershire sauce work well as soy-free seasoning. For things like miso, check for those made with rice and chickpeas.

In place of soy, use:

- Soy sauce: coconut aminos, Maggi sauce, Worcestershire sauce

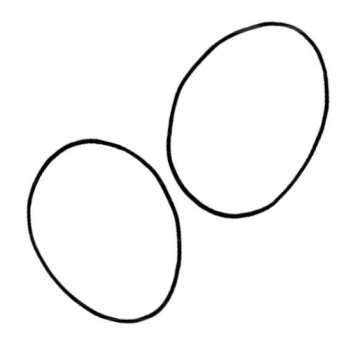

SUGARS

Though sugars are not usually allergens, many people are moving toward alternatives to the traditional refined white and brown sugars. For most recipes—except cakes, which are more reliant on exact chemical reactions—the alternatives work perfectly and have more flavor! You can also tweak how much you use if you want less sweetness. For dry sugars you can use a 1-to-1 ratio, so 1 cup (250 mL) of sugar can be replaced with 1 cup (250 mL) of coconut or date sugar. Liquid sugars should be halved so that 1 cup (250 mL) of sugar is replaced with ½ cup (125 mL) of honey, maple syrup, coconut syrup, or agave syrup.

In place of traditional refined sugar, use:

- Sugars: coconut sugar, date sugar, honey
- Syrups: maple syrup, coconut syrup, agave syrup

READ BEFORE YOU COOK!

LEARN THESE FIRST!

... you'll need them as you go through the book.

How to Cook Eggs · 30
How to Cook Bacon · 34
How to Mash Potatoes · 36
How to Cook Pasta · 39
How to Cook Rice · 42
How to Roast a Chicken · 45
How to Make Salad Dressing · 48
How to Make Bread · 51

HOW TO COOK EGGS

Eggs are such a versatile food! They're a good source of protein and a great addition to a bunch of recipes: Avocado Toast (page 74), Caesar Salad (page 108), or even BBQ Best Burgers (page 130). On the following pages, we've given you instructions on how to prepare them in a few different ways. Once you feel confident, you can move on to Omelets (page 88).

Note: When you're cracking eggs, crack them into a shallow **bowl** first and then transfer to your main bowl to ensure that no bits of shell accidentally fall into the dish you are preparing.

HARD-BOILED EGGS

Eggs that are fully cooked in their shell. They're great for popping into your lunch box, or for making egg salad or Deviled Eggs (page 122). With their shells on, they'll keep in the fridge for up to 7 days, so make a few ahead of time for a ready-made snack.

Place 1–2 eggs per person in a small **pot** of cold water and cover with a lid. Bring to a **boil** over high heat. Once the water is boiling, turn off the heat and set a **timer** for 8 minutes. Meanwhile, prepare a medium **bowl** with water and lots of ice. This is called an ice bath. It helps to stop the cooking and to cool down the eggs quickly. When the timer goes off, carefully lift the eggs out of the hot water with a slotted spoon and transfer them to the ice bath.

Turn off the stove!

LET'S EAT

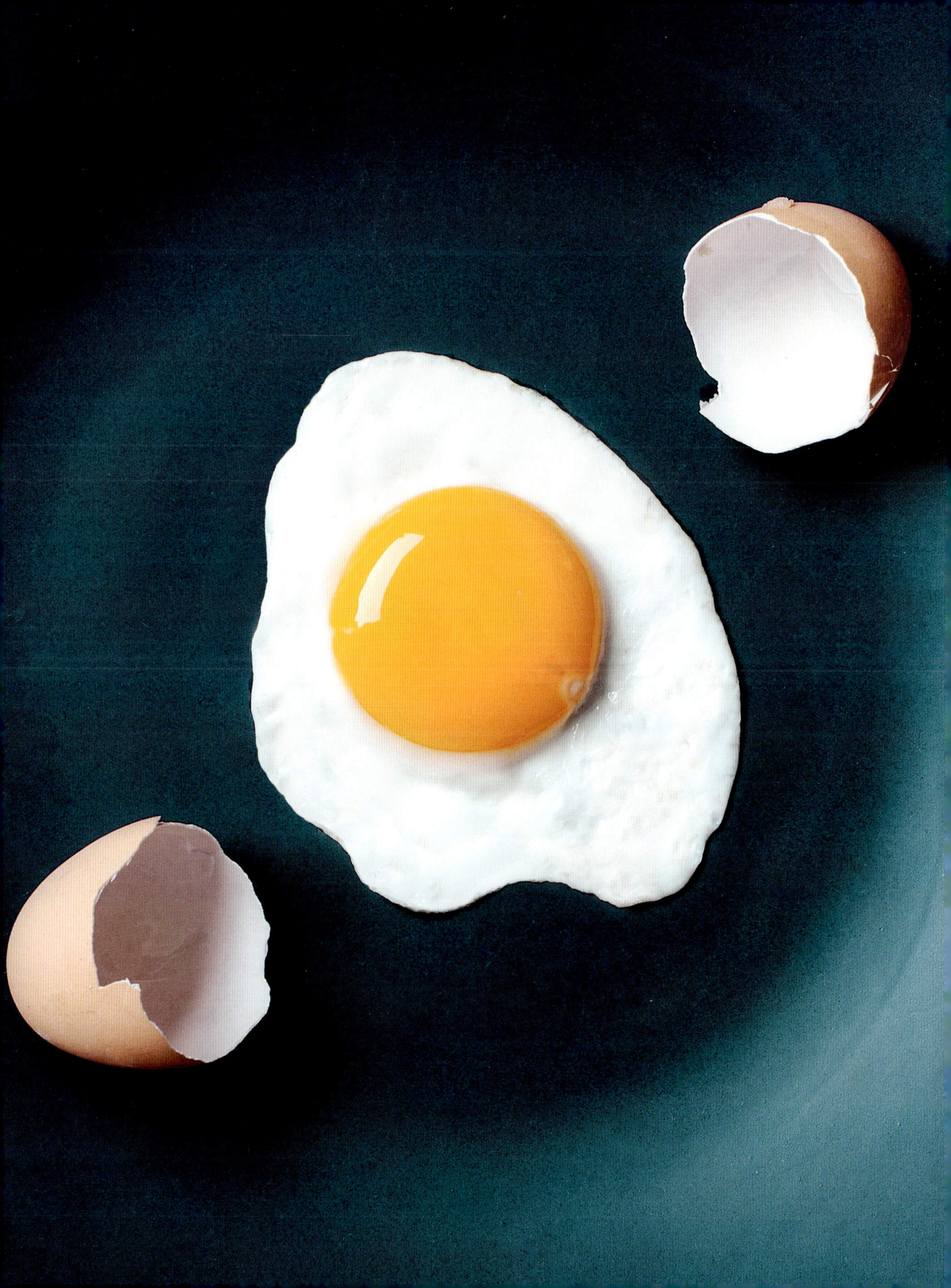

Let the eggs sit for 10–15 minutes. Lay a piece of **paper towel** on a work surface. Remove the eggs from the water and put them on the paper towel. Gently tap the top and bottom of each egg to crack the shell. Lay the egg on its side and gently roll it back and forth, cracking the sides. Gently peel off the shell. You'll find that the shell has a membrane or skin under it that will separate from the egg white. Once you get under that, peeling is much easier. Eggs are MUCH easier to peel if they have been left to chill in the fridge overnight, so if you're using these for Deviled Eggs (page 122), for example, you may want to **boil** them the night before you want to use them.

SOFT-BOILED EGGS

Eggs that are partially cooked in their shell. The white is solid and cooked, but the yolk remains a bit runny or jammy. These are excellent in ramen or on toast.

Place 1–2 eggs per person in a small **pot** of cold water and cover with a lid. Bring to a **boil** over high heat. Once the water is boiling, turn off the heat and set a **timer** for 5 minutes. Meanwhile, prepare a medium **bowl** with water and lots of ice. This is called an ice bath. It helps to stop the cooking and to cool down the eggs quickly. When the timer goes off, carefully lift the eggs out of the hot water with a slotted spoon and transfer them to the ice bath.

Turn off the stove!

Let the eggs sit for 15 minutes. Lay a piece of **paper towel** on a work surface. Remove the eggs from the water and put them on the paper towel. Gently tap the top and bottom of each egg to crack the shell. Lay the egg on its side and gently roll back and forth, cracking the sides. Gently peel off the shell.

SCRAMBLED EGGS

Scrambled eggs are exactly that—you mix the white and the yolks all together into one fluffy eggy mix. Crack 2 eggs per person and put them in a medium **bowl**. Add salt and pepper **to taste** and 1 Tbsp (15 mL) of water per person. Using a fork or a **whisk**, beat the eggs together until completely blended and fluffy.

In a medium **frying pan** over medium-high heat, heat 2 tsp (10 mL) of olive oil or butter for every 4 eggs. Add the eggs and, starting from the outside, gather the eggs toward the center and rotate the pan around to move the running eggs. Keep gathering and moving the eggs around until they are cooked all the way through, about 3–4 minutes. Remove from the heat and serve.

SUNNY SIDE UP

These are fried eggs that show the yolk in the middle of the cooked whites. In a medium nonstick **frying pan** over medium-low heat, heat 1 tsp (5 mL) of olive oil or butter for every 2 eggs. Crack 1–2 eggs per person and slide them carefully into the pan. Add salt and pepper **to taste**. Cook the eggs until all of the white is cooked. It will change from clear to white. The edges will be crispy, the whites will be cooked through, and the yellow will be runny. This will take about 5 minutes. Remove from the heat and serve.

OVER EASY

These eggs are like sunny side up eggs, but they're flipped over midway through the frying time to cook both sides of the egg evenly. In a medium nonstick **frying pan** over medium heat, heat 1 tsp (5 mL) of olive oil or butter for every 2 eggs. Crack 1–2 eggs per person and slide them carefully into the pan. Add salt and pepper **to taste**. Cook until most of the white is **set**, about 2 minutes. Slide a **spatula** under the egg and carefully flip it over. Cook for another minute and remove from the heat. The longer you cook the egg, the more cooked the yolk will be. If you do not like a runny yolk, pop it at the start.

Charlie Says

Which came first, the chicken or the egg? Doesn't matter, they're both delicious!

LEARN THESE FIRST!

HOW TO COOK BACON

Cooking bacon in the oven is great for several reasons. First, it prevents the splattering of grease all over the stove. Second, it's less messy, so the cleanup is much easier. Lastly, it allows you to prepare something else at the same time. For example, you can prepare a Caesar Salad (page 108) while the bacon is cooking.

2-3 STRIPS OF BACON PER PERSON

Preheat the oven to 400°F (200°C). **Line** a **baking sheet** with **parchment paper**. Line a plate with **paper towel**.

Lay the bacon on the **parchment paper** in a single layer. Place the **baking sheet** in the center of the oven and cook the bacon until browned, 15–20 minutes. You don't need to turn it while it's cooking.

Using **oven mitts**, carefully remove the **baking sheet** from the oven and transfer the bacon slices to the prepared plate.

Turn off the oven!

Allow the bacon grease to cool before cleaning it up as it will be very hot.

Félix Says

Mmmmm... bacon...

LET'S EAT

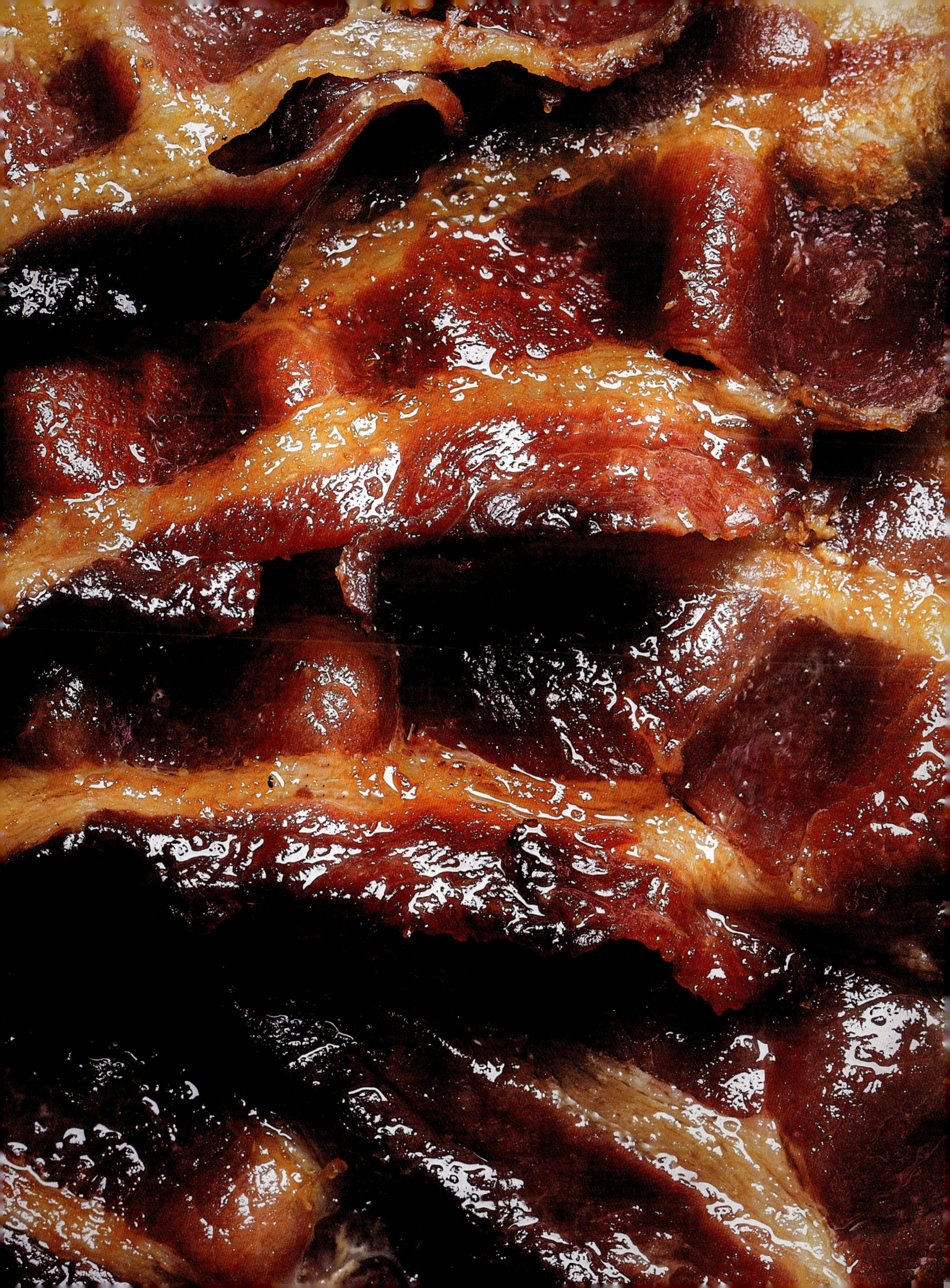

HOW TO MASH POTATOES

Did you know mashed potatoes freeze really well? Cooking a big batch of potatoes and storing them in the freezer is a great way to cut down on the time it takes to make a meal, which is a big help on school nights. Double or triple this recipe so you can stock extras away.

SERVES 4

For perfect potatoes, the chef's rule is: *the higher the fat content in your milk and butter, the fluffier your mash.* A **potato ricer** will give you a perfectly smooth and creamy texture. Of course, if you need a nondairy version, you can swap the butter for olive or avocado oil and replace the milk with chicken or veggie stock and they'll still be super delicious.

Note: Russet and Yukon Gold are two great and versatile potatoes. Both produce light and fluffy mashed potatoes.

2 lb (900 g) potatoes
¼ cup (60 mL) unsalted butter, cut in cubes, or avocado oil or olive oil
½ cup (125 mL) milk or chicken stock or veggie stock
Salt and pepper

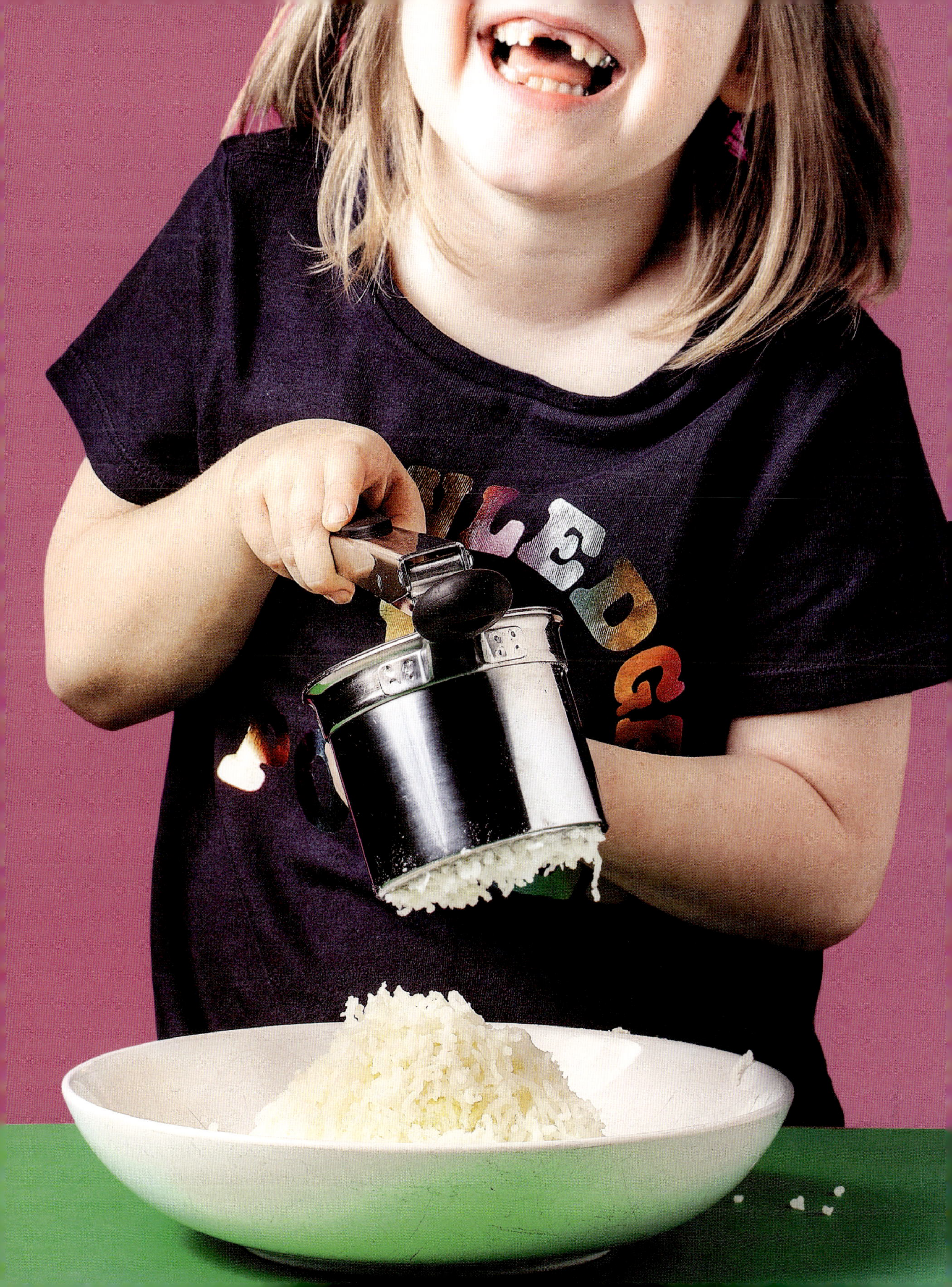

Fill a large **pot** halfway with cold water. Peel the potatoes. Carefully cut them lengthwise down the middle. Place them flat side down and slice lengthwise down the middle again. Turn and cut the potato widthwise into three or four cubes. Add them to the cold water. (Immersing cut potatoes in cold water prevents them from oxidizing, turning brown.)

Place the **pot** on the stove over high heat and bring to a **boil**. Lower the heat and cook, uncovered, until you can easily stick a fork into the potatoes, 10–15 minutes. Using a sieve or colander, drain the potatoes and let them cool in the sieve for a minute or two.

Place a **potato ricer** over the pot you cooked the potatoes in.

Using a fork or spoon, place a scoop of potatoes into the **potato ricer** and press down the lever. Repeat this until all the potatoes are mashed. If you don't have a ricer, use a **potato masher** to mash the potatoes.

Over a low heat, **fold** the butter and milk (or oil and stock) into the potatoes until combined. Do not overmix as the potato starches will activate and the potatoes will become sticky, glue-like, and unpleasant. We want fluffy mashed potatoes!

Turn off the heat.

Season with salt and pepper **to taste**.

HOW TO COOK PASTA

Cooking pasta properly isn't difficult, but it's important to find the perfect amount of doneness: too little cooking and you get hard, starchy, raw bites; too much cooking and you get mushy goop. The in-between stage is called *al dente*—that's an Italian term that means "to the teeth," so you want the noodles to have just a bit of resistance to your teeth. Pasta packaging has a recommended time that you can use for guidance for perfectly cooked pasta!

SERVES 4

1 lb (450 g) pasta
Salt

Bring a large **stock pot** of water to a **boil** over high heat. You want lots of water so that you can stir the pasta well and it cooks evenly. If you don't have enough water, you run the risk of the pasta pieces sticking together as they cook and ending up clumpy and uncooked. This is especially true of long pastas like spaghetti and linguini.

Season the water with a healthy five-finger pinch of salt. You want the water to be salty. This changes the boiling point of the water to make it hotter and seasons the pasta at the same time.

When the water is **boiling**, add the pasta, stir well, and set a **timer** for the cooking time listed on the package instructions. Stir every few minutes to prevent the pasta pieces from sticking or clumping together.

Once the pasta is done cooking, drain it over the sink in a **colander** or **sieve**.

Turn off the stove!

Return the pasta to the **pot** and immediately add whichever sauce you're using. For a cold pasta salad, rinse the pasta really well with cold water for 4–5 minutes and then drain in the **colander**. **Toss** it in a **bowl** with your favorite dressing.

To store leftover pasta, add a bit of olive oil to stop it from **setting** and sticking together and place in an airtight **container** in the fridge for up to 4 days.

LEARN THESE FIRST!

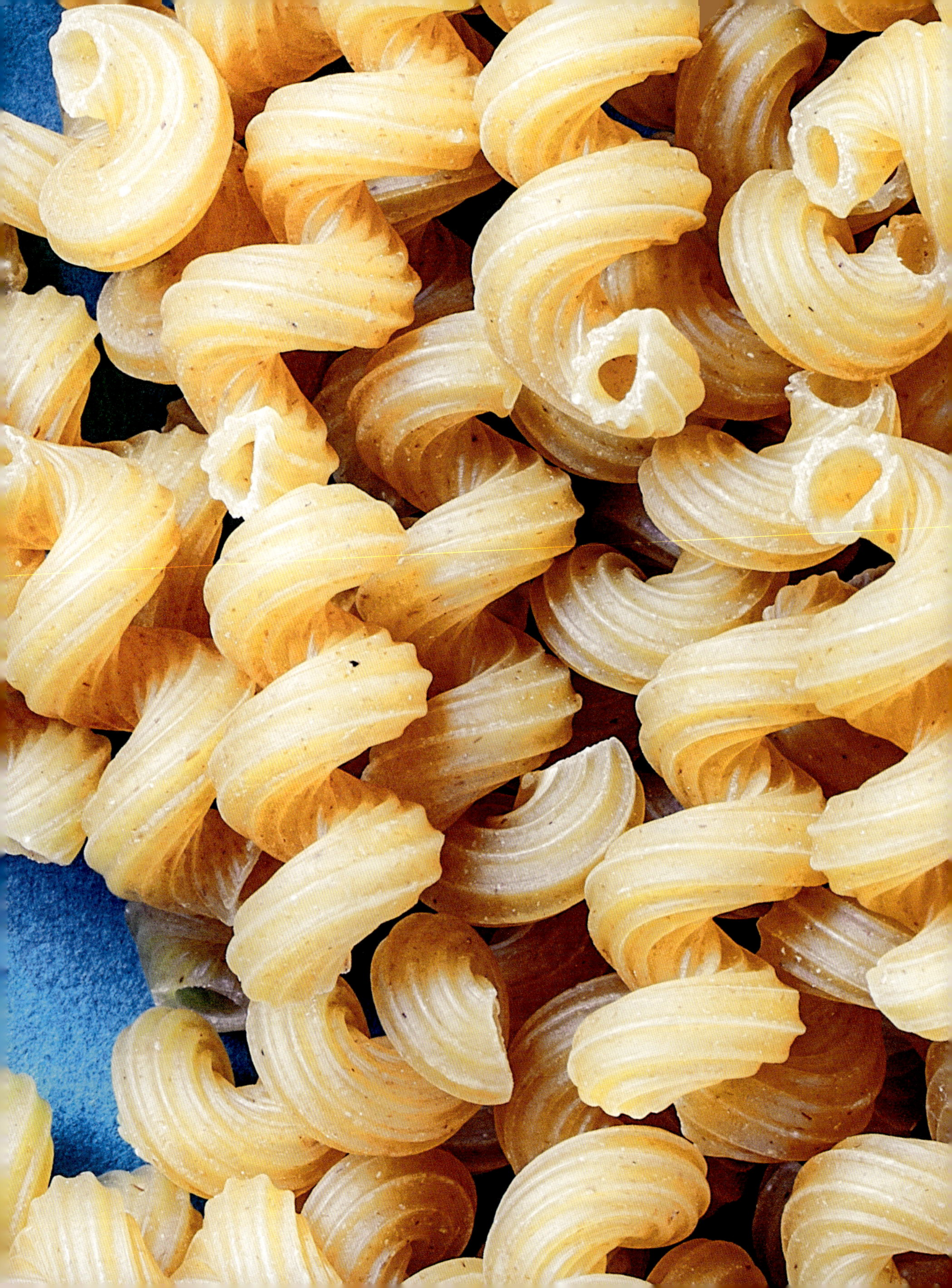

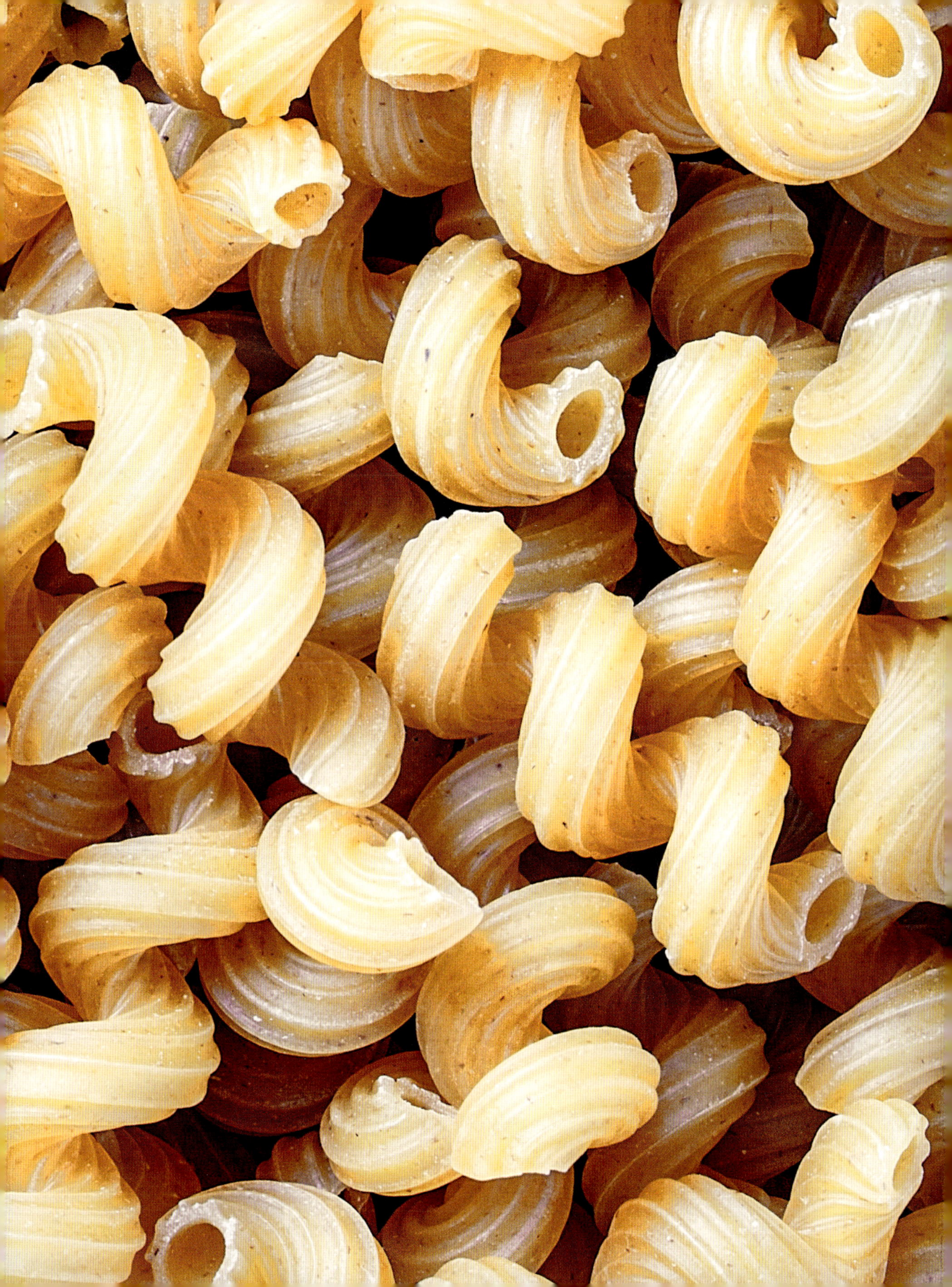

HOW TO COOK RICE

Most rice packages have instructions that work best for the kind of rice you're making, but here are some basic guidelines that will help you make perfect rice every time. Note: 1 cup (250 mL) of uncooked rice will give you about 3 cups (750 mL) of cooked rice.

SERVES 2-4

1 cup (250 mL) uncooked rice

Be sure to check the cooking time for the kind of rice you're making. Brown rice can take up to an hour to be fully cooked, while some basmati rice varieties are done in 15 minutes. Timing is important so that your rice is hot and ready when you need it.

Be sure to rinse your rice! Yes, that's right. Cleaning your rice removes some of the extra starch and will make it lighter and fluffier.

Measure your rice and place it in a medium **pot** or the **bowl** of a **rice cooker**. Fill the pot or bowl with cold water and swish the rice around with your hand. You will see the water turn cloudy with the starch. Strain the rice through a **sieve** to remove all the water, and then repeat this process at least two more times until the water turns clear (you'll usually need to rinse it three or four times). After the final straining, cook the rice as described below.

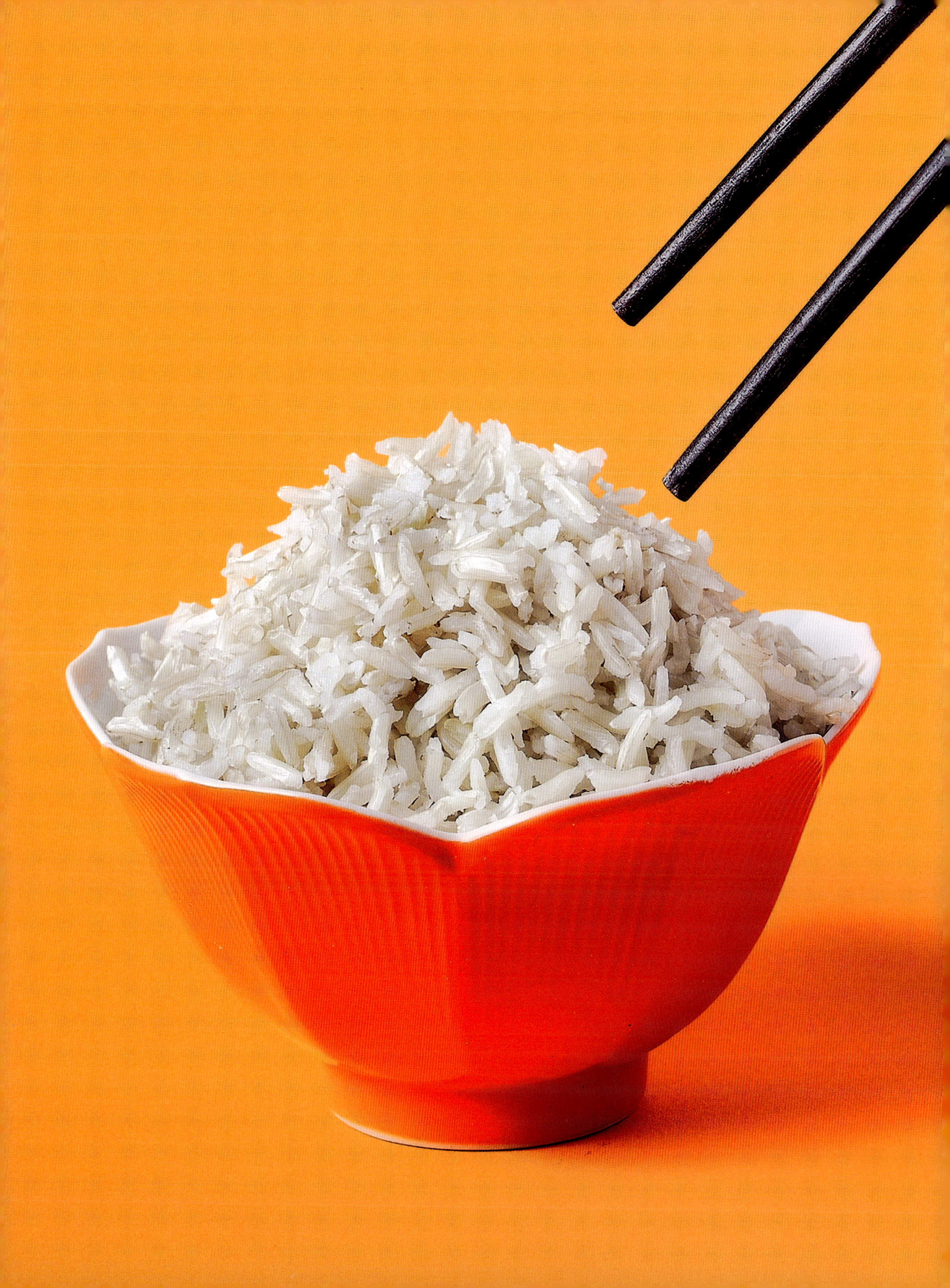

On the stove top

Measure your rice and water according to the package instructions, and place both in a **pot** with a tight-fitting lid.

Place the pot on high heat to bring the water and rice up to a full rolling **boil**. Then turn the temperature down to the lowest setting and place the lid on the pot.

Set a **timer** for the cooking time given on your rice package and DO NOT remove the lid until the timer goes off.

Once the **timer** goes off, take the pot off the heat, turn off the heat, and remove the lid from the pot. Fluff the rice up with a fork and serve.

In a rice cooker

Measure your rice and water according to the package instructions, and place both in your rice cooker.

Follow the rice cooker instructions.

As soon as your rice is done, fluff your rice with a fork and serve.

HOW TO ROAST A CHICKEN

Roast chicken may seem like an impossibly difficult thing to cook, but honestly, it's one of the easiest meals ever. Just a few steps and then pop it in the oven. That's it! Keeping things clean is the most important part of cooking chicken. Be sure to work on a plastic **cutting board** that can be cleaned with hot water and disinfect any areas or tools that come in contact with raw chicken. Now wash your hands. No, really, wash them again—before and after you touch raw chicken. Note: You'll need a **meat thermometer** and a 9 × 13-inch (23 × 33 cm) roasting pan with sides at least 1 inch (2.5 cm) high.

SERVES 2-4

- 1 (4–6 lb/1.8–2.7 kg) whole chicken, thawed (if frozen)
- 1 organic lemon
- 1 organic garlic bulb
- 2 Tbsp (30 mL) olive oil
- 2 tsp (10 mL) ground sage
- 2 tsp (10 mL) sea salt
- 1 tsp (5 mL) freshly ground black pepper

Preheat the oven to 425°F (220°C).

Drain any liquid from inside your chicken and place it breast side up in a roasting pan with sides at least 1 inch (2.5 cm) high.

Cut the lemon into 4 pieces. Take the garlic bulb and cut it widthwise so every clove is cut in half. Open the chicken's legs and push the lemons and garlic bulb into the chicken's cavity—that's the big open space inside.

Pour the olive oil over the outside of the chicken and spread it evenly over the chicken with your hands. Now wash your hands.

LEARN THESE FIRST!

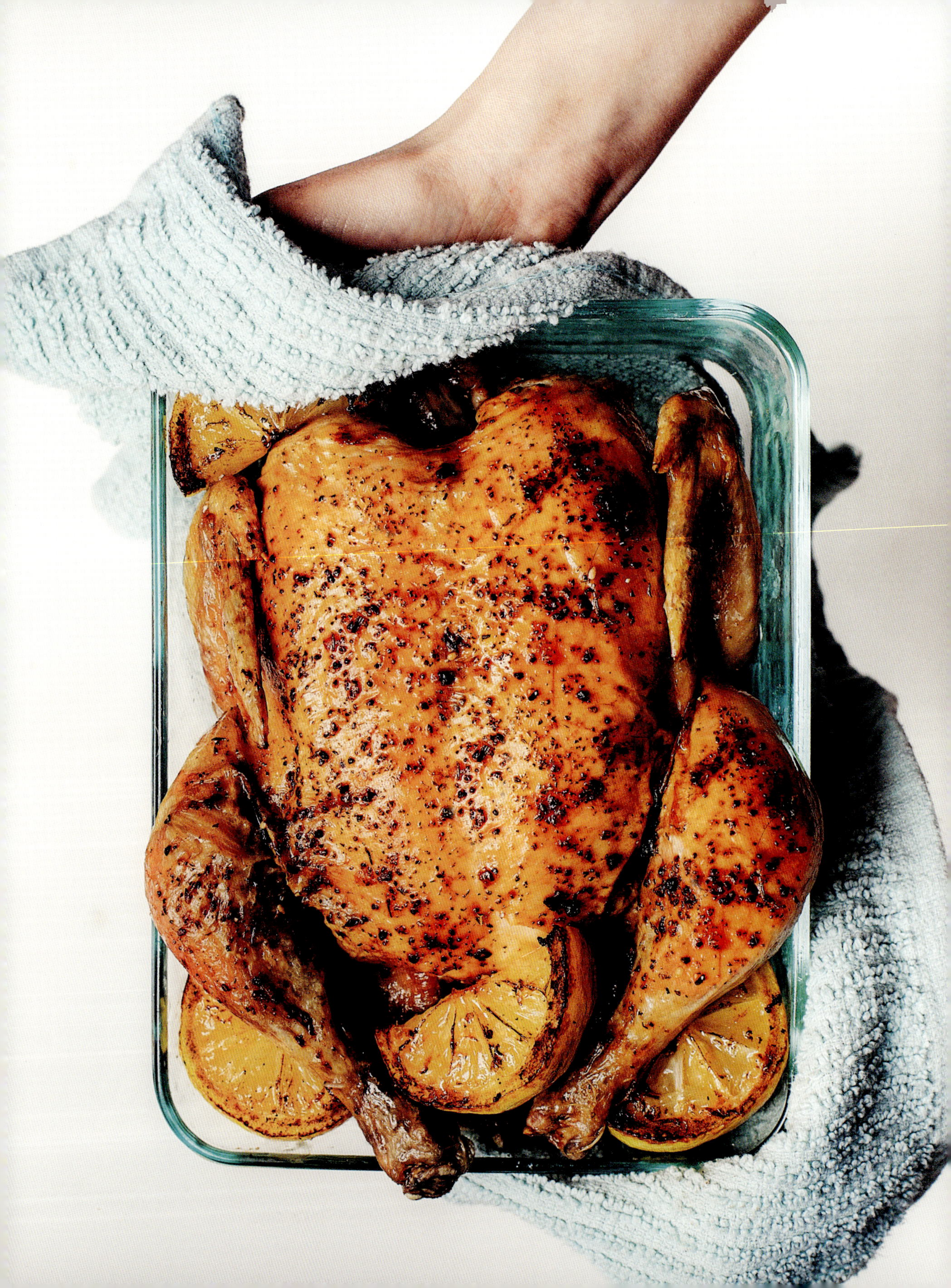

Sprinkle the sage, salt, and pepper over the outside of the chicken. Use your hands to rub these all around the chicken evenly. Now wash your hands again.

Place the chicken in the pan on the middle rack of the oven and set your **timer** for 30 minutes. When the timer goes off, turn the oven heat down to 375°F (190°C) and let it roast for another 45 minutes.

Check the chicken for doneness with a **meat thermometer**. Using **oven mitts**, remove the roasting pan from the oven so that you can reach all parts of the chicken safely. Place the sensor portion of the thermometer into the thickest part of the chicken's thigh. The chicken is cooked when the thermometer reads at least 165°F (74°C). Double-check the temperature by inserting it in the fattest part of the breast as well. If the chicken isn't done after this amount of time, put it back in the oven and check the temperature every 10–15 minutes until it's done.

Once the chicken is fully cooked, using **oven mitts**, remove it from the oven and place the roasting pan on a heat-proof surface to let the chicken rest for at least 10 minutes. This lets all the juices settle into the meat.

Turn off the oven!

Now the chicken is ready to eat! If you're going to store the chicken in the fridge for using in other recipes, be sure it cools completely to room temperature first, then remove the meat from the bones and store in an airtight **container** in the fridge.

Chloë Says

Learn this! You'll need it for a bunch of recipes.

LEARN THESE FIRST!

HOW TO MAKE SALAD DRESSING

Once you know the basic recipe for salad dressings, it's really easy to mix it up and create all kinds of different flavors. **Toss** it with your favorite salad blend and you have an instant side dish. Top that salad with some Roast Chicken (page 45) and serve with some Easy Bread Rolls (page 150) and you have a perfect lunch or quick supper.

MAKES 1–1½ CUPS (250–375 ML) OF DRESSING

The key ingredients in any dressing are good quality oil, acid (vinegar or citrus juice), Dijon mustard, sweetener, and sea salt. See Switch Up the Flavor! for how much of these to use.

Just place all the ingredients in a jar, screw on the top, and give it a good shake to combine. That's it! These dressings will keep for up to 5 days in an airtight jar in the fridge.

Switch Up the Flavor!

VERY BERRY

½ cup (125 mL) fresh or frozen (thawed) raspberries, strawberries, or blackberries mashed with a fork
½ cup (125 mL) good quality olive oil
3 Tbsp (45 mL) red wine vinegar
1 Tbsp (15 mL) Dijon mustard
1 Tbsp (15 mL) maple syrup
1 tsp (5 mL) sea salt

LEMON POPPY SEED

½ cup (125 mL) plain Greek yogurt
½ cup (125 mL) good quality olive oil
3 Tbsp (45 mL) freshly squeezed lemon juice (1–2 lemons)
1 Tbsp (15 mL) Dijon mustard
1 Tbsp (15 mL) honey
1 Tbsp (15 mL) poppy seeds
1 tsp (5 mL) sea salt

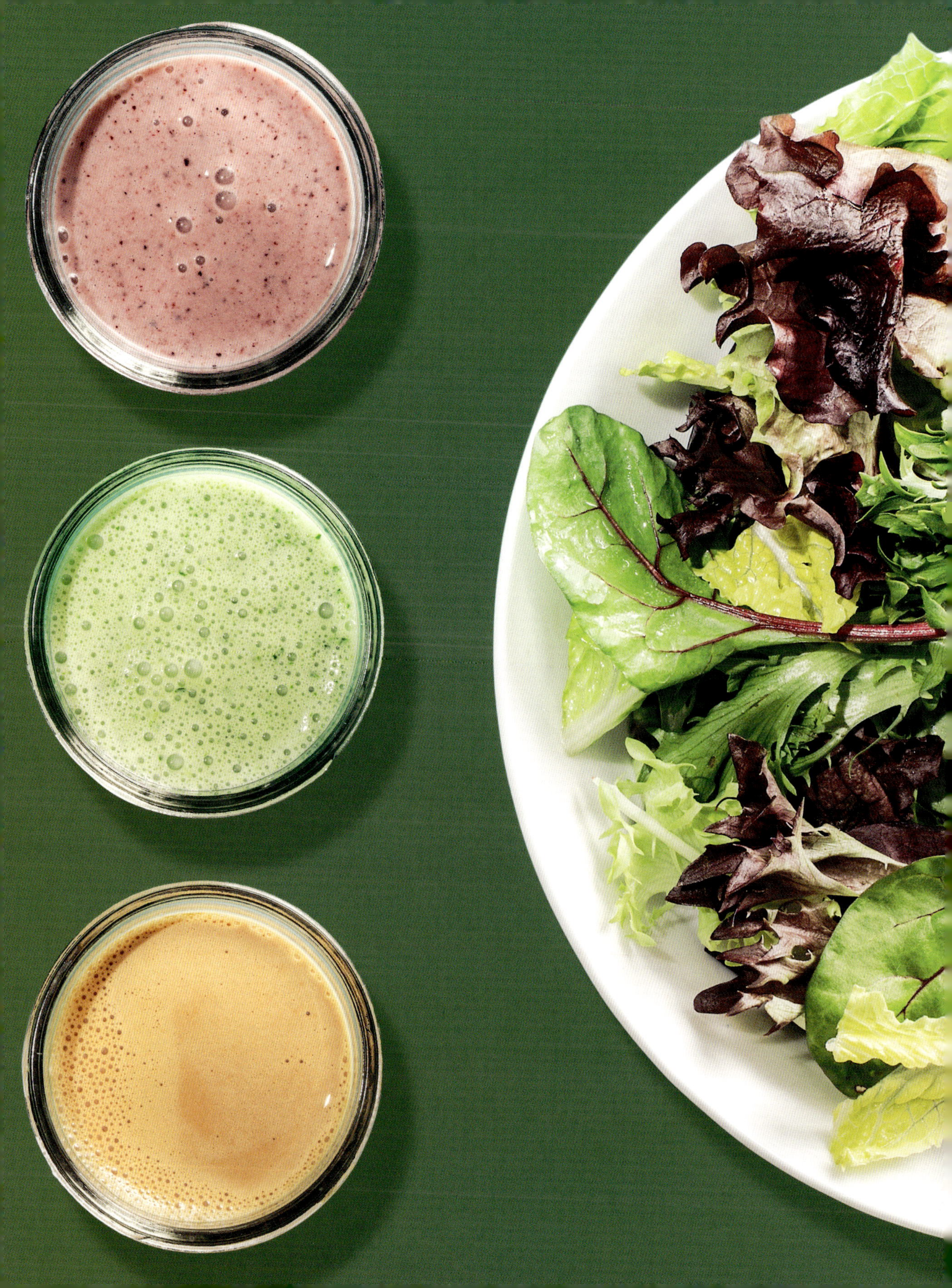

TOASTED SESAME

½ cup (125 mL) good quality olive oil
¼ cup (60 mL) toasted sesame oil
¼ cup (60 mL) tamari or coconut aminos
3 Tbsp (45 mL) apple cider vinegar
1 Tbsp (15 mL) Dijon mustard
1 Tbsp (15 mL) maple syrup
1 tsp (5 mL) sea salt

BALSAMIC

½ cup (125 mL) good quality olive oil
¼ cup (60 mL) balsamic vinegar
1 Tbsp (15 mL) Dijon mustard
1 Tbsp (15 mL) brown sugar
1 tsp (5 mL) sea salt

HERBY GREEN GODDESS

½ cup (125 mL) chopped fresh herbs (any combination of dill, basil, thyme, cilantro, and flat-leaf or curly leaf parsley)
½ cup (125 mL) good quality olive oil
¼ cup (60 mL) plain Greek yogurt
3 Tbsp (45 mL) apple cider vinegar
1 Tbsp (15 mL) Dijon mustard
1 Tbsp (15 mL) honey
1 clove garlic, minced
1 tsp (5 mL) sea salt

CILANTRO LIME

½ cup (125 mL) chopped cilantro
½ cup (125 mL) good quality olive oil
¼ cup (60 mL) plain Greek yogurt
¼ cup (60 mL) freshly squeezed lime juice (2–3 limes)
1 Tbsp (15 mL) Dijon mustard
1 Tbsp (15 mL) honey
1 tsp (5 mL) sea salt

HOW TO MAKE BREAD

This method of bread-making is no-knead and loosely based on the sourdough method. Adding sugar to the yeast helps to activate it. If the yeast does not bubble, either the water is the wrong temperature (usually too hot) or the yeast is no longer active. If it doesn't bubble up, start again using fresh yeast and make sure the temperature is correct; otherwise the dough will not rise properly. Always store dry yeast in the fridge or freezer (cool, dark place).

MAKES 1 LOAF

1¾ cups (435 mL) warm water (100°F–110°F/38°C–43°C), **divided**
2¼ tsp (11 mL) instant yeast
1 tsp (5 mL) sugar
3 cups (750 mL) all-purpose flour
1 Tbsp (15 mL) sea salt

In a small **bowl**, place 1 cup (250 mL) of the warm water, the yeast, and the sugar. Stir gently. Allow to sit for 10 minutes until thick and bubbly. At this point, if the yeast is not active and the mixture is not thick and bubbly, start over. This way you will not waste flour.

In a large **bowl**, mix the flour and salt well. Add the bubbly yeast water and the remaining warm water. Using a rubber **spatula**, stir gently to combine. The dough will be soft and sticky. Cover the bowl with a clean, dry **tea towel** for 10 minutes to let the dough rest in a warm spot.

Uncover the **bowl**. Using a **spatula**, fold the dough over several times to mix in all the flour bits. Cover the bowl with the **tea towel** and let rest again in a warm spot until doubled in size, 45–60 minutes.

Uncover the **bowl** again. Run your hands under water. Using wet hands, scoop the dough up, turn it a quarter turn, and plop it back into the bowl. Repeat this process three more times, turning a quarter turn every time. The dough will be sticky and ribbonlike.

Lightly grease a 5 × 8-inch (12.5 × 20 cm) loaf pan. Lay the dough, seam side down, in the pan and cover with the **tea towel**. Let rise in a warm spot until doubled in size again, 45–60 minutes.

LEARN THESE FIRST!

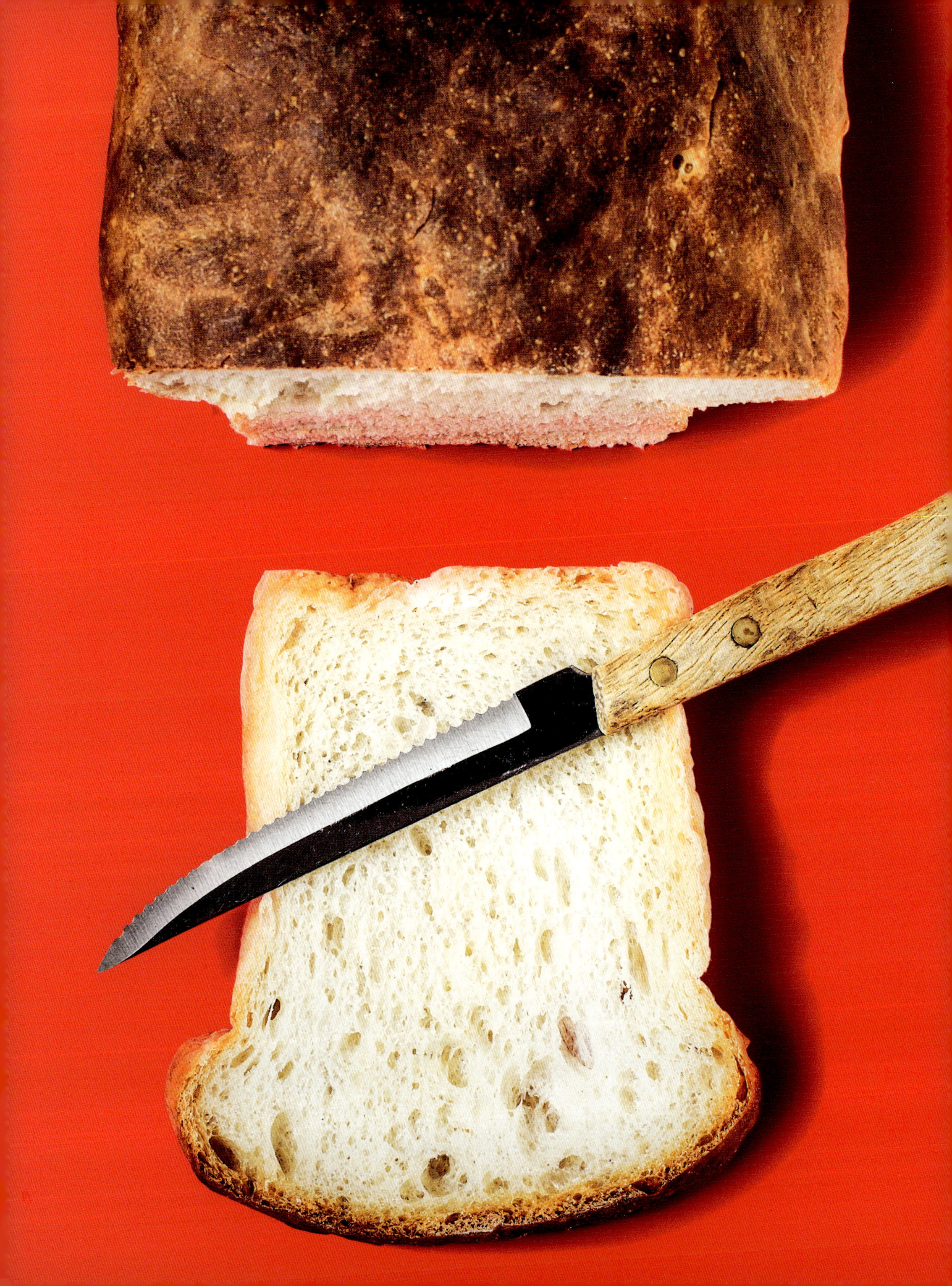

Position the rack in the center of the oven. Preheat the oven to 450°F (230°C).

Bake the bread for 35–40 minutes or until the top is golden brown and crusty.

Turn off the oven!

Using **oven mitts**, place the loaf pan on a **cooling rack**. Let the bread sit in the loaf pan for at least 30 minutes. Turn out the loaf and let stand for another 30 minutes before cutting into it.

This bread will keep in a plastic bag or airtight **container** in the fridge for 5–7 days.

William Says

Slather this with butter and Quick Jam (page 72) and it's better than cake . . . almost.

LEARN THESE FIRST!

RISE & SHINE!

. . . come on, sleepyhead, it's time for breakfast.

Smoothies • 56
Granola Bars • 60
Easy Puff Pastries • 62
Magnificent Muffins • 65
Scones • 68
Quick Jam • 72
Avocado Toast • 74
Pancakes • 76
French Toast • 79
Waffles • 82
Yogurt Parfaits • 86
Omelets • 88
Sweet or Savory Bread Pudding • 90

SMOOTHIES

Smoothies are a great grab-n-go breakfast when you need to get out the door, and perfect for an after-school or in-between-meals snack. For an extra-cold smoothie with a super-creamy texture, use frozen banana chunks. Peel a banana, cut it into 1-inch (2.5 cm) chunks, place them on a **cookie sheet**, and pop them in the freezer until frozen. Transfer them to a large freezer bag to keep on hand for smoothies.

SERVES 2

The key ingredients to any smoothie are frozen fruit, liquid yogurt (plain or vanilla, dairy or coconut), banana, and extra flavoring like berries. See Switch Up the Flavor! for how much of these to use.

Place all the ingredients in a **blender** and mix until smooth.

Switch Up the Flavor!

MIXED BERRY

2 cups (500 mL) mixed frozen berries
1 cup (250 mL) orange juice
½ cup (125 mL) yogurt of choice
1 banana or 4 frozen banana chunks
1 tsp (5 mL) vanilla

MANGO MADNESS

1½ cups (375 mL) frozen mango
½ cup (125 mL) frozen raspberries
½ cup (125 mL) orange juice
½ cup (125 mL) almond milk
½ cup (125 mL) yogurt of choice
1 banana or 4 frozen banana chunks

CHOCOLATE PEANUT BUTTER CUP

1 cup (250 mL) milk of choice
1 cup (250 mL) ice cubes
½ cup (125 mL) yogurt of choice
¼ cup (60 mL) peanut butter
1 banana or 4 frozen banana chunks
2 Tbsp (30 mL) cocoa powder

LET'S EAT

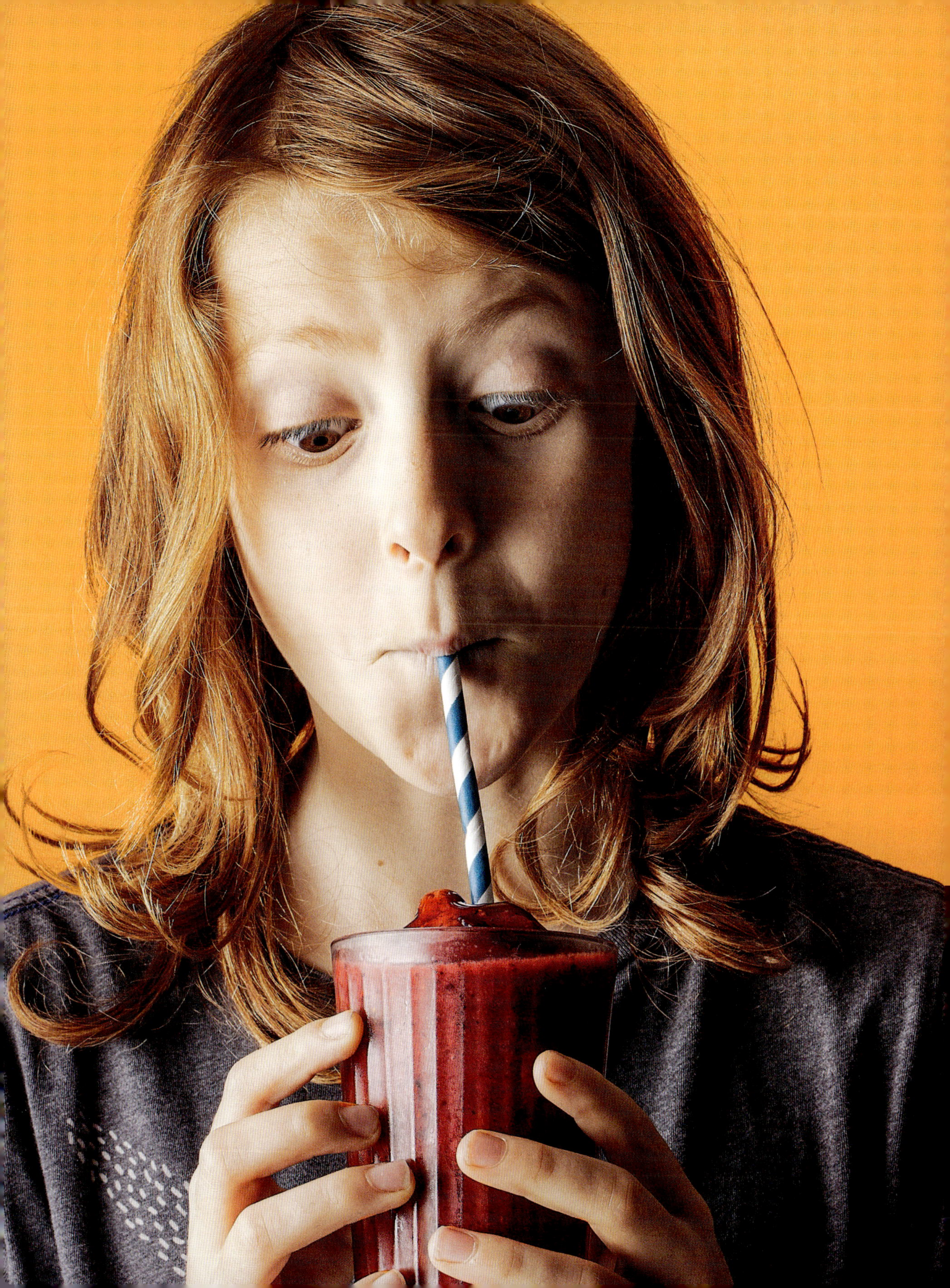

PUMPKIN SPICE

2 cups (500 mL) pumpkin purée
1 cup (250 mL) coconut milk
½ cup (125 mL) yogurt of choice
1 frozen banana or 4 frozen banana chunks
1 Tbsp (15 mL) pumpkin spice

BLUEBERRY SPICE

2 cups (500 mL) frozen blueberries
1 cup (250 mL) almond milk
½ cup (125 mL) yogurt of choice
1 banana or 4 frozen banana chunks
2 tsp (10 mL) ground cinnamon

SUPER GREEN

1½ cups (375 mL) frozen mango
½ cup (125 mL) frozen spinach
½ cup (125 mL) orange juice
½ cup (125 mL) almond milk
½ cup (125 mL) yogurt of choice
1 Tbsp (15 mL) green or blue spirulina powder
1 banana or 4 frozen banana chunks

Georgia Says

I love to add spinach and kale for an extra green kick.

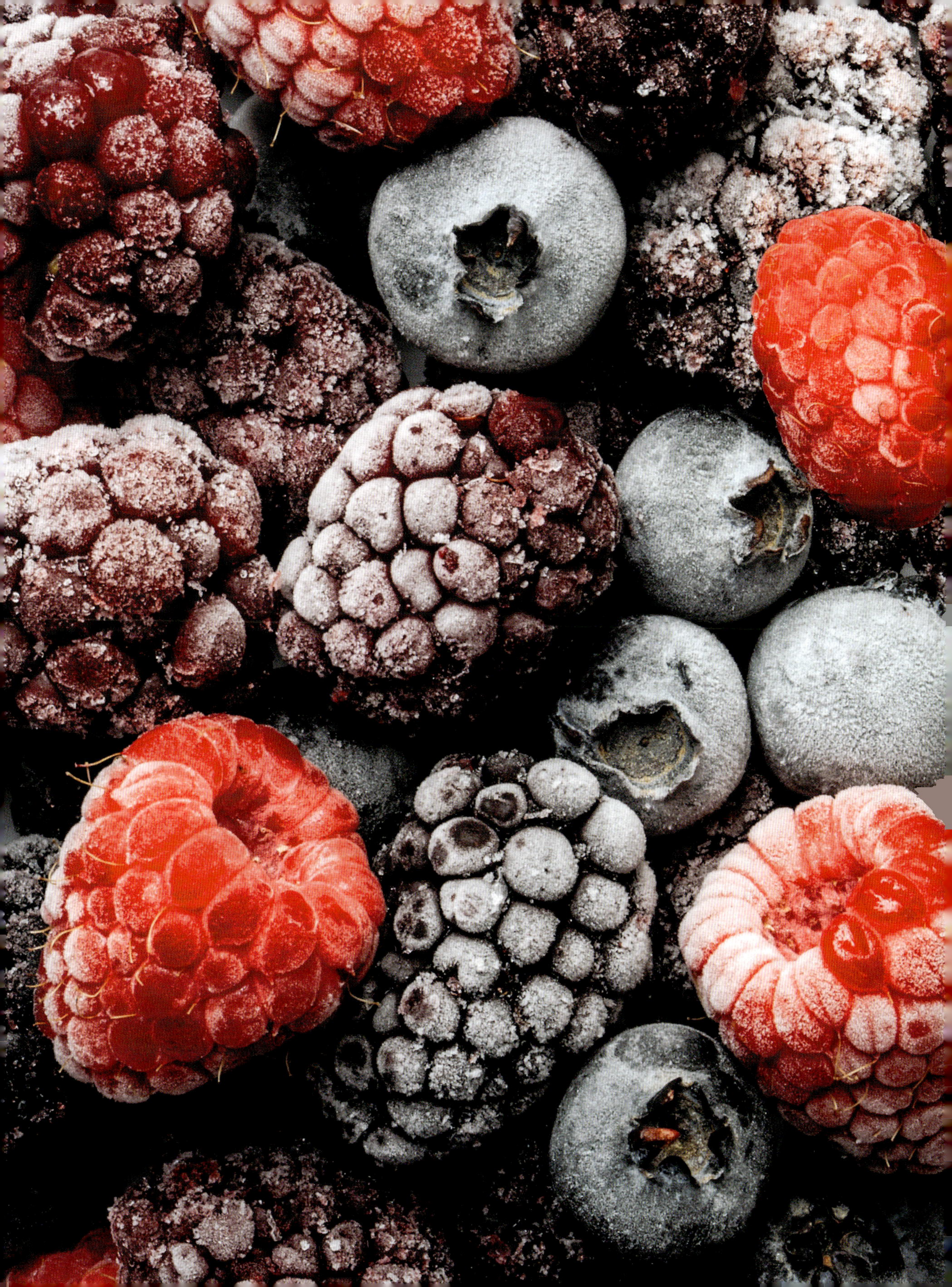

GRANOLA BARS

These bars are quite versatile. We keep a jar of trail mix on the counter for snacking, and right before we refill it, we empty its contents into a **bowl** and make these delicious bars.

MAKES 12 BARS

- ⅓ cup (80 mL) honey
- ¼ cup (60 mL) unsalted butter or coconut oil
- ¼ cup (60 mL) packed brown sugar
- ¼ tsp (1 mL) sea salt (optional)
- ½ tsp (2.5 mL) vanilla extract
- 2½ cups (625 mL) old-fashioned rolled oats
- 1 cup (250 mL) add-ins (chopped nuts, chopped dried fruits like apricot, mango, or dates, seeds like pumpkin or sunflower seeds)
- ½ cup (125 mL) mini chocolate chips (any kind)

Line the bottom of a 9 × 9-inch (23 × 23 cm) baking pan with **parchment paper**.

In a small **pot**, mix the honey, butter, sugar, salt (if using), and vanilla together. Warm over medium heat, stirring frequently, until bubbles start to form and all the sugar is dissolved.

Turn off the heat!

Set the pot aside to cool slightly on a pot holder or cool part of the stove top.

In a large **bowl**, stir the oats with the add-ins and chocolate chips to combine. Pour the honey mixture over the oats and stir well to combine everything.

Transfer the mixture to the prepared pan and spread it all round evenly, getting right into the corners. Place another piece of **parchment** on top and press down firmly for about a minute.

Place in the fridge, uncovered, for at least 2 hours. Remove from the fridge, remove the **parchment**, and cut into 12 equal bars.

These will keep in an airtight **container** at room temperature for up to 1 week.

LET'S EAT

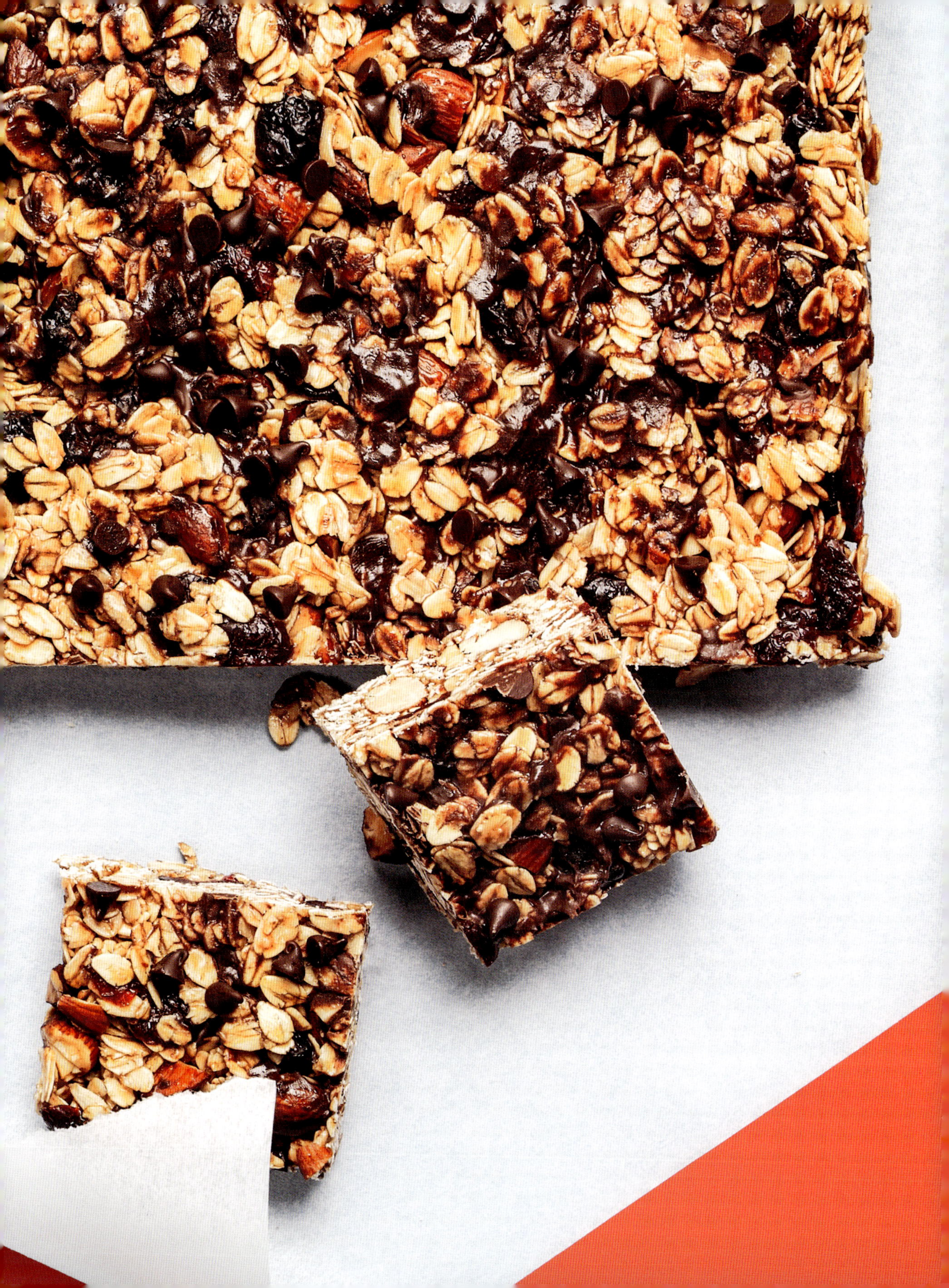

EASY PUFF PASTRIES

These easy Danish-style puff pastries make yummy breakfast snacks. If you can't eat dairy, a cashew-based cream cheese will work just as well as dairy cream cheese.

SERVES 6-8

- 1 cup (250 mL) cream cheese, at room temperature
- ¼ cup (60 mL) ground almonds (optional)
- 2 Tbsp (30 mL) granulated sugar
- 2 cups (500 mL) small-diced fruit (see Try These Toppings!)
- ¼ cup (60 mL) packed brown sugar
- 2 tsp (10 mL) cornstarch
- 1 tsp (5 mL) vanilla extract
- 1 egg
- 1 tsp (5 mL) water
- 1 sheet pre-rolled puff pastry, thawed
- 2 Tbsp (30 mL) icing sugar

Preheat the oven to 400°F (200°C). Line a large cookie sheet with parchment paper.

Using a stand mixer or hand mixer, beat the cream cheese, ground almonds (if using), and granulated sugar in a medium bowl until light and fluffy. Set aside.

Place the fruit, brown sugar, cornstarch, and vanilla in a medium bowl and stir to combine. Set aside.

Using a fork, lightly beat the egg with the water in a small bowl. Set aside.

Place the puff pastry on the prepared cookie sheet and use a knife or pizza cutter to cut it into 12-16 even pieces. Move the pieces so they have at least ½ inch (1.25 cm) of space between them. Using a sharp knife, score a ½-¾-inch (1.25-2 cm) border around each piece with a knife—that means draw on the pastry with a knife without cutting all the way through.

Place about 1½ Tbsp (23 mL) of cream cheese filling on each piece of pastry and use the back of a spoon to spread it lightly, avoiding the border. Top the cream cheese with about 2 Tbsp (30 mL) of fruit filling.

Use a pastry brush to brush the bare borders of each pastry with the egg mixture. Place the cookie sheet on

LET'S EAT

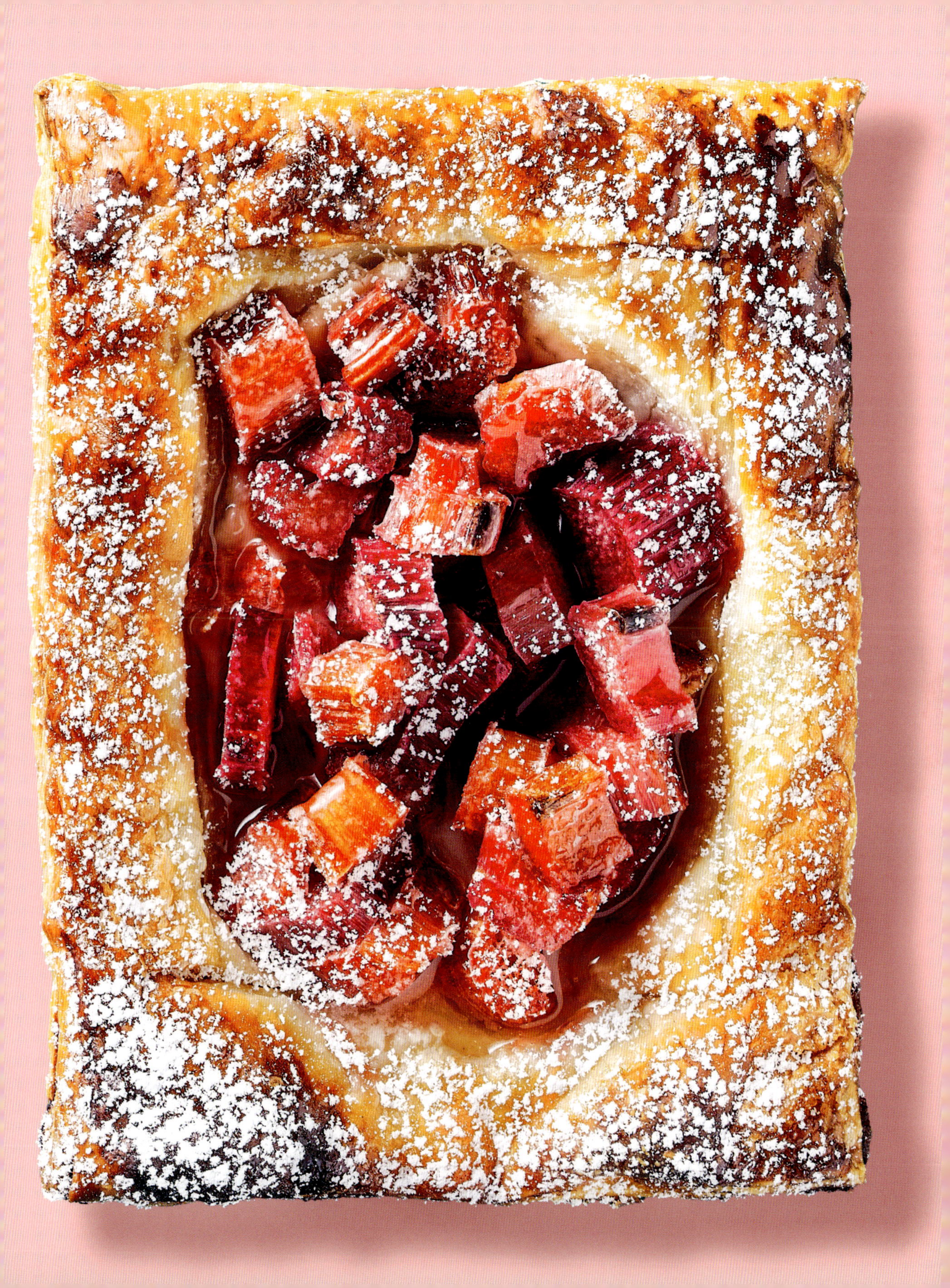

the center rack in the oven and bake until the borders are puffed and golden, 15–18 minutes. Using **oven mitts**, remove the baking sheet from the oven and slide the **parchment paper** with the pastries on it from the cookie sheet onto a **cooling rack**. Turn off the oven. Let the pastries cool for 5 minutes.

Place the icing sugar in a small sieve and shake it over the pastries to dust them.

Try These Toppings!

- You can use apples, cherries, blueberries, rhubarb, or strawberries for the fruit.
- Or skip the fruit and use 1 cup (250 mL) of **shredded** ham and 1 cup (250 mL) of shredded cheese.

Georgia Says

If you don't like cheese, just use the fruit filling on its own.

LET'S EAT

MAGNIFICENT MUFFINS

This recipe is a great base for a multitude of muffin flavors. Blueberry, lemon poppy seed, double chocolate . . . see Mix It Up! for which spices and fruits or chocolate chips to use. Pick your favorites or mix it up day by day. These whip up in about 40 minutes, so they're great for whenever you want a quick snack.

MAKES 12 MUFFINS

2 cups (500 mL) all-purpose flour
1 cup (250 mL) rolled oats
2 tsp (10 mL) baking powder
½ tsp (2.5 mL) baking soda
½ tsp (2.5 mL) sea salt
Spice (see Mix It Up!)
1 cup (250 mL) milk
2 eggs
1 cup (250 mL) unsalted butter, melted
½ cup (125 mL) granulated sugar
Fruit or chocolate chips (see Mix It Up!)

Preheat the oven to 375°F (190°C). **Line** the cups of a 12-cup **muffin pan** with paper liners.

Place the flour, oats, baking powder, baking soda, salt, and spice in a large **bowl** or **stand mixer**. Mix lightly to combine.

Pour the milk into a large measuring cup and add the eggs. Stir with a fork to break up the egg yolks and mix them into the milk. Add the melted butter (it's ok if it's still a bit warm) and give it all a stir to combine.

Pour the wet mixture into the dry mixture and mix on medium speed for 1 minute or stir with a **wooden spoon** until just combined. The mixture will be lumpy and that's ok! Add the sugar and fruit or chocolate chips and stir gently to mix them in.

Spoon the batter evenly into the muffin cups. Place the **muffin pan** on the middle rack in the oven and bake until a toothpick or wooden skewer inserted in the center of a muffin comes out clean and the tops are nicely browned, about 30 minutes. Take the muffins out of the oven.

RISE & SHINE!

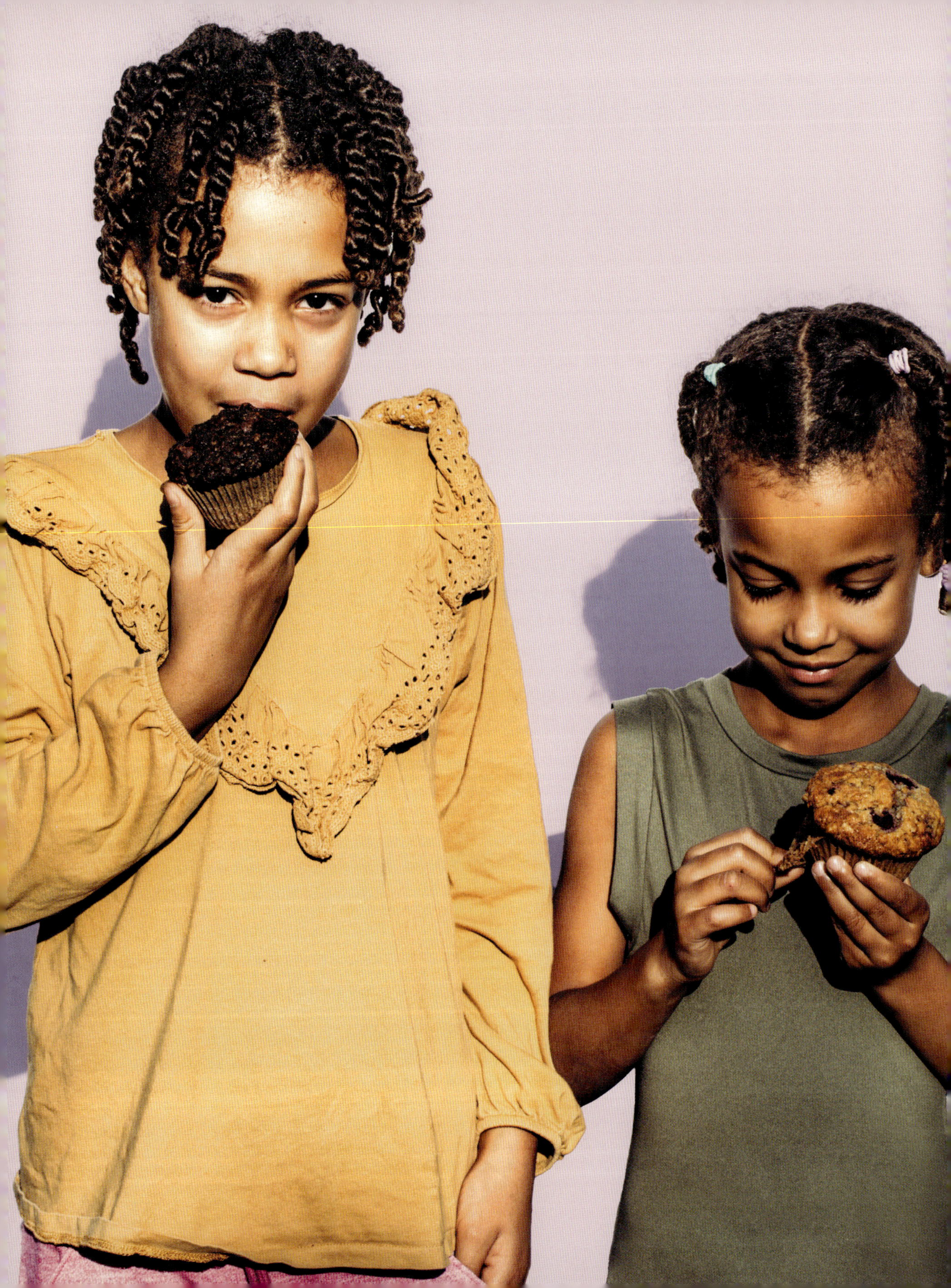

Turn off the oven!

Place the **muffin pan** on a **cooling rack**. Let the muffins cool in the pan for at least 15 minutes before removing.

Muffins will stay fresh in an airtight **container** at room temperature for up to 3 days or you can freeze them in a freezer bag for up to 3 months.

Mix It Up!

BLUEBERRY

2 cups (500 mL) frozen blueberries
1 Tbsp (15 mL) ground ginger

RASPBERRY

2 cups (500 mL) frozen raspberries
1 Tbsp (15 mL) ground cinnamon

PEACH

2 cups (500 mL) medium-**diced** frozen peach slices
2 tsp (10 mL) ground cinnamon
1 tsp (5 mL) ground ginger

DOUBLE CHOCOLATE

1½ cups (375 mL) semisweet chocolate chips
2 Tbsp (30 mL) cocoa powder

LEMON POPPY SEED

¼ cup freshly squeezed lemon juice
2 Tbsp lemon zest
2 Tbsp poppy seeds

Alice Says

The double chocolate muffins are the BEST!

SCONES

Scones are quick and easy and can be made in a gazillion different flavor combinations. Cold unsalted butter is the key to lots of fluffy, light layers. Keep a stick or two in your freezer so that you always have some on hand.

MAKES 8 SCONES

Scones
2 cups (500 mL) all-purpose flour
¼ cup (60 mL) granulated sugar
1 Tbsp (15 mL) baking powder
½ tsp (5 mL) sea salt
½ cup + 1 Tbsp (140 mL) whipping cream (30%–36% fat), plus more for brushing
1 large egg
2 tsp (10 mL) vanilla extract
6 Tbsp (90 mL) unsalted butter, frozen
Extra (see Add These Extras!)
2 Tbsp (30 mL) coarse golden sugar (for sweet scones)

Glaze
1 cup (250 mL) icing sugar
1–2 Tbsp (15–30 mL) milk of choice
1 tsp (5 mL) flavoring of choice (see Add These Extras!)

Preheat the oven to 400°F (200°C). Line a large cookie sheet with parchment paper.

Place the flour, granulated sugar, baking powder, and salt in a large mixing bowl and mix together.

In a separate bowl, whisk together the cream, egg, and vanilla until fully combined. Add the wet ingredients to the dry ingredients and stir lightly to combine. Use a box grater to grate the frozen butter into the mixture. Add any extras you want to use and stir again to combine all of the ingredients. You should see the pieces of butter in the dough. These are what make the deliciously fluffy layers!

Lightly flour your work surface. Dump the dough mixture out onto the flour and pull the dough together to form a ball. Flatten the ball with your hands into a 7-inch (18 cm) circle. Use a knife to cut the dough like a pizza into 8 slices and place the pieces on the prepared cookie sheet, leaving at least 1 inch (2.5 cm) between them.

LET'S EAT

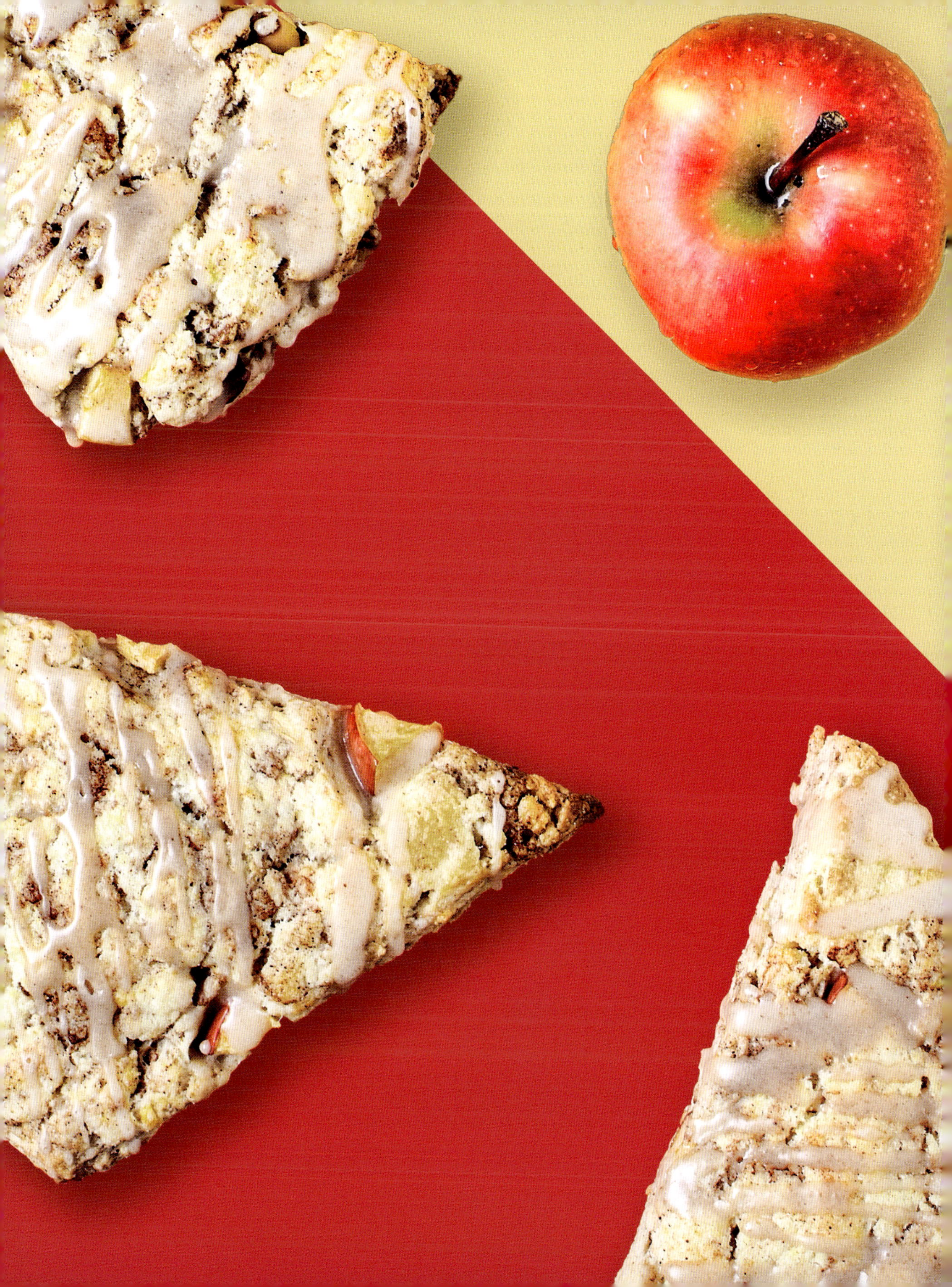

Place the **cookie sheet** in the freezer for 5–10 minutes to recool the butter. Trust us, this makes for GREAT scones.

Take the **cookie sheet** out of the freezer and use a **pastry brush** to brush some whipping cream across the tops of the scones. You'll need about 2 Tbsp (30 mL) of cream for this. If you're making sweet scones, sprinkle slightly less than 1 tsp (5 mL) of coarse golden sugar over top each scone.

Bake until the tops are lightly browned, approximately 18–22 minutes. You can break one open to check and see if they are done. The inside should feel nice and moist but not be doughy or wet. Using **oven mitts**, remove from the oven.

Turn off the oven!

Slide the **parchment paper** and scones onto a **cooling rack** to cool. If you're using a glaze, **whisk** the icing sugar with the milk and flavoring and pour over the cooled scones.

You can freeze the unglazed scones in an airtight freezer bag for up to 3 months, and glazed scones can be kept at room temperature in an airtight **container** for up to 5 days.

William Says

I like to eat scones with plenty of butter and jam, or just some good quality molasses!

LET'S EAT

Add These Extras!

DRIED FRUIT

Mix in 1 cup (250 mL) of dried berries (blueberries, currants, raisins, cherries) and 1 tsp (5 mL) of ground cinnamon. Make the glaze with maple syrup as flavoring.

FRESH BERRY

Add 1 cup (250 mL) fresh berries to the scone mix. Make the glaze with orange juice as flavoring.

APPLE CINNAMON

Using a **vegetable peeler**, peel and core a fresh, crispy apple, then cut it into small **dice**. Mix in 1 cup (250 mL) of the apple pieces and 1 Tbsp (15 mL) ground cinnamon. Make the glaze with maple syrup as flavoring.

LEMON POPPY SEED

Zest 1 medium, organic lemon. Mix in the zest along with 2 tsp (10 mL) poppy seeds. Make the glaze with lemon juice as flavoring.

CHEESE AND HERB

Omit the sugar and add 1 cup (250 mL) of cheddar cheese instead. Add 1 Tbsp (15 mL) of fresh chopped herbs like rosemary, thyme, or oregano for seasoning. Skip the glaze.

CRANBERRY ORANGE

Zest 1 medium orange. Mix in 1 Tbsp (15 mL) of the zest along with 1 cup (250 mL) of sweetened dried cranberries. Make the glaze with orange juice as flavoring.

CHOCOLATE

Mix in 1 cup (250 mL) semisweet, milk, or white chocolate chips and 1 tsp (5 mL) cocoa powder. Make the glaze with vanilla as flavoring.

PUMPKIN SPICE

Reduce the whipping cream to ¼ cup (60 mL). Mix in ¼ cup (60 mL) pumpkin purée and 1 Tbsp (15 mL) of pumpkin spice seasoning. Make the glaze with maple syrup as flavoring.

RISE & SHINE!

QUICK JAM

You can stir up this jam in minutes and keep it in an airtight **container** in the fridge for up to 3 weeks, or in the freezer for up to 3 months. If you're using fresh fruit, wash it, remove any pits, and then peel and roughly chop the fruit. If you're using frozen, simply measure it from the bag. This jam does not have any preservatives in it, and it's not canned, so it can't sit on your shelf unopened for months at a time.

MAKES ABOUT 2 CUPS (500 ML) OF JAM

1 lb (450 g) fresh or frozen fruit
1 cup (250 mL) granulated sugar
1 Tbsp (15 mL) lemon juice

In a medium **pot**, combine the fruit with the sugar and lemon juice and cook over medium-high heat, stirring regularly. Remove from the heat once all the fruit has broken down and the mixture has thickened, about 20 minutes. It will thicken more as it cools.

Turn off the stove.

Carefully pour the jam into a clean 8 oz (1 cup/250 mL) mason jar and let stand at room temperature for an hour until it is cool enough to place in the fridge. Seal with a lid and store in the fridge for up to 3 weeks or the freezer for up to 3 months. Use within 10 days once opened.

Chloë Says

Spreading the jam is SO ASMR!

LET'S EAT

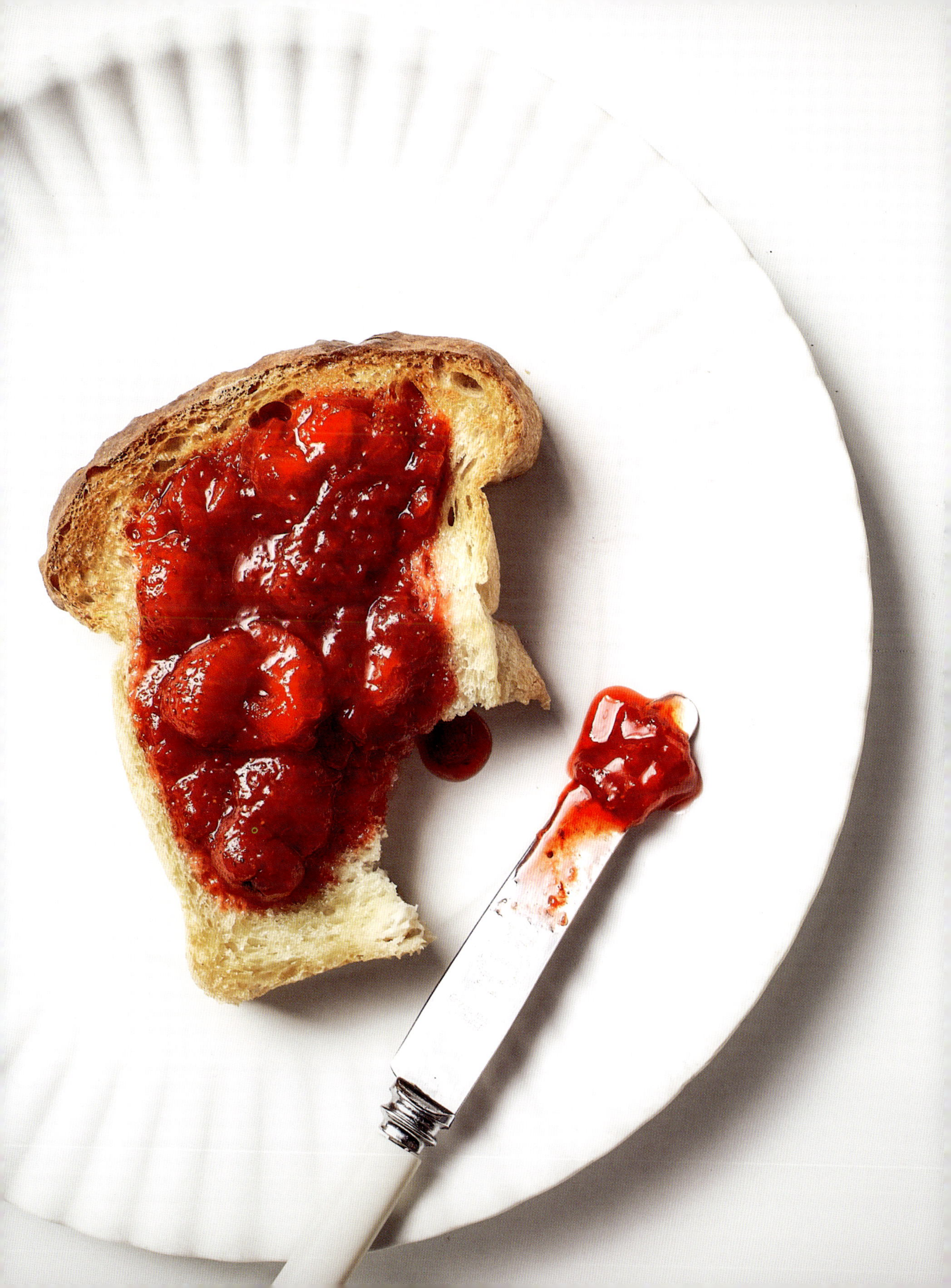

AVOCADO TOAST

This recipe can easily be doubled or tripled. Avocado toast makes a great after-school snack or weekend lunch, and throw a fried egg on it and BAM!—breakfast is served! Quartering the avocado makes it easier to remove the pit.

SERVES 2

1 ripe avocado
Sea salt and freshly ground black pepper
1 Tbsp (15 mL) lemon or lime juice (1 lemon or lime)
2 slices of bread
Handful of toppings

Quarter the avocado and remove the seed. Scoop the avocado flesh into a shallow **bowl**. Use a fork to mash it up until it's chunky and a bit creamy. Season **to taste** with salt, pepper, and lemon or lime juice (you may not want to use the full 1 Tbsp/15 mL we've listed, or you may want to use a bit more).

Toast the bread to your desired consistency. Place it on a plate and divide the avocado between both slices of bread. Add your chosen toppings and serve.

Try These Toppings!

- Sliced tomatoes
- A fried egg
- Sliced ham
- Bacon
- Smoked salmon
- Sesame seeds
- Chili flakes
- Taco seasoning

Félix Says

Ew, avocados . . . *stops to think* . . . unless it's with taco seasoning; then it tastes like tacos!

LET'S EAT

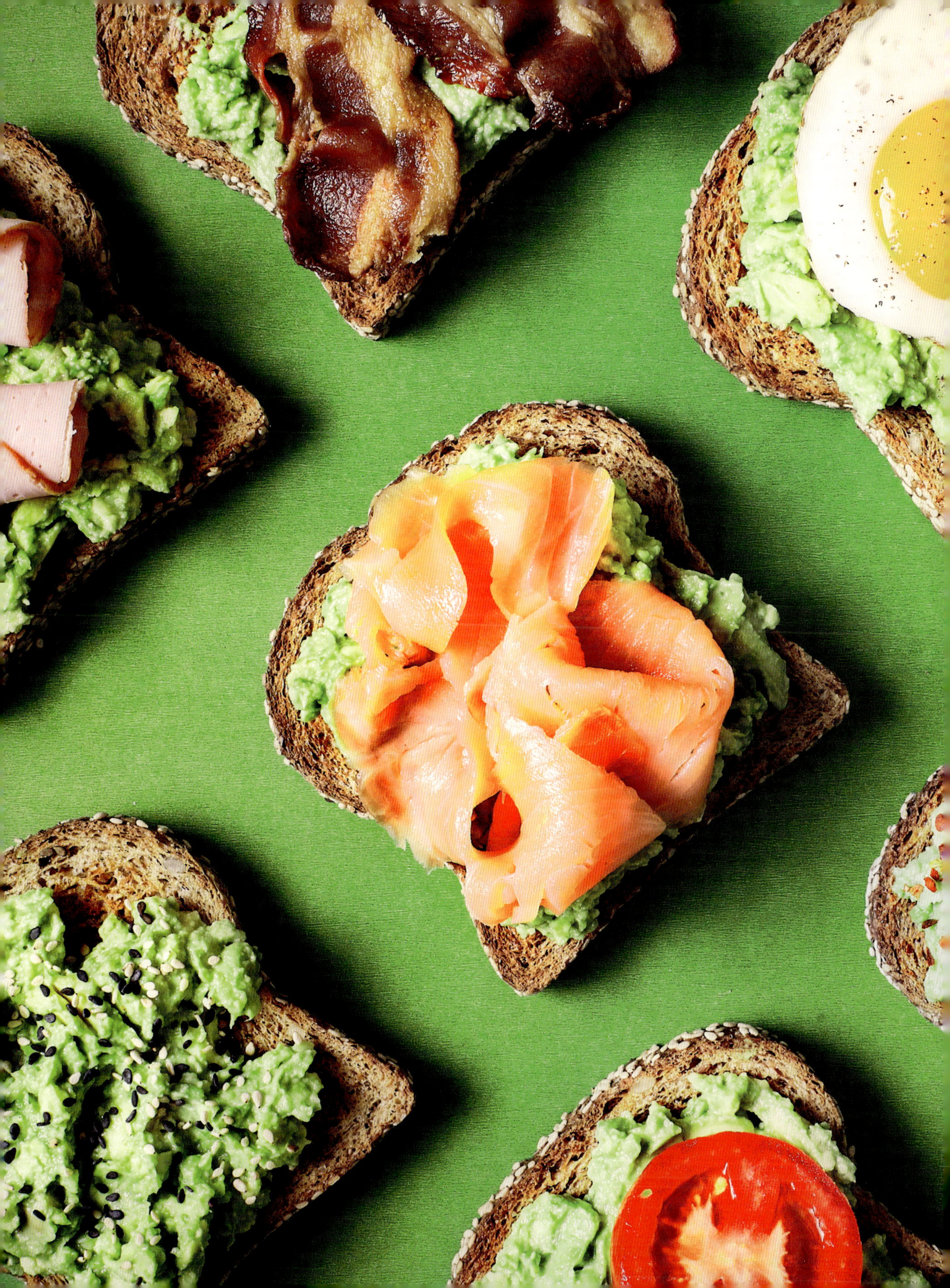

PANCAKES

An **electric griddle** is a wonderful tool for making pancakes as it will let you make five to six at once. You can, of course, make them in a **frying pan** on the stove, but it will take you a bit longer. Extra pancakes can be frozen and then reheated in the toaster. Or you can bottle the extra batter and keep it in the fridge to make pancakes the next day.

SERVES 4

- 1½ cups (375 mL) all-purpose flour
- 1 tsp (5 mL) baking powder
- 1 tsp (5 mL) baking soda
- ½ tsp (2.5 mL) sea salt
- 1½ cups (375 mL) whole milk or buttermilk
- 2 large eggs
- 2 Tbsp (30 mL) olive oil
- 1 tsp (5 mL) vanilla extract
- Cooking oil, for the frying pan
- 2 cups (500 mL) tasty extras, if using (see Add These Extras!)
- Butter and maple syrup, for serving

Preheat the oven to 200°F (95°C). **Line** a **cookie sheet** with **parchment paper**.

In a **mixing bowl**, combine the flour, baking powder, baking soda, and salt. **Whisk** in the milk, eggs, olive oil, vanilla, and your filling of choice, if using (see Switch Up the Flavor!). The batter should be slightly lumpy, not perfectly smooth. Let the batter sit at room temperature for at least 10 minutes and up to 30 minutes before you make the pancakes.

Heat a large **frying pan** over medium-low heat on the stove or set your **griddle** pan to medium-low. Coat the pan or griddle with just enough oil so that the surface is shiny but not so much that there is a pool of oil. You don't want to deep-fry the pancakes. Use a ½-cup (125 mL) measuring cup to scoop the batter out of the **bowl** and pour it in the pan. Let the pancakes sit for one minute and then add ¼ cup (60 mL) of any extras (if using) to each pancake. Let the pancakes cook until the edges start to look done and bubbles form across the entire pancake, about 2–3 minutes per side. Flip the pancakes over and cook on the other side.

Place the pancakes on the prepared cookie sheet and keep them warm in the oven until you're ready to serve them.

Turn off the oven and the stove!

Serve the pancakes with butter and maple syrup.

LET'S EAT

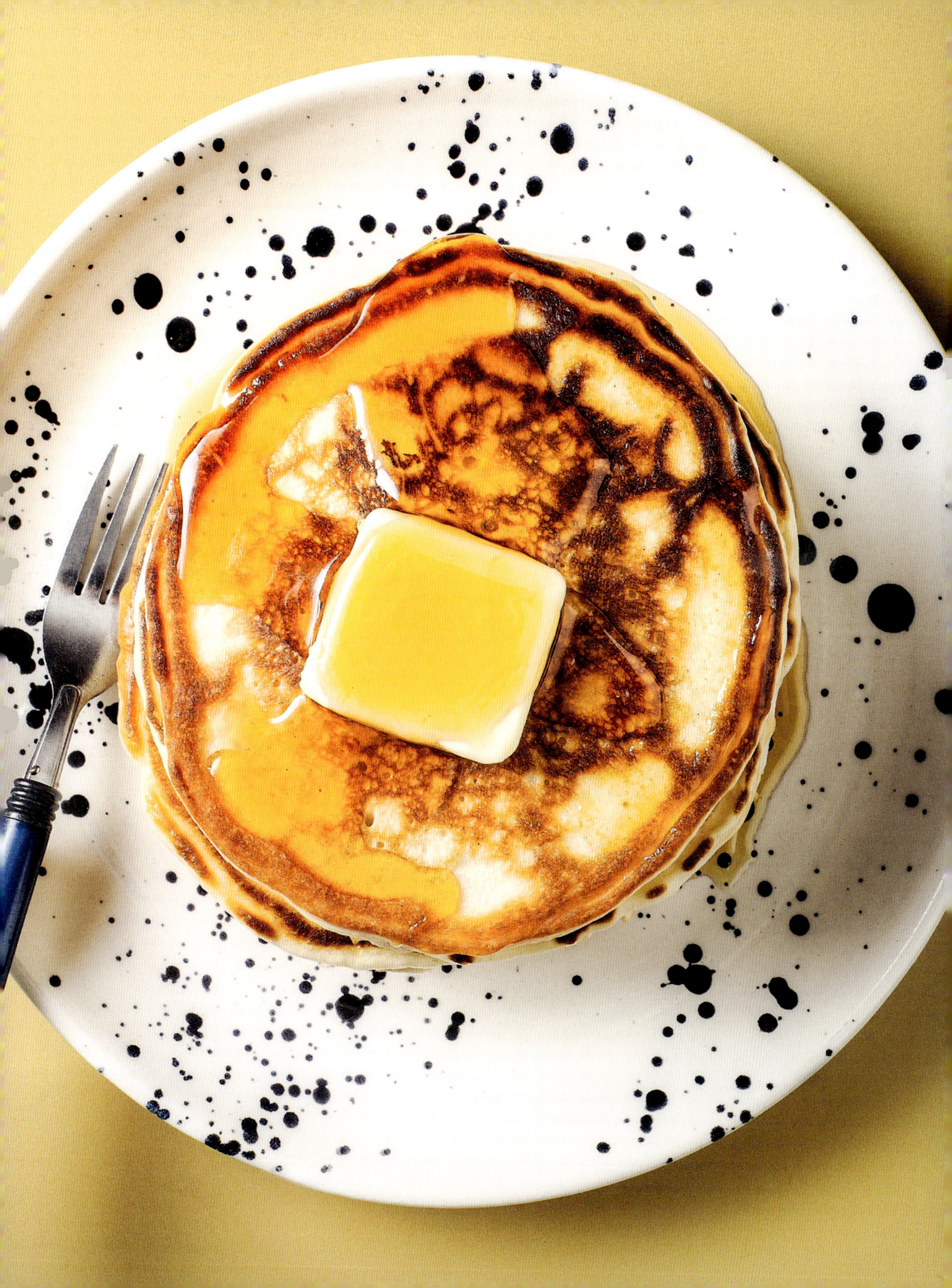

Add These Extras!

2 cups (500 mL) fresh blueberries
2 cups (500 mL) sliced strawberries
2 cups (500 mL) chocolate chips
2 cups (500 mL) banana slices

Switch Up the Flavor!

LEMON RICOTTA

Add ¼ cup (60 mL) ricotta, 1 Tbsp (15 mL) lemon zest, and 1 Tbsp (15 mL) freshly squeezed lemon juice to the wet ingredients.

PUMPKIN SPICE

Add ¼ cup (60 mL) pumpkin purée and 1 Tbsp (15 mL) pumpkin spice to the wet ingredients.

DOUBLE CHOCOLATE

Add ¼ cup (60 mL) cocoa to the dry ingredients and use 1 cup (250 mL) semisweet, milk, or white chocolate chips as your tasty extras.

FRENCH TOAST

French toast is a family favorite in our house, and every so often it makes an appearance for dinner. Félix started his cooking adventures by learning how to make this classic breakfast item, a task that was made even easier with the use of an electric griddle.

SERVES 2-4

4 eggs
¼ cup (60 mL) milk of choice
½ tsp (2.5 mL) vanilla extract
½ tsp (2.5 mL) ground cinnamon
Pinch of sea salt
2 Tbsp (30 mL) unsalted butter, divided
8 slices of bread (while brioche works well here, any bread will do!)
Maple syrup, jam, or honey, for topping
Toppings (see Try These Toppings!)

In a shallow **bowl**, use a fork to **whisk** the eggs, milk, vanilla, cinnamon, and salt until combined.

On an **electric griddle** or in a large non-stick **frying pan**, melt 1 Tbsp (15 mL) of the butter for every 2 slices of bread over medium heat. Place 2 slices of bread in the egg mixture and let the mixture soak for a few seconds. Place the eggy bread in the pan. Cook until each side is golden brown, 2-3 minutes per side.

Remove from the pan and set aside on a plate. Continue until all the bread is cooked.

Turn off the stove!

Top with maple syrup, jam, or honey and any additional toppings.

Try These Toppings!

Use about ¼ cup (60 mL) of toppings in total for every 2 pieces of French toast:

- Fruits like berries, sliced bananas, and sliced peaches
- Crushed nuts
- Unsalted butter
- Icing sugar
- Whipped cream

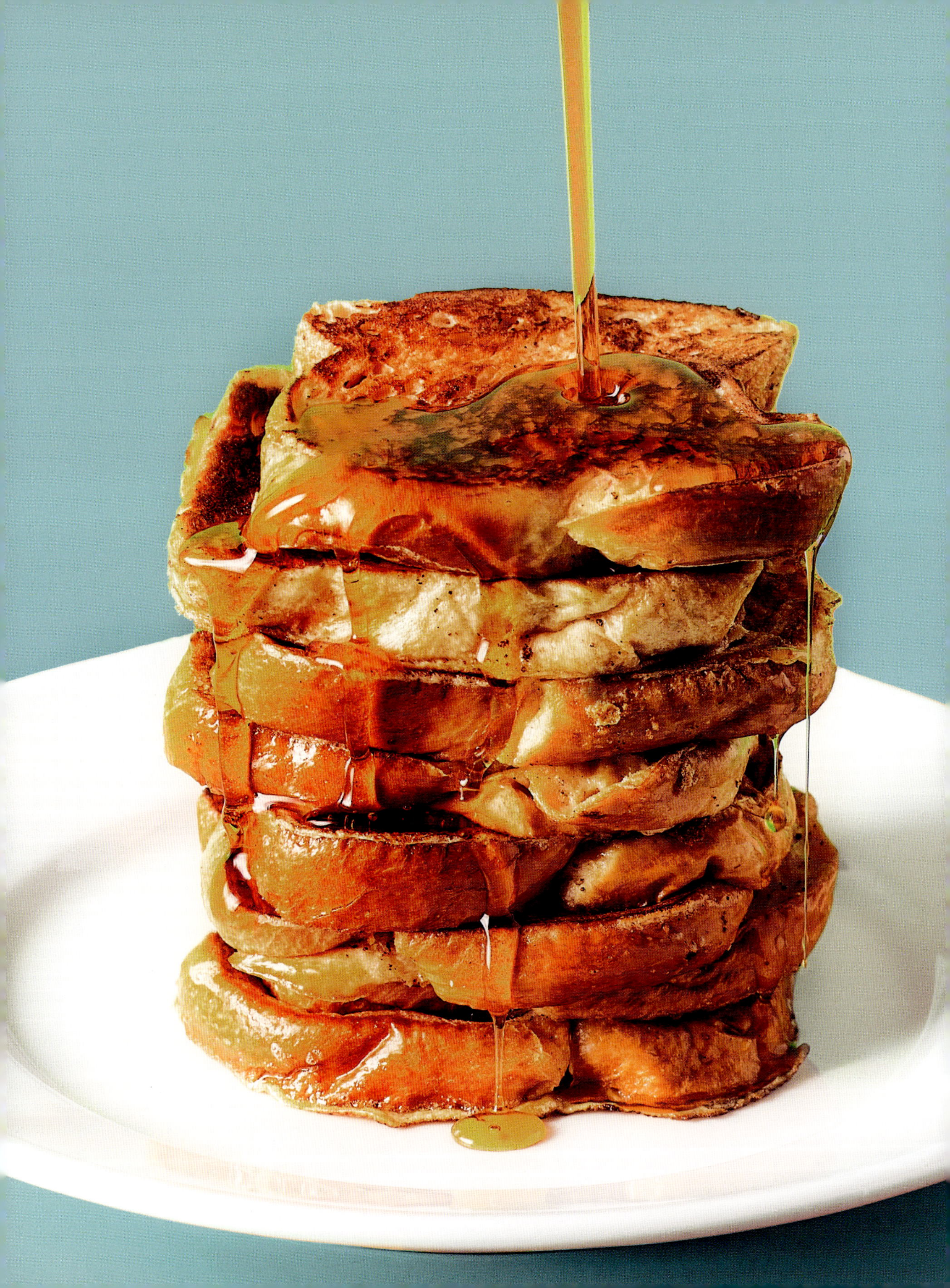

Take It to the Next Level!

STUFFED FRENCH TOAST

You can level up your French toast by stuffing two pieces with jam and then dipping them in your egg mixture. When you cut into the middle, you'll have a warm, sweet surprise!

SERVES 2-4

4 eggs
¼ cup (60 mL) milk of choice
½ tsp (2.5 mL) vanilla extract
½ tsp (2.5 mL) ground cinnamon
Pinch of sea salt
8 slices of bread (while brioche works well here, any bread will do!)
8 Tbsp (120 mL) jam or 4 tsp (20 mL) granulated sugar + 4 tsp (20 mL) ground cinnamon
2 Tbsp (30 mL) unsalted butter, **divided**
Maple syrup, jam, or honey, for topping
Toppings (see Try These Toppings!)

In a shallow **bowl**, use a fork to **whisk** the eggs, milk, vanilla, cinnamon, and salt until combined.

Cut the crusts off the bread and use a **rolling pin** to roll out the bread slightly. You want all the slices to be a similar size. Place 2 Tbsp (30 mL) of jam or 1 tsp (5 mL) of sugar and 1 tsp (5 mL) ground cinnamon together in the center of 4 of the slices, leaving a border around each slice, and place another slice on top. Pinch the sides and seal all around the bread. Dip the sandwiches in the egg mixture and cook over medium heat for about 2 minutes per side.

Turn off the stove!

Top with maple syrup, jam, or honey and any additional toppings.

Félix Says

The best part is adding strawberries and whipped cream with the maple syrup!

RISE & SHINE!

WAFFLES

Some people wonder what the difference between pancakes and waffles is. Really, it's in the way the eggs are handled. In pancakes, you whip everything up together; in waffles, you separate the eggs and whip the whites into a fluffy cloud that gives waffles their "crispy on the outside, light and fluffy on the inside" awesomeness. You'll need a **waffle iron** to make these.

SERVES 6 (2 WAFFLES EACH)

2 cups (500 mL) all-purpose flour
1 Tbsp (15 mL) brown sugar
1 tsp baking powder
1 tsp baking soda
Pinch of sea salt
6 eggs
1 Tbsp (15 mL) granulated sugar
2⅓ cups (580 mL) milk
½ cup (125 mL) unsalted butter, melted and cooled

Place the flour, brown sugar, baking powder, baking soda, and salt in a large **mixing bowl** and stir to combine.

Separate the eggs. The easiest way to do this is to have three **bowls** ready and break an egg cleanly into one of them. Then place your hand over another bowl, palm facing up. Pour the egg from the dish into your cupped hand so that you catch the yolk and let the whites fall through your fingers into a bowl. Place the yolk in one of the waiting bowls and then pour the whites into your **stand mixer** or a large bowl. Repeat for all 6 eggs.

Whisk the egg whites and granulated sugar together in a **stand mixer** or with an electric **whisk** until you reach **stiff peaks**.

Use a hand **whisk** to mix the egg yolks into the milk and add the melted butter. Add all of this to the dry ingredients and give it all a stir. It should look a lot like pancake batter.

Scoop the stiff egg whites into the batter and **fold** them in so that the batter is light and fluffy and you can still see streaks of the whites. You don't want them to disappear.

Follow the directions for your **waffle iron** to cook the waffles. Be sure to unplug the iron when you're done.

Store any extra waffles in a freezer bag or other airtight **container** in the freezer.

LET'S EAT

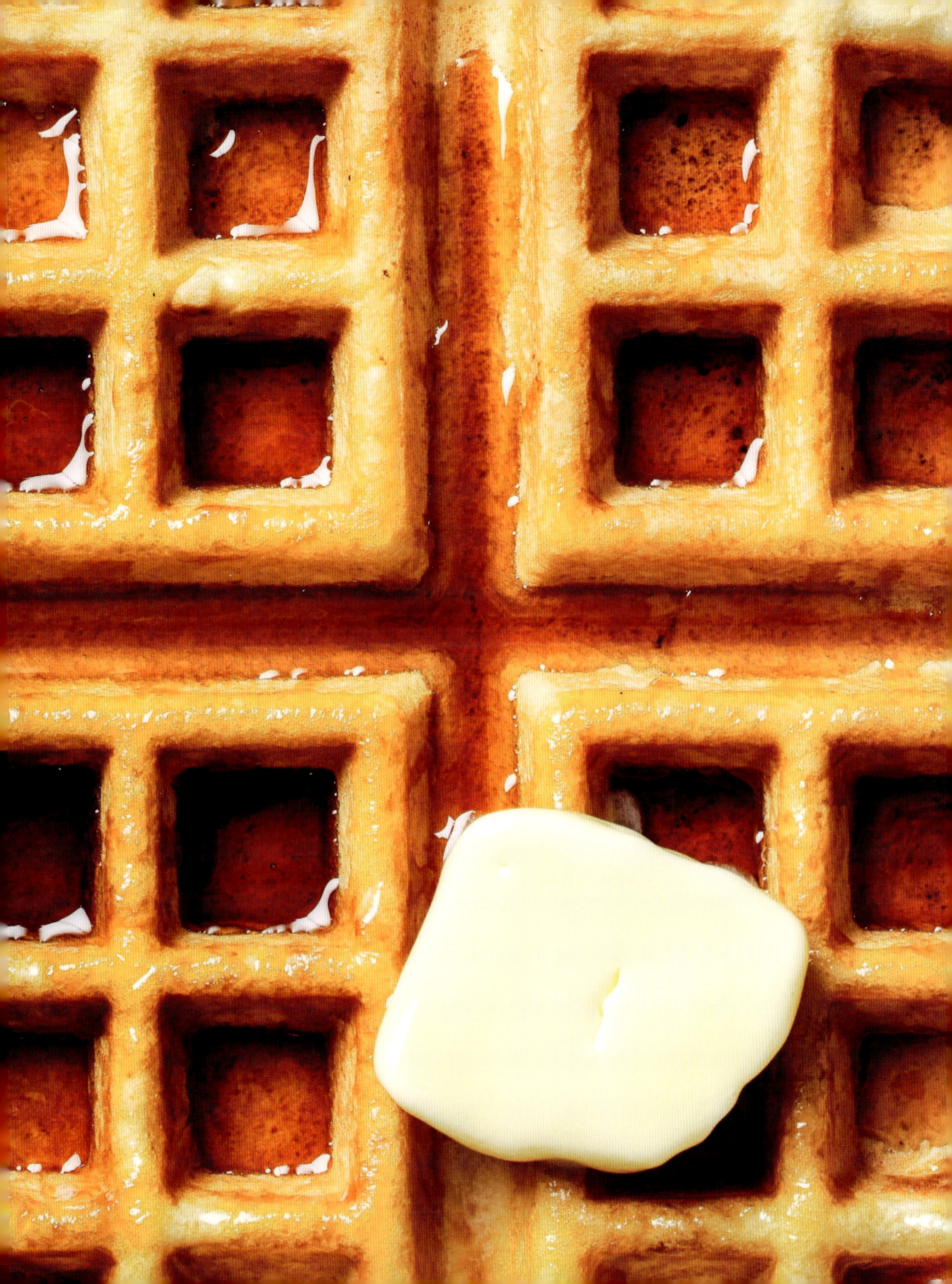

Switch Up the Flavor!

CHOCOLATE

Add 2 Tbsp (30 mL) cocoa powder to your flour mixture.

CHEESE

Remove the sugars and add 1 cup (250 mL) of **grated** cheddar or Swiss cheese to your batter before **folding** in the egg whites. These are awesome topped with a fried egg (page 33), Pajama Pants Pulled Pork (page 170), or Roast Chicken (page 45).

RAINBOW

You can make the waffles all one color by adding a few drops of food coloring to the mix before **folding** in the egg whites OR you can get creative! Try dividing the batter out into a few smaller **bowls** before you fold in the egg whites and mixing in a few drops of different-colored food coloring into each. Divide the egg whites across those bowls and fold in. When you're placing the batter into the **waffle iron**, add different-colored scoops together to create a rainbow of color inside.

William Says

If you keep leftover waffles in the freezer, you can pop them into the toaster and have warm waffles whenever you want.

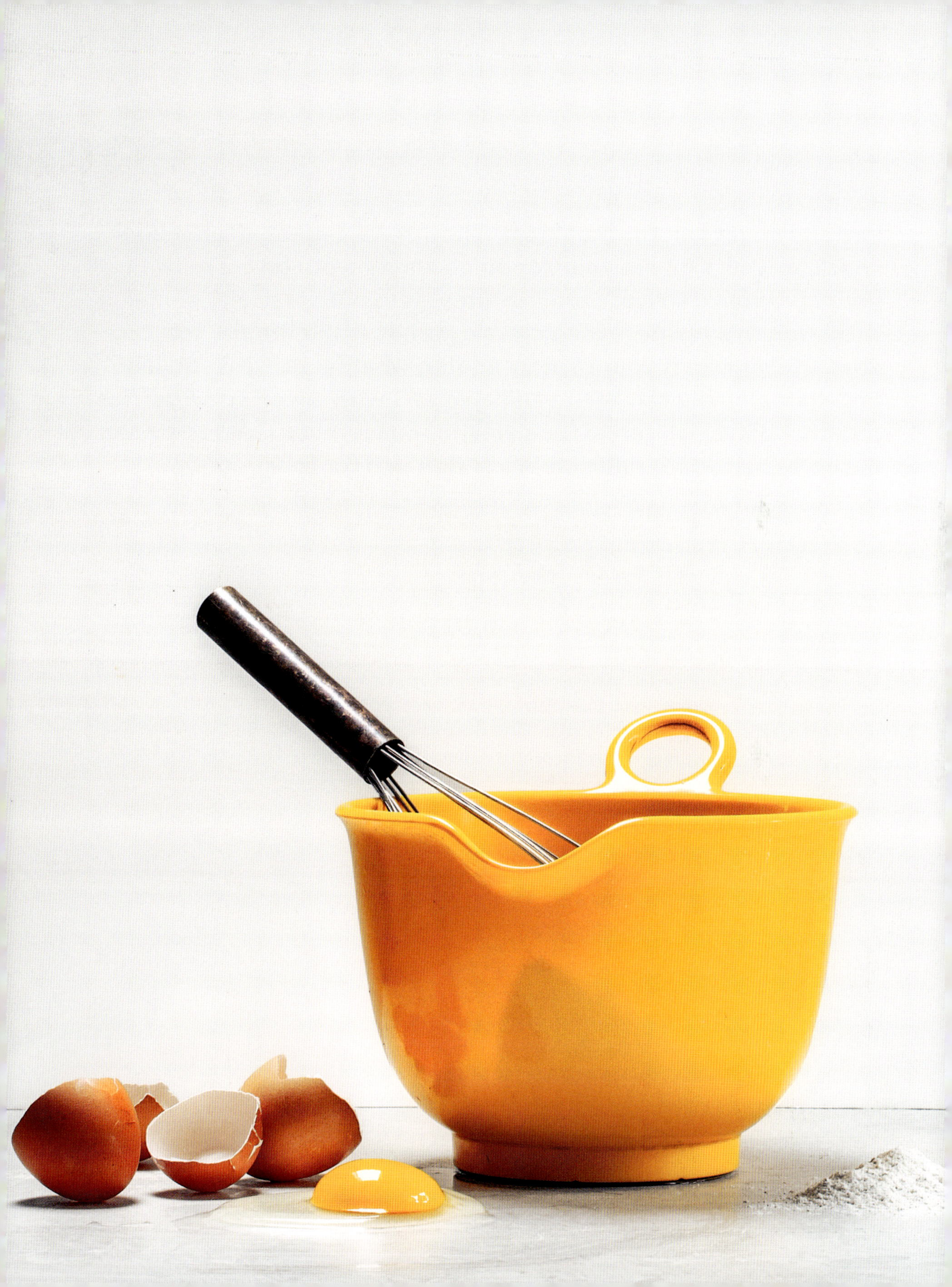

YOGURT PARFAITS

Parfaits aren't just for breakfast. They make a great after-school snack as well. Choose your toppings and fill your layers with your favorite fresh and crunchy bites—let your creativity shine! Although this recipe is for a classic parfait with granola, you can absolutely make it your own by adding whatever cereal you like. For example, you can layer vanilla yogurt with sliced strawberries and chocolate rice cereal for a Neapolitan combo. This recipe can easily be halved for one serving or doubled for four servings.

MAKES 2 PARFAITS

- 2 cups (500 mL) yogurt of choice
- 1 cup (250 mL) granola or muesli
- 1 cup (250 mL) prepared fresh fruit of choice or Quick Jam (page 72)

In two tall glasses, start layering by adding ¼ cup (60 mL) of yogurt, then 2 Tbsp (30 mL) cereal and 2 Tbsp (30 mL) fruit or jam. Repeat the process for the remaining ingredients, ending with fruit.

If you're using plain yogurt and want to add some sweetness, add 2 tsp (10 mL) of honey, maple syrup, or jam to each layer of yogurt.

Berries work well for the fruit layer, as do stone fruits like peaches and apricots cut into a medium **dice** (if you're using frozen fruit, dice it and then let it thaw before adding to the parfaits).

Chloë Says

Creating the layers is so satisfying!

LET'S EAT

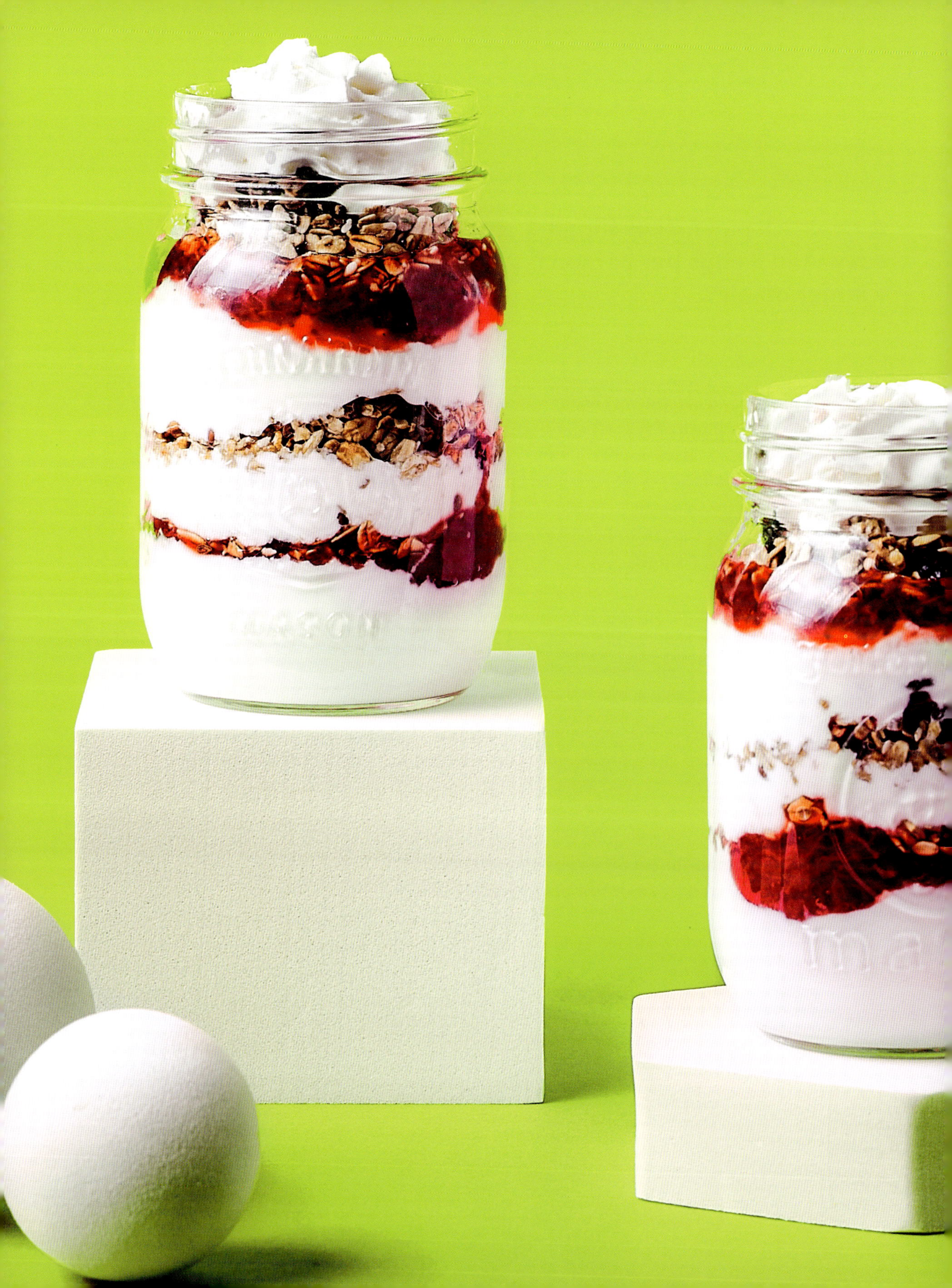

OMELETS

A nonstick pan makes flipping omelets super easy. Add 3 eggs per person if you want to make a larger omelet.

SERVES 2

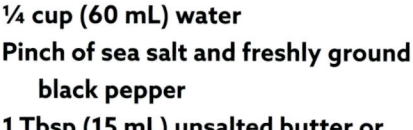

4 eggs
¼ cup (60 mL) water
Pinch of sea salt and freshly ground black pepper
1 Tbsp (15 mL) unsalted butter or olive oil
⅔ cup (165 mL) filling (see Favorite Fillings!)

Crack the eggs and place them in a medium mixing bowl. Add the water, salt, and pepper. Whisk with a fork until well combined and frothy.

Place a medium nonstick frying pan over medium-low heat and add the butter or oil. When the butter is melted, or the oil is hot, add the eggs. Let them sit for a minute for the bottom to set. Then, using a rubber or wooden spatula, gently gather the eggs toward the center of the pan, tilting it around to fill any gaps in the egg mixture.

When the center is still a bit runny, add your fillings evenly across the omelet. Let it cook for another minute or two or just until any cheese begins to melt and the eggy surface has solidified.

Fold the omelet in half and cook for another minute to melt the cheese and heat the fillings inside. Slide the omelet onto a plate and turn off the heat. If you aren't comfortable with folding the omelet in half, simply place a tight-fitting lid on the frying pan and cook on low heat until the center of the omelet is cooked.

Turn off the stove!

Favorite Fillings!

- Cubed ham
- Grated cheese
- Fried onions
- Tomatoes
- Spinach
- Cream cheese
- Smoked salmon
- Fresh herbs

LET'S EAT

Félix Says

These are fun as you don't have to add veggies to them!

SWEET OR SAVORY BREAD PUDDING

Bread pudding is a super-versatile dish that can be either sweet or savory. Prepare a savory version—called a Strata—the night before you want to eat it and just pop it into the oven an hour before breakfast, or go for a sweet pudding that you can prepare in the morning and bake for dessert while dinner is on the table.

SERVES 6-8

Basic recipe
1 (12 oz/340 g) loaf French bread
10 large eggs
3 cups (750 mL) milk
1 tsp (5 mL) sea salt
Sweet or savory flavorings

Sweet
½ cup (125 mL) granulated sugar
2 tsp (10 mL) vanilla extract
2 cups (500 mL) extras (see Switch Up the Flavor!)

Savory
1 Tbsp (15 mL) Dijon mustard
1 clove garlic, minced
1 cup (250 mL) grated cheese
3 cups (750 mL) extras (see Switch Up the Flavor!)
Olive oil or unsalted butter, to grease the pan

LET'S EAT

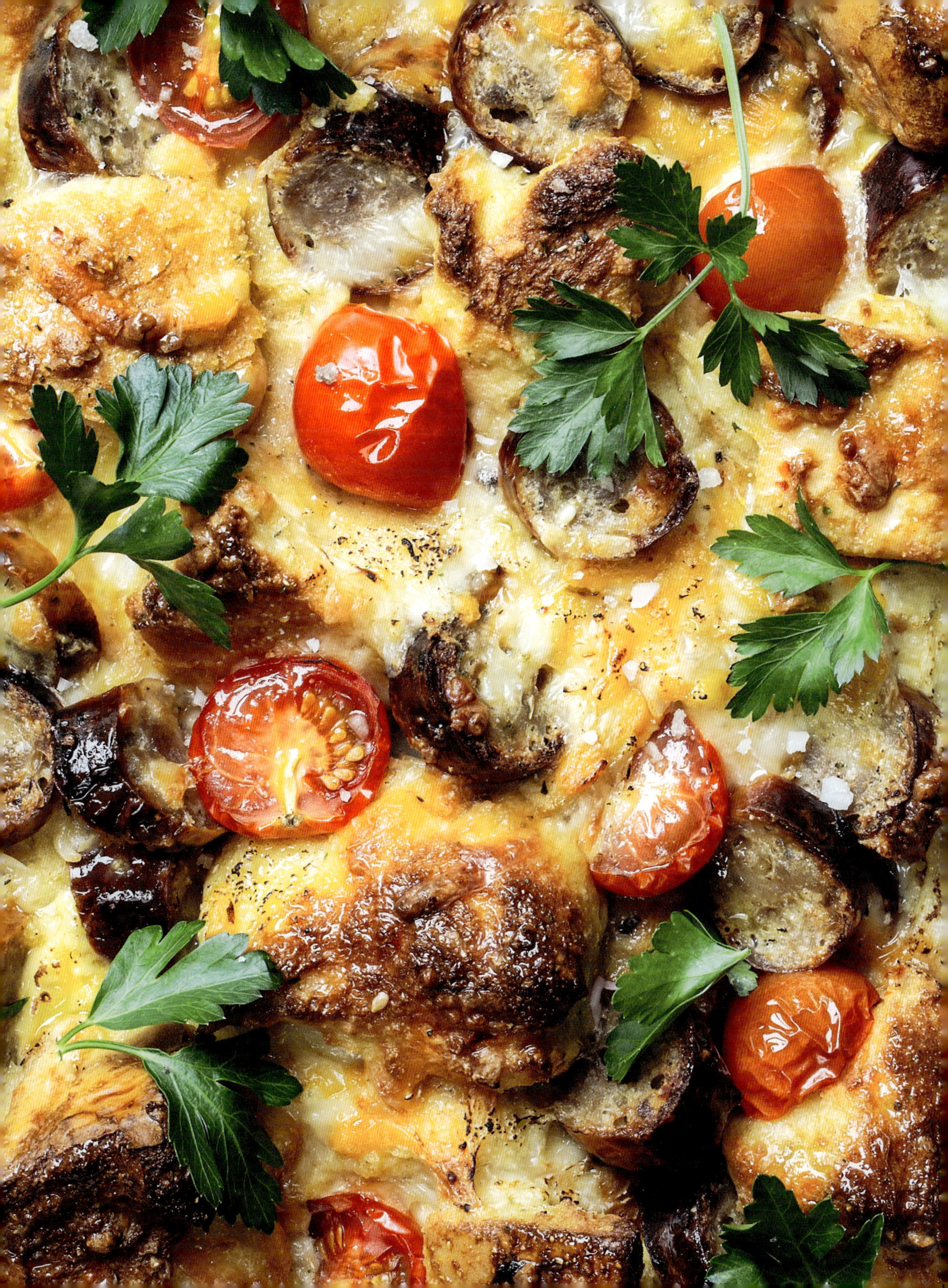

Tear the bread into 1-inch (2.5 cm) chunks and set aside.

Crack the eggs and place them in the **bowl** of a **stand mixer**. Add the milk and salt and, using the **whisk** attachment, **whisk** on high for 2–3 minutes or until the mixture is really whipped up and has become light yellow and very frothy. Remove the bowl from the mixer, add your flavorings and extras of choice and the bread chunks, and give the mixture a stir by hand so that everything is mixed in.

If you don't have a **stand mixer**, you can use a hand **whisk** to beat the eggs, milk, and sea salt together in a **mixing bowl**. **Whisk** for 3–4 minutes or until the mixture gets frothy and turns a pale yellow. Add the flavorings, extras, and bread chunks and give another stir to bring it all together.

Cover the **bowl** with plastic wrap and place in the fridge for at least 1 hour and up to overnight.

When you're ready to bake, preheat the oven to 350°F (180°C). Grease a 9 × 13-inch (23 × 33 cm) **baking dish** with olive oil or butter.

Pour your mixture into the dish and bake, uncovered, until the top is golden brown and the center is completely cooked through, 50–60 minutes. You can check for doneness by inserting a wooden skewer or knife in the center. If it comes out clean, the pudding is ready. If it's not cooked, pop it back in the oven for another 10 minutes and check again. Using **oven mitts**, remove from the oven.

Turn off the oven!

Let the dish cool on the counter for 5 minutes before serving.

Serve sweet bread pudding with your ice cream of choice. Serve savory bread pudding with ketchup, HP sauce, or your hot sauce of choice.

Switch Up the Flavor!

SWEET

If you have large ingredients like apples, cut them into medium **dice** before measuring them and mixing them in. Feel free to mix up any combination that sounds good to you. Here are a few of our favorites to get you started.

- 2 cups (500 mL) apples and 1 Tbsp (15 mL) ground cinnamon
- 2 cups (500 mL) pears and 1 Tbsp (15 mL) ground ginger
- 2 cups (500 mL) fresh or frozen berries and 1 Tbsp (15 mL) ground cinnamon
- 2 cups (500 mL) dried fruit and 1 Tbsp (15 mL) nonalcoholic rum flavoring
- 2 cups (500 mL) bananas, 2 Tbsp (30 mL) brown sugar, and 1 Tbsp (15 mL) nonalcoholic rum flavoring
- 2 cups (500 mL) rhubarb, 1 Tbsp (15 mL) ground ginger, and 2 Tbsp (30 mL) brown sugar

SAVORY

If you have large ingredients, cut them into medium **dice** before measuring and mixing them in. Feel free to mix up any combination that sounds good to you. Here is our favorite formula to get you started: 1 cup (250 mL) diced meat, 1 cup (250 mL) diced mixed vegetables, and 1 cup (250 mL) diced cheese.

Meat
- Cooked ham
- Bacon
- Cooked chicken
- Cooked ground beef
- Pulled pork (page 170)
- Sausage

Veggies
- Cherry tomatoes
- Chopped tomatoes
- Olives
- Corn kernels
- Red pepper
- Broccoli
- Spinach
- Fried onions
- Fresh herbs

Cheese
- Cheddar cheese
- Swiss cheese
- Goat's cheese
- Parmesan
- Asiago
- Cream cheese

RISE & SHINE!

KEEP IT FRESH!

. . . go eat your fruits and veggies.

Iced Tea • 96
Pineapple Cream Cheese Dip
  with Fruit Skewers • 98
Veggie Dip • 102
Guacamole • 104
Carrot and Apple Salad • 106
Caesar Salad • 108
Potato Salad • 110
Spring Roll Salad • 112
Honey-Roasted Carrots • 115
Sesame Roasted Broccoli • 118

ICED TEA

Homemade iced tea is so much tastier than store-bought—and really easy to make! The tea will keep in a sealed pitcher in the fridge for up to 1 week.

SERVES 6

12 cups (3 L) water
8 bags decaffeinated black tea
1 cup (250 mL) liquid honey
Ice cubes, for serving

Put the water in a large **pot** and place it on the stove over high heat. Bring the water to a **boil** and then turn off the heat. Place the tea bags and honey in the water, give it all a stir, and set aside on a pot holder or cool part of the stove top to cool completely.

Once the tea has cooled completely, remove the tea bags and pour the tea into ice cube–filled glasses to serve or store in a pitcher in the fridge until ready to drink.

Switch Up the Flavor!

MINT

Add ½ cup (125 mL) of loosely packed mint leaves to the water with the tea bags.

BERRY

Add 1 cup (250 mL) of frozen or fresh berries to the water with the tea bags and honey. Once the water is completely cooled, remove the tea bags and use a **potato masher** or fork to smash the berries up. Let the tea sit another 20 minutes or so and then strain it through a **sieve** into a pitcher.

PEACH

Omit the honey and add one 14 oz (398 mL) can of peaches in syrup (and their syrup) with the tea bags. Once the water is completely cooled, remove the tea bags and use a **potato masher** or fork to smash the peaches up. Let the tea sit for another 20 minutes or so and then strain it through a **sieve** into a pitcher.

ALOHA

Add one 14 oz (398 mL) can of pineapple pieces in juice (and their juice) and one 14 oz (400 mL) can of coconut milk to the water with the tea bags and honey. Once the water is completely cooled, remove the tea bags and use a **potato masher** or fork to smash the pineapple up. Let the tea sit for another 20 minutes or so and then strain it through a **sieve** into a pitcher.

Charlie Says

You can make super-simple iced teas by adding fruit-flavored tea bags and honey to the water instead of the black tea bags.

PINEAPPLE CREAM CHEESE DIP WITH FRUIT SKEWERS

This dip is quick and easy to make and is a perfect addition for a party fruit or veggie tray. The fruit skewers are also really good dipped in chocolate sauce or sweet whipped cream.

MAKES 3 CUPS (750 ML) OF DIP AND 24 SKEWERS

- Assorted fruit for fruit skewers (strawberries, melon, grapes, apples, bananas, and kiwi work nicely)
- 24 (12-inch/30 cm long) wooden kitchen skewers
- 1 (14 oz/398 mL) can pineapple chunks in juice
- 1 (16 oz/450 g) package cream cheese, softened at room temperature for at least 1 hour
- ¼ cup (60 mL) icing sugar
- 1 tsp (5 mL) ground cinnamon
- 2 tsp (10 mL) vanilla extract

If you're using berries or grapes, wash them carefully and pat dry with **paper towel**. If you're using apples, melons, kiwis, or bananas, cut them into large bite-size pieces.

Make the skewers by carefully feeding the pieces of fruit onto the sticks, leaving at least 2 inches (5 cm) at the dull end to use as a handle. Arrange the skewers on a serving platter.

Open the can of pineapple. Place a **sieve** over a **bowl** or cup and pour the can of pineapple in. Use the back of a spoon to squeeze most of the juice out through the sieve. Save the juice for another recipe or drink it—it's delicious!

Place the pineapple, cream cheese, icing sugar, cinnamon, and vanilla in either a **stand mixer** fitted with the paddle attachment or a medium **mixing bowl** and beat until all of the ingredients are well combined and the dip is light and fluffy.

LET'S EAT

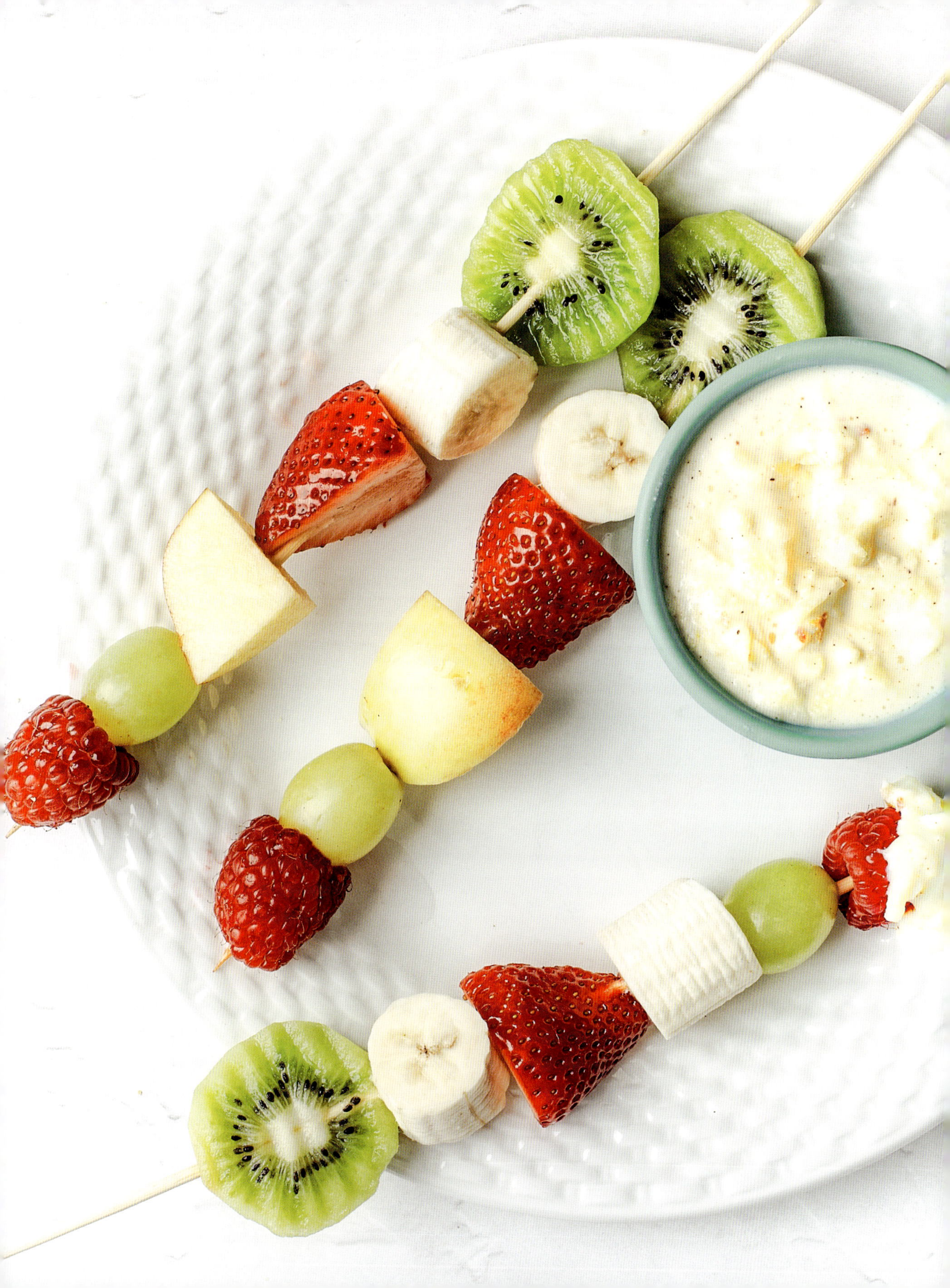

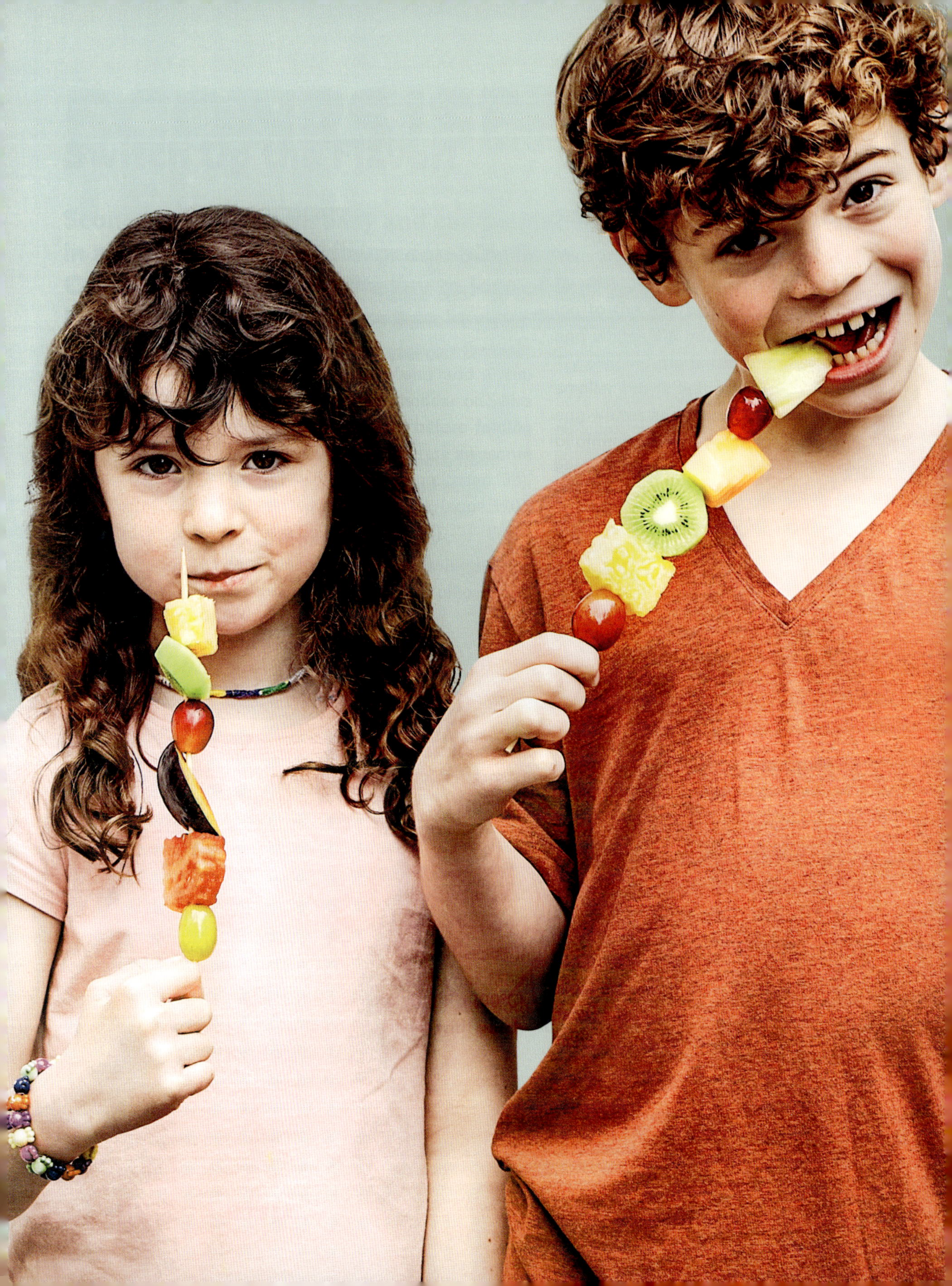

Pour the dip into a serving **bowl**, place the bowl on the platter with the fruit skewers, and either serve immediately or cover with plastic wrap and place in the fridge until you're ready to eat. The dip will keep in an airtight **container** in the fridge for up to 3 days. Fruit skewers will stay fresh in the fridge overnight on a plate wrapped in plastic wrap.

Mix It Up!

If you replace the sugar, cinammon, and vanilla with 1 tsp (5 mL) onion powder, 1 tsp (5 mL) garlic powder, and 1-2 tsp (5-10 mL) of sriracha, you get a great savory dip for chicken skewers, vegetables, or chips.

Alice Says

Try grilling the fruit skewers on the BBQ for a couple of minutes on each side—flavorama!!

KEEP IT FRESH!

VEGGIE DIP

This dip is great for a veggie snack plate or as a dip in packed lunches. Although you can totally eat it immediately, it's way better to wait at least 30 minutes to let the flavors blend, so make some and stash it in the fridge for when you want a quick snack.

MAKES 2 CUPS (500 ML) OF DIP

1 cup (250 mL) sour cream
1 cup (250 mL) mayonnaise
¼ tsp (1 mL) smoked paprika
¼ tsp (1 mL) garlic powder
Pinch of sea salt and freshly ground black pepper

Combine all the ingredients in a medium **bowl**. Cover with plastic wrap and refrigerate it for at least 30 minutes and up to overnight.

Serve with your favorite vegetables like cucumbers, peppers, carrots, radishes, celery, broccoli florets, etc. For a quick on-the-go snack, you can put about 2 Tbsp (30 mL) in a mason jar and place cut-up veggies on top. Secure with a lid and bring it with you.

Chloë Says

I love to bring this on a picnic with my friends.

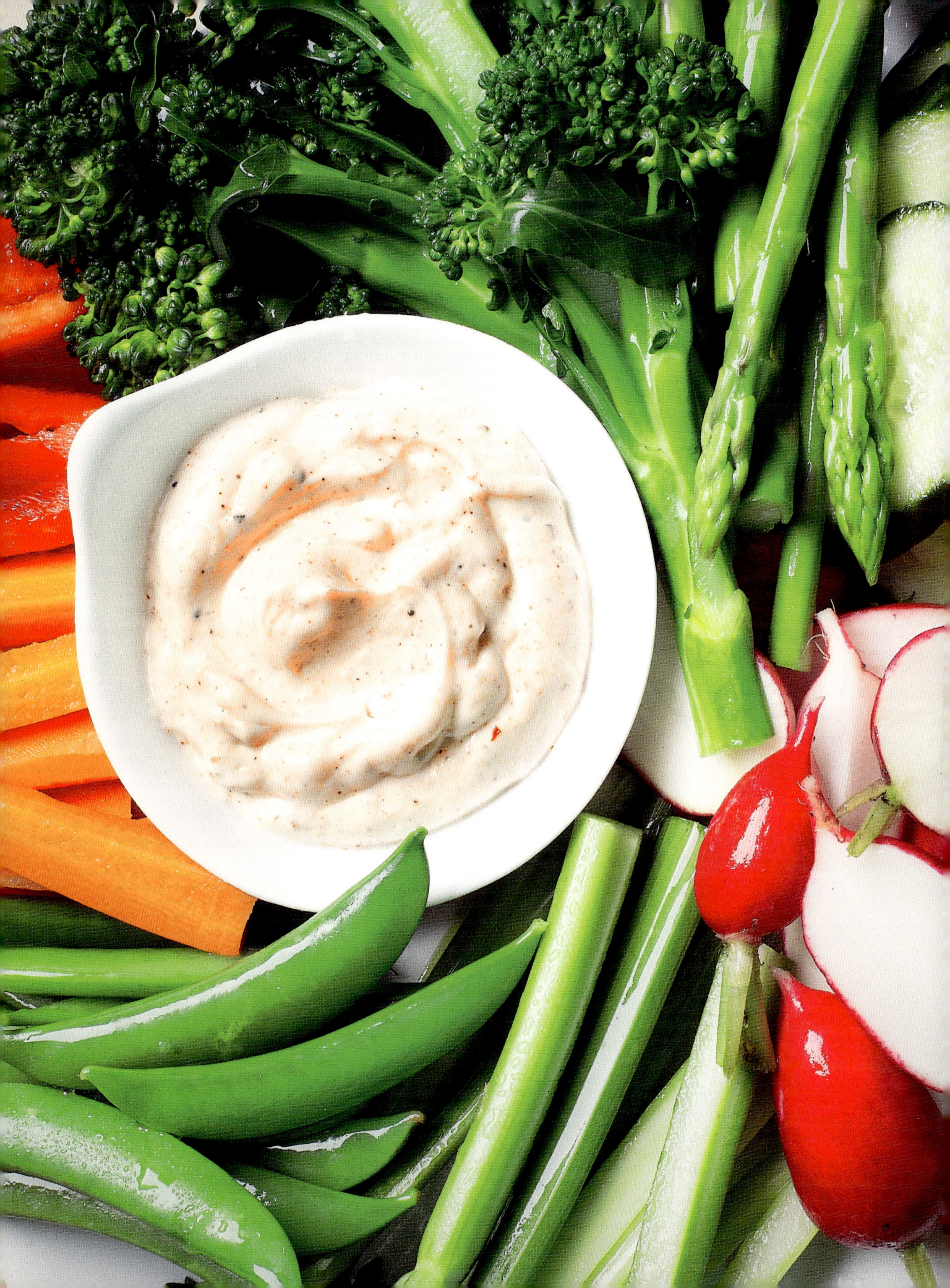

GUACAMOLE

This is an easy and fresh dip that is quick to mix together. It goes perfectly with the Loaded Nachos (page 146), Easy Peasy Taco Tuesday (page 134), a large plate of chopped fresh veggies, or even just a bowl of tortilla chips.

SERVES 4

3 ripe avocados
2 Tbsp (30 mL) freshly squeezed lime juice (about 2 limes)
½ small red onion, finely diced
2 Roma tomatoes, finely diced
2 garlic cloves, minced
1 Tbsp (15 mL) taco seasoning
1 tsp (5 mL) ground cumin (optional)
½ tsp (2.5 mL) sea salt
Handful of cilantro leaves, chopped up a bit

Quarter the avocados and remove the seeds. Scoop the avocado flesh into a medium-sized mixing bowl. Use a fork to mash it up and then mix the lime juice in.

Add the onions and tomatoes to the avocado and mix to combine. Add the garlic, taco seasoning, cumin, salt, and cilantro. Give it all a good stir to mix together and it's ready to serve. Guacamole will keep for 3 days in the fridge in an airtight container.

William Says

Don't trust a purple shark when it tells you that the guacamole stocks are falling. Instead, make double so there's more for ME!

LET'S EAT

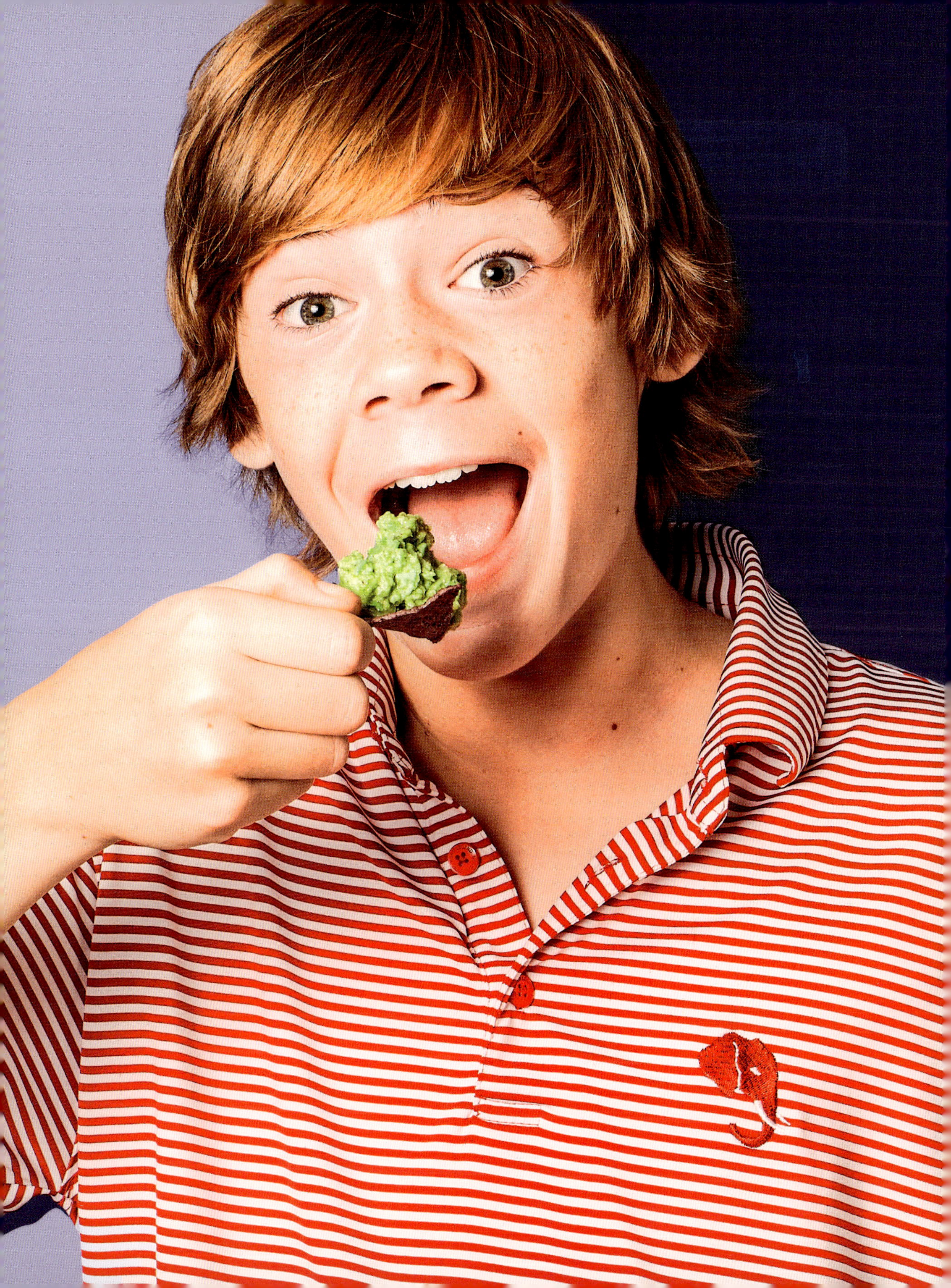

CARROT AND APPLE SALAD

This deliciously herby, sweet salad goes perfectly with Best Burgers (page 130), Falafel Veggie Burgers (page 127), Chicken Pot Pie (page 175), and Sticky Teriyaki Baked Salmon (page 132).

SERVES 6

3 apples (Granny Smith are best)
4 large carrots
4 large bunches curly leaf parsley
1 cup (250 mL) chopped almonds or pecans (optional)
2 Tbsp (30 mL) apple cider vinegar
Pinch of sea salt

Wash and then **grate** the apples (you don't need to peel and core them first) and the carrots with a box or cheese **grater** and place in a large **bowl**. Watch your fingers, as graters can be quite sharp.

Grab the bunches of parsley by the leaves and cut off the larger portion of the stems. Discard these stems. Roughly cut the remaining leafy bits into smaller chunks and add to the apples and carrots in the **bowl**. If you're new to using a **knife**, you can use a pair of kitchen scissors to snip the parsley. Add the nuts (if using).

Add the vinegar and then the salt to the salad and mix well to combine. Serve immediately.

Take It to the Next Level!

Turn this into a perfect one-dish lunch by mixing in 2 cups (500 mL) of cooked quinoa or brown rice.

LET'S EAT

Georgia Says

I eat this salad every day . . . No, really. I'm not kidding.

CAESAR SALAD

Caesar salad is a perfect side for just about any main dish. You can also toss in some Hard-Boiled Eggs (page 30), Roast Chicken (page 45), or Sticky Teriyaki Baked Salmon (page 132) for a yummy lunch or supper. While store-bought dressings work, our easy homemade version is miles better!

SERVES 4-6

Salad
5 strips bacon
1 small head romaine lettuce
¼ cup (60 mL) finely grated Parmesan cheese
½ cup (125 mL) croutons

Dressing
2 garlic cloves, pushed through a garlic press (or ¼ tsp/1 mL garlic powder)
1 cup (250 mL) mayonnaise
½ cup (125 mL) grated Parmesan cheese
2 Tbsp (30 mL) freshly squeezed lemon juice (1 lemon)
1 tsp (5 mL) anchovy paste or fish sauce (or 1 Tbsp/15 mL capers)
1 tsp (5 mL) Dijon mustard
1 tsp (5 mL) Worcestershire sauce
¼ tsp (1 mL) sea salt
¼ tsp (1 mL) freshly ground black pepper

Cook the bacon (see page 34) and let it cool. Once it's completely cool, cut it into medium dice.

Wash and dry the lettuce. It's important that you dry the lettuce completely or the dressing won't stick to the salad, and you'll be left with watery dressing. Use a tea towel to dry it.

Roughly chop the lettuce into bite-size pieces.

In a large bowl, combine the lettuce, Parmesan, diced bacon, and croutons.

In a small bowl, whisk the dressing ingredients together. Pour the dressing over the salad and toss well.

Make It Vegan!

To make this vegan, omit the bacon and use 2 Tbsp (30 mL) nutritional yeast instead of the Parmesan cheese. For the dressing, substitute 1 cup (250 mL) Vegenaise for the mayonnaise and 3 Tbsp (45 mL) nutritional yeast for the Parmesan, add 1 Tbsp (15 mL) roughly chopped capers instead of the anchovy paste, and use vegan Worcestershire sauce.

LET'S EAT

Chloë Says: Best salad ever!

POTATO SALAD

Who doesn't love potato salad? This recipe makes a great lunch dish all on its own, and it also pairs well with Sesame Roasted Broccoli (page 118), Roast Chicken (page 45), and BBQ Best Burgers (page 130).

SERVES 4–6

2 lb (900 g) new potatoes
¾ cup (185 mL) plain yogurt or sour cream
¼ cup (60 mL) medium-diced green onions
¼ tsp (1 mL) garlic powder
¼ tsp (1 mL) onion powder
Pinch of sea salt and freshly ground black pepper

Scrub the potatoes well. Pat them dry with a tea towel. Fill a large pot with water.

Cut each potato in half. Place the potatoes in the pot of water. Cover and bring to a boil over high heat. Uncover and cook until fork-tender (the fork slides into the potato easily), 10–15 minutes.

Turn off the stove!

Meanwhile, in a large bowl, mix together the yogurt, green onions, garlic powder, onion powder, salt, and pepper.

Place a sieve over a large bowl and use it to drain the potatoes. Let them sit in the sieve for 5 minutes to cool. Add the potatoes to the large bowl with the yogurt mixture and stir to combine.

Cover and chill in the fridge for 1 hour before serving so the flavors have time to come together. Can be stored in an airtight container for up to a week.

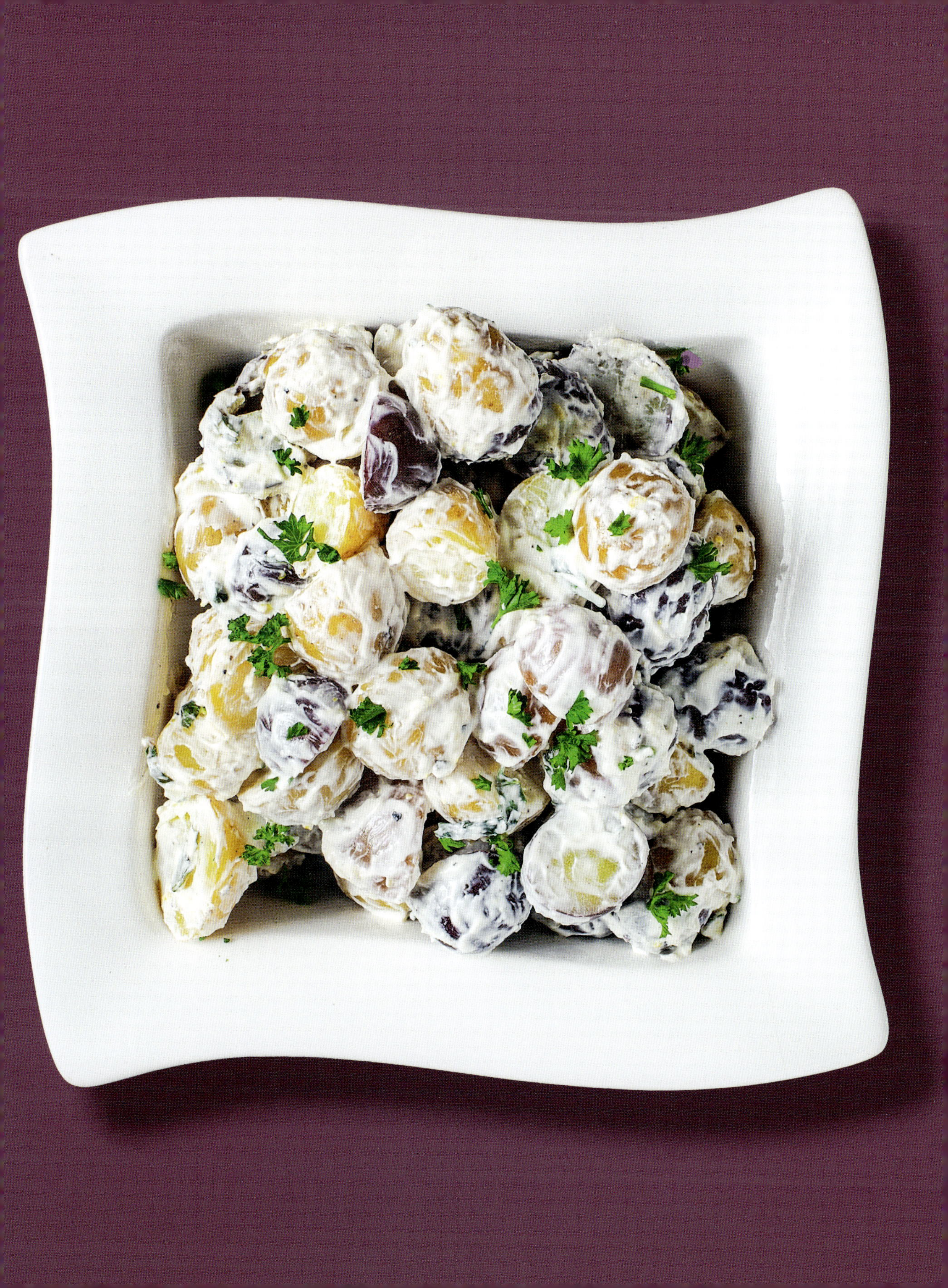

SPRING ROLL SALAD

This is a great big bowl of yum! A deconstructed version of Vietnamese salad rolls, this dish comes together quickly and makes a perfect lunch. Omit the chicken and you have a good side dish for Sticky Soda Pop Ribs (page 142) or Best Burgers (page 130).

SERVES 4

- 1 (1 lb/450 g) package of vermicelli noodles
- Dressing (see Mix It Up!)
- 2–3 large handfuls of bite-size salad greens
- 2 cups (500 mL) shredded Roast Chicken (page 45)
- 1 cup (250 mL) grated carrots
- 1 cup (250 mL) bean sprouts
- 1 red bell pepper, cut into matchsticks
- 1 yellow bell pepper, cut into matchsticks
- ½ cucumber, cut into matchsticks
- ½ cup (125 mL) chopped fresh cilantro leaves
- ½ cup (125 mL) chopped fresh mint leaves
- ½ cup (125 mL) chopped peanuts or almonds (optional)
- Large handful of sugar peas

Cook the rice noodles according to the package instructions. Once they're cooked, transfer them to a sieve and rinse them under cold running water until completely chilled.

Turn off the stove!

Transfer the noodles to a large mixing bowl, pour over the dressing, and toss to combine. Add the remaining ingredients and toss the salad all together. Serve chilled.

The salad can be stored in an airtight container in the fridge for 3–4 days.

Mix It Up!

Instead of roast chicken, you can use 2 cups (500 mL) cooked shrimp, 2 cups (500 mL) medium-rare steak sliced into strips, or 2 cups (500 mL) medium-firm tofu chopped into ½-inch (1.25 cm) cubes.

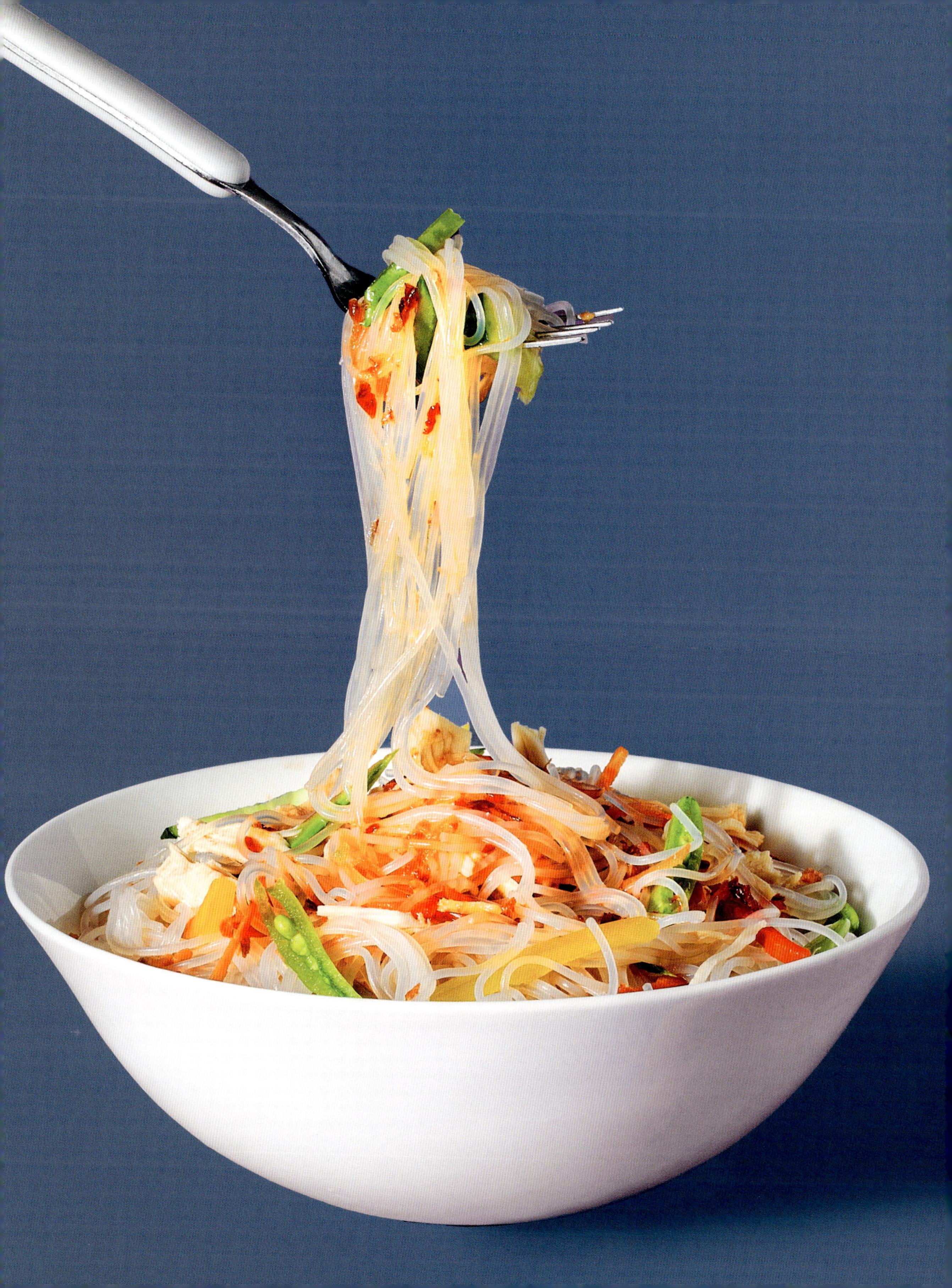

NUOC CHAM DRESSING

¼ cup (60 mL) water
¼ cup (60 mL) granulated sugar
2 Tbsp (30 mL) freshly squeezed lime juice (1–2 limes)
1–2 Tbsp (15–30 mL) sambal oelek chili sauce
1 Tbsp (15 mL) fish sauce
2 tsp (10 mL) toasted sesame oil

Place the water and sugar in a small **pot**. Set the pot over medium heat and bring to a **boil**. Stir the sugar around until it completely dissolves and remove the pot from the heat. Add the remaining ingredients, stir, and set aside on a pot holder or cool part of the stove top to cool completely before using.

PEANUT OR SUNFLOWER BUTTER DRESSING

½ cup (125 mL) peanut or sunflower butter
½ cup (125 mL) orange juice
2 cloves garlic, **minced**
2 Tbsp (30 mL) freshly squeezed lime juice (1–2 limes)
2 Tbsp (30 mL) tamari or coconut aminos
2 Tbsp (30 mL) maple syrup
1 Tbsp (15 mL) toasted sesame oil
1 Tbsp (15 mL) fish sauce
1–2 tsp (5–10 mL) sriracha or hot sauce (optional)

Mix the peanut or sunflower seed butter and orange juice together in a small **pot**. Place the pot over medium heat until the butter melts. **Whisk** gently to combine with the orange juice. Remove the pot from the heat and stir in the rest of the ingredients. Set aside on a pot holder or cool part of the stove top to cool completely.

Charlie Says

Nuoc cham is a bit spicy—try the peanut butter dressing instead.

LET'S EAT

HONEY-ROASTED CARROTS

Carrots never tasted this good before! These make a delicious side dish for Crispy Sesame Chicken (page 136), Sticky Teriyaki Baked Salmon (page 132), or Roast Chicken (page 45).

SERVES 4

- 1 lb (450 g) carrots
- 2 Tbsp (30 mL) unsalted butter
- 2 Tbsp (30 mL) liquid honey
- 1 tsp (5 mL) celery or caraway seeds (optional)
- ½ tsp (2.5 mL) sea salt

Preheat the oven to 400°F (200°C). **Line** a large **baking sheet** with **parchment paper**.

Peel the carrots and cut their tops and bottoms off. Cut the carrots in half lengthwise, and then cut each of those halves in half lengthwise. Cut each of the carrot sticks in half widthwise. You should have a bunch of carrot sticks now. Place the sticks in a medium-sized **mixing bowl** and set aside.

Place the butter and honey in a small **pot** and set the pot over low heat to melt the butter. Stir to combine the butter and honey. Add the celery or caraway seeds (if using) and pour the liquid over the carrot sticks. Add the salt and **toss** all the carrots around to cover them evenly.

Dump the carrots out onto the prepared **baking sheet** and arrange them so that they aren't overlapping. Place the **baking sheet** in the oven and bake until the carrots are tender and starting to turn golden, 25–35 minutes. The roasting time will depend on how big your carrots are. Using **oven mitts**, remove from the oven, turn off the heat, and serve immediately.

KEEP IT FRESH!

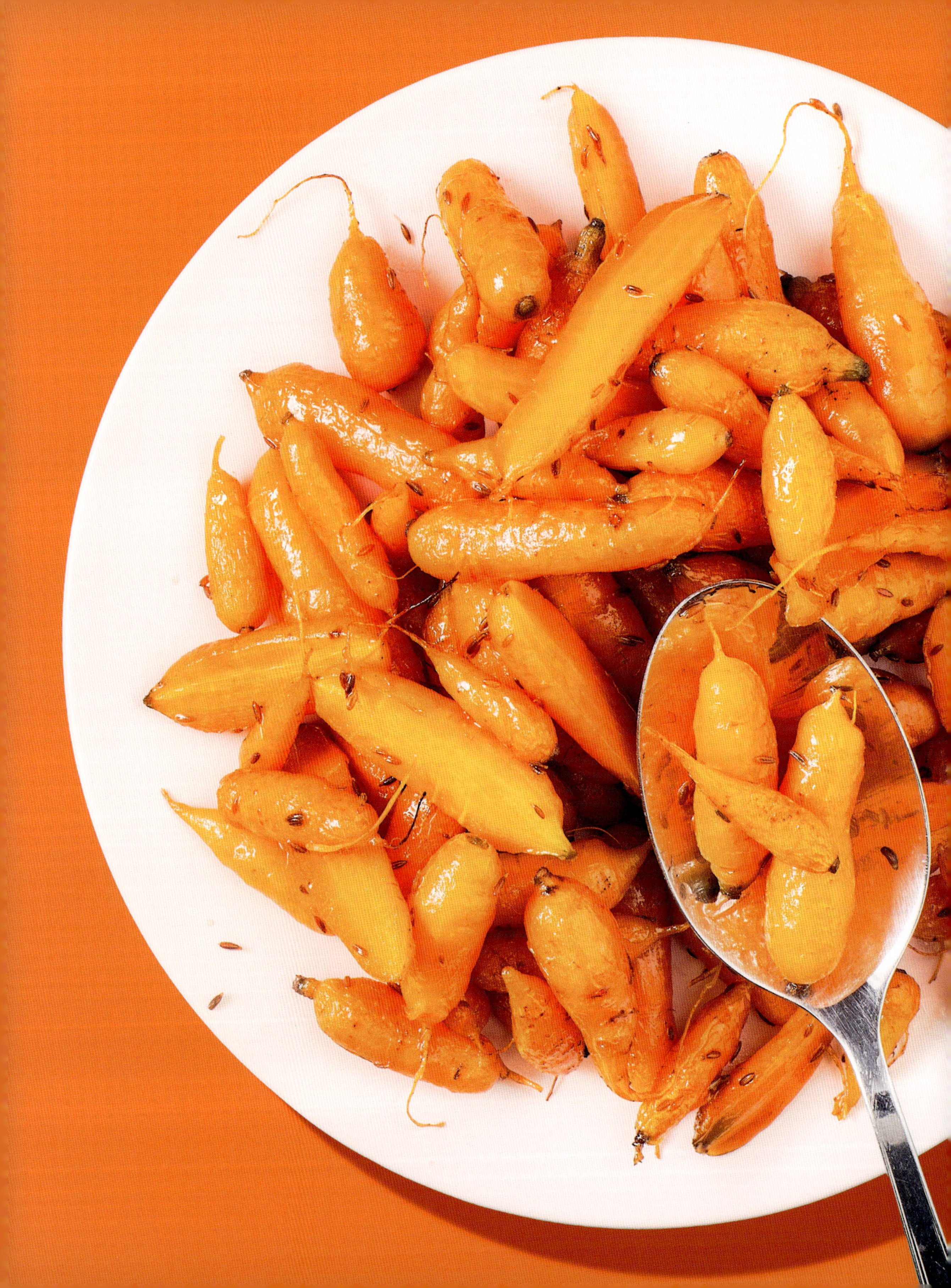

Switch Up the Flavor!

SESAME

Add 1 tsp (5 mL) sesame oil to the butter and honey. Omit the celery/caraway seeds. Sprinkle the cooked carrots with sesame seeds.

SPICY

Add 2 tsp (10 mL) sriracha to the butter and honey, and sprinkle the cooked carrots with ½ cup (125 mL) chopped curly or flat-leaf parsley.

Alice Says

Eat these at EVERY meal!

KEEP IT FRESH!

SESAME ROASTED BROCCOLI

This is a fun alternative to boiled or steamed broccoli. The sesame oil gives a punch of flavor to the broccoli and the roasting gives it a nice crispy edge. We love to eat this with Sticky Teriyaki Baked Salmon (page 132) and steamed rice. (Note: Florets are the flowering stems that make up the top, dark green part of the broccoli.)

SERVES 4

- 1 large head of broccoli, washed, cut into florets, and stems sliced, OR 1 bag frozen florets
- 2 Tbsp (30 mL) sesame oil
- 2 Tbsp (30 mL) canola or vegetable oil
- 2 Tbsp (30 mL) sesame seeds
- ¼ tsp (1 mL) sea salt
- ¼ tsp (1 mL) freshly ground black pepper

Preheat the oven to 400°F (200°C). **Line** a large **baking sheet** with **parchment paper** or a **silicone mat**.

In a large **bowl**, mix together the broccoli, sesame oil, canola oil, and sesame seeds. **Toss** to coat the broccoli completely. Transfer to the prepared **baking sheet** and arrange in a single layer.

Bake until the broccoli is softened and starting to brown and crisp along the edges, 15–22 minutes. Using **oven mitts**, carefully remove the **baking sheet** from the oven and sprinkle the broccoli with the salt and pepper. Turn off the heat. Toss and serve.

Félix Says

This is so yummy with roast chicken or mixed into pasta.

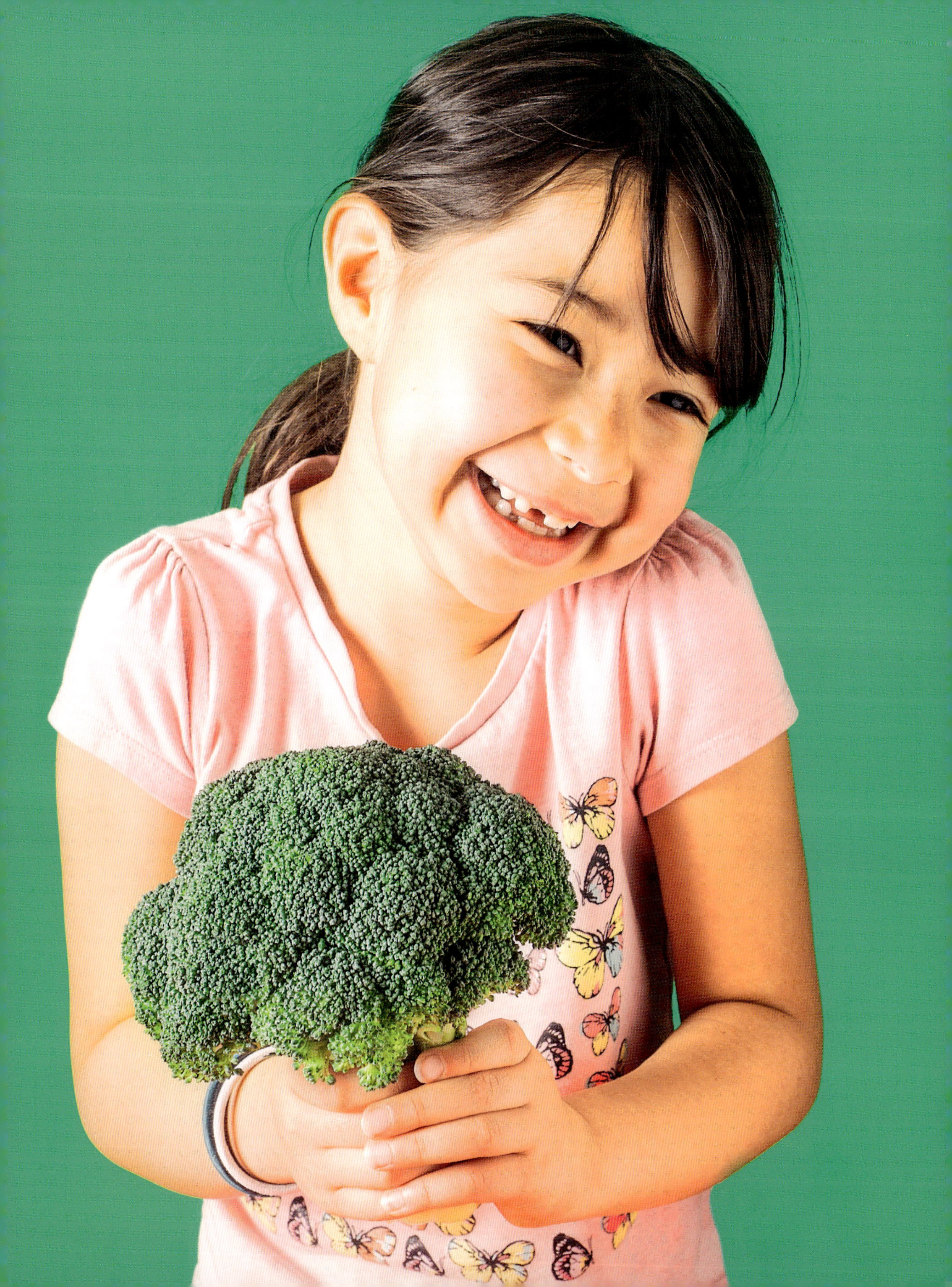

MAKE IT THE MAIN EVENT!

... find your new favorites here.

Deviled Eggs • 122
Coconut Shake 'n' Bake • 124
Falafel Veggie Burgers • 127
Best Burgers • 130
Sticky Teriyaki Baked Salmon • 132
Easy Peasy Taco Tuesday • 134
Crispy Sesame Chicken • 136
Pizza Your Way • 139
Sticky Soda Pop Ribs • 142
Loaded Nachos • 146

DEVILED EGGS

No matter how many deviled eggs we make, there never seem to be enough! The eggs can be boiled and kept in the fridge for up to 3 days before they get the deviled treatment. You can skip the butter if you're dairy free.

SERVES 6

- 12 large, hard-boiled eggs (see page 30)
- ⅓ cup (80 mL) mayonnaise
- 2 Tbsp (30 mL) unsalted butter, softened to room temperature
- 1 Tbsp (15 mL) Dijon mustard
- 2 tsp (10 mL) apple cider vinegar
- 1 tsp (5 mL) brown sugar
- ½ tsp (2.5 mL) sea salt
- ½ tsp (2.5 mL) freshly ground black or white pepper
- Toppings (see Try These Toppings!)

Follow the instructions on page 32 to peel the eggs.

After all of the eggs are peeled, slice them in half lengthwise. Use a teaspoon to remove the yolks and place the yolks in a medium-sized mixing bowl. Place the egg whites on a platter or plate, round side down, and set aside.

Add the mayonnaise, butter, Dijon mustard, apple cider vinegar, sugar, salt, and pepper to the egg yolks and mash them all together until the mixture is smooth. Place a spoonful of the mixture back into the waiting egg whites and top with a sprinkle of toppings as desired.

Try These Toppings!

- Paprika
- Cooked bacon slices (see page 34), cut into 1-inch (2.5 cm) pieces
- Nori
- Sesame seeds
- Chives
- Tobiko
- Jalapeños
- Pickles
- Crispy onions

LET'S EAT

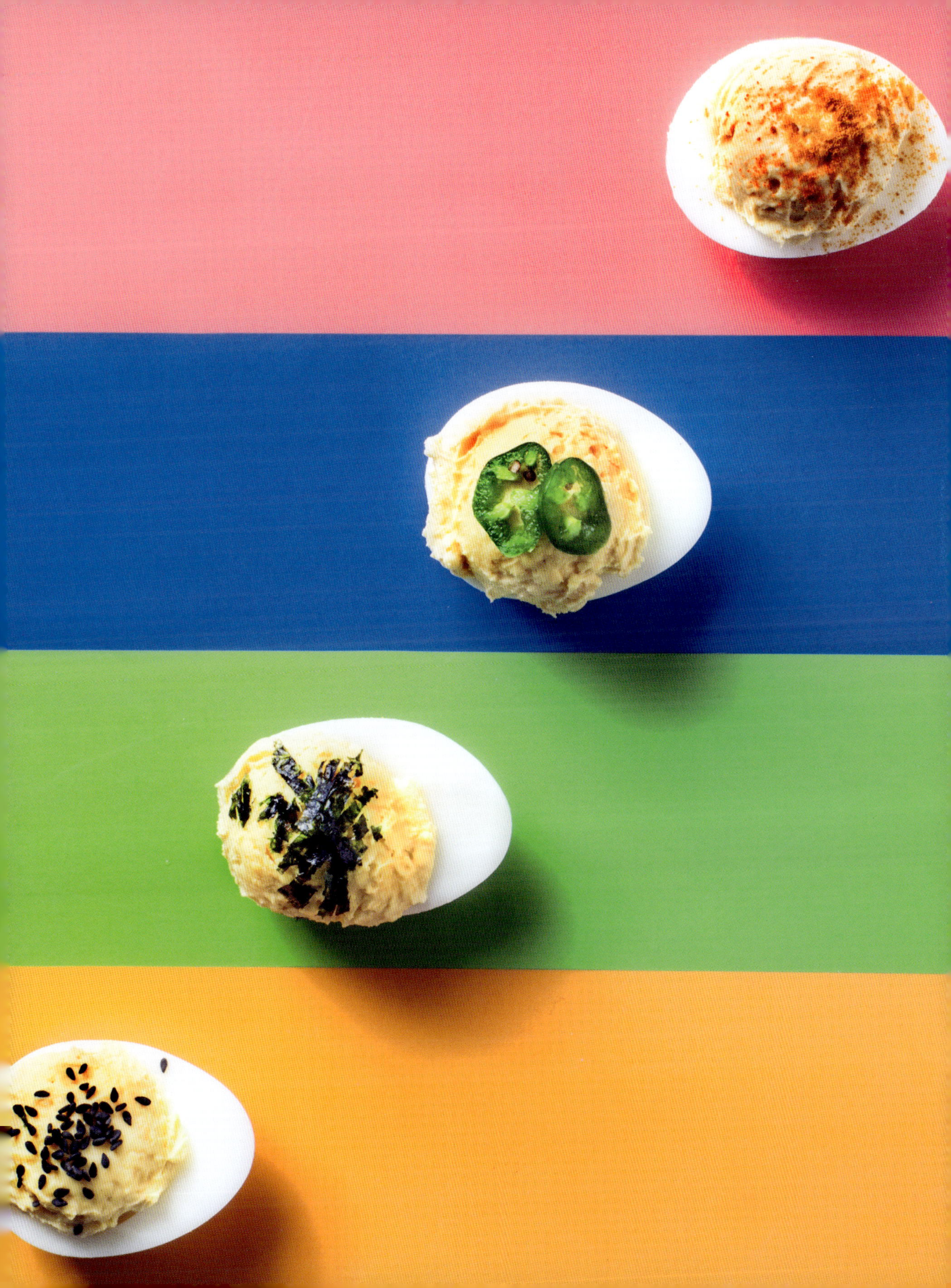

COCONUT SHAKE 'N' BAKE

This is a modern twist on the classic store-bought formula. Now you can make it from scratch and have fun doing it at the same time! All you have to do is pop your seasoning in a bag, throw in your chicken, give it a shake, and BAM!—perfectly seasoned and crispy coated chicken ready to be baked to perfection.

SERVES 4

- 2 large eggs
- ½ cup (125 mL) Italian bread crumbs or panko
- ¼ cup (60 mL) unsweetened shredded coconut
- ¼ tsp (1 mL) curry powder
- ¼ tsp (1 mL) sea salt
- ¼ tsp (1 mL) freshly ground black pepper
- 1 lb (450 g) chicken fillets

Preheat the oven to 375°F (190°C). **Line** a large **baking sheet** with **parchment paper** or a **silicone mat**.

Crack the eggs and place them in a shallow **bowl** large enough to hold a chicken fillet. **Whisk** until combined. In a large ziplock bag or medium-sized bowl, combine the bread crumbs, coconut, curry powder, salt, and pepper.

Working with 1 fillet at a time, dunk them completely in the egg mixture and then shake off any excess. Now place them in the dry ingredients and coat on both sides. You can pat the mixture down slightly to help it stick. Transfer to the prepared **baking sheet**.

Place the **baking sheet** on the top rack of the oven and bake until the chicken is golden brown, 15–18 minutes.

Using **oven mitts**, remove the **baking sheet** from the oven and let the chicken cool for a few minutes before serving.

Turn off the oven!

LET'S EAT

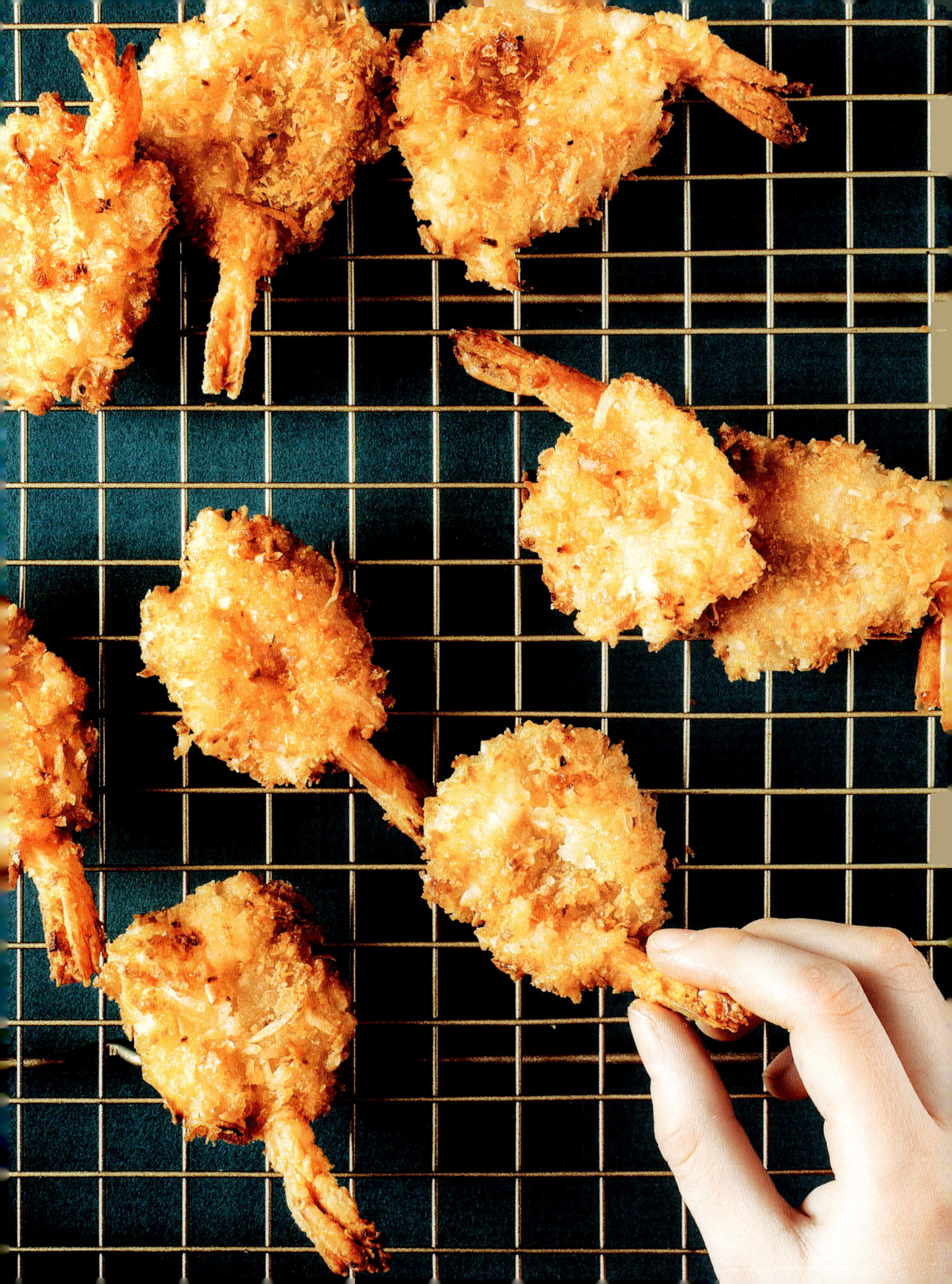

Shake It Up!

The shake-style rub in this recipe works well on prawns (deveined and tail on), pork cutlets, and even firm tofu as well as chicken. Do NOT save any leftovers once it has come in contact with raw meat; anything left over needs to go in the compost immediately.

Use 1 lb (450 g) of your chosen protein. Follow the same recipe and bake as follows.

- Shrimp: 8–10 minutes
- Tofu: 8–10 minutes
- Pork cutlets: 15–18 minutes

FALAFEL VEGGIE BURGERS

Falafel is usually served as fried balls wrapped in pita, but we think it makes the perfect veggie burger when topped with your favorite fixings. Note that you need to start these the night before you plan to eat them. Don't be tempted to use canned chickpeas to save time, though, as they are super-soaked and will make for mushy burgers.

MAKES 6-8 BURGERS

1 cup (250 mL) dried chickpeas
1 small onion, cut into 6-8 pieces
1 cup (250 mL) curly leaf parsley, roughly torn
1 cup (250 mL) cilantro, roughly torn
2 garlic cloves, minced
2 Tbsp (30 mL) freshly squeezed lemon juice (approx)
2 Tbsp (30 mL) sesame seeds
1 tsp (5 mL) ground cumin
1 tsp (5 mL) sea salt
2 Tbsp (30 mL) almond or chickpea flour (approx)
½ tsp (2.5 mL) baking soda
¼ cup (60 mL) vegetable or avocado oil, divided
6-8 burger buns of choice
Condiments of choice (ketchup, mustard, mayo . . .)

Place the chickpeas in a large bowl, cover completely with cold water, and let soak overnight.

The next morning, drain the chickpeas in a sieve and discard the water. You'll have 3 cups (750 mL) of soaked chickpeas.

Place the chickpeas, onions, parsley, cilantro, garlic, lemon juice, sesame seeds, cumin, and salt in a food processor fitted with the steel blade and use the pulse function several times until all the ingredients are combined into a rough mixture.

Dump the mixture into a large bowl and add the flour and baking soda. Stir all the ingredients together, cover the bowl with plastic wrap, and put it in the fridge for at least 30 minutes and up to overnight.

When you're ready to make the burgers, preheat the oven to 425°F (220°C). Line a baking sheet with parchment paper.

MAKE IT THE MAIN EVENT!

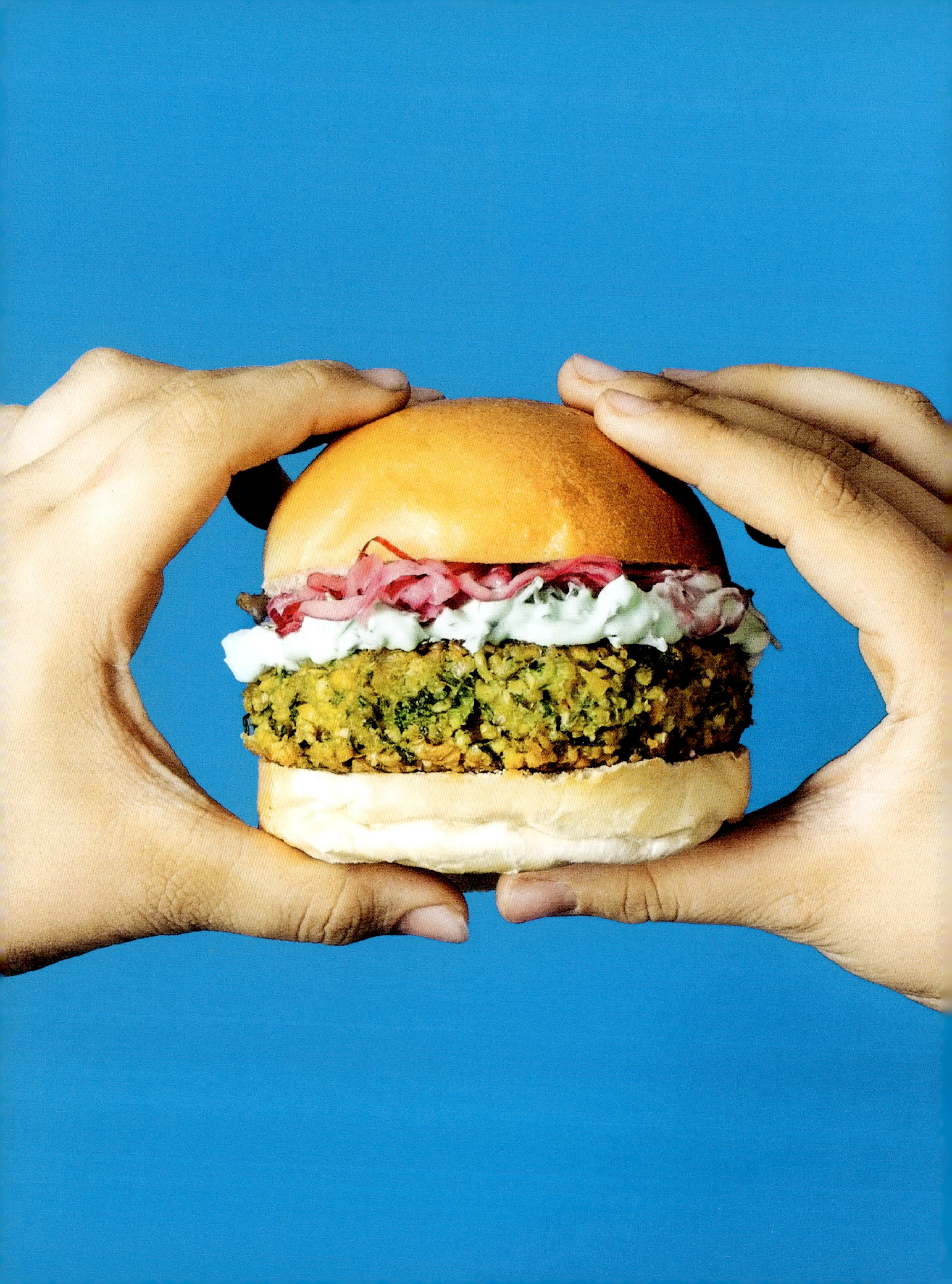

Use a ½-cup (125 mL) measuring cup to scoop the mixture into six to eight evenly sized piles and form patties that are 1 inch (2.5 cm) thick. If the mixture is too wet and mushy, add another 1 Tbsp (15 mL) of flour. If it's too dry, add another 1–2 Tbsp (15–30 mL) lemon juice.

Place the patties on the prepared **baking sheet** and brush the tops with half the oil, making sure there is a good amount on each patty. Bake for 15 minutes. Flip the patties over, brush them with the remaining oil, and bake for another 15 minutes. The patties should be crispy and golden on the outside but still tender on the inside.

Serve the falafel burgers on buns with your favorite condiments. On the bottom half of each bun, layer a condiment like mustard, then add lettuce and tomato, followed by a cooked patty, cheese, and pickles. On the underside of the top bun, spread another condiment like ketchup and place it on the burger. You can add as many or as few of the condiments and add-ons (like lettuce and tomatoes) as you like!

William Says

Even if you're not a vegetarian, you'll love these!

MAKE IT THE MAIN EVENT!

BEST BURGERS

The ultimate canvas to paint with all of your favorite toppings! Do you like pickles on your burger? Avocado? How about a fried egg? Or you can get crazy and add the works! No matter what you put on top, these burgers will quickly become a favorite in your recipe rotations. You can swap the beef for ground chicken, turkey, or lamb if you prefer.

SERVES 4

- 1 lb (450 g) ground beef
- 2 Tbsp (30 mL) BBQ Sauce (page 174, or store-bought)
- 1 tsp (5 mL) sea salt
- 1 tsp (5 mL) freshly ground black pepper
- 4 burger buns
- Condiments of choice (ketchup, mustard, mayo . . .)
- 4 lettuce leaves
- 4 slices of tomatoes
- 4 slices cheese
- 8 slices pickles

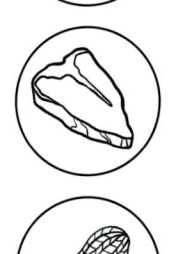

In a medium **bowl**, combine the beef, BBQ sauce, salt, and pepper. Make four evenly sized patties about ½ inch (1.25 cm) thick. Press your thumb down in the center of the each, about halfway down the patty. This will help the patty stay flatter as it cooks.

In a large **frying pan**, cook the patties over medium heat for about 4 minutes per side. Remove the pan from the heat and leave the patties there to stay warm.

Toast the buns by placing them open side up in the oven with the broiler on low. Broil until they're just starting to turn golden. Using **oven mitts**, remove from the oven. On the bottom half of each bun, layer a condiment like mustard, then add lettuce and tomato, followed by a cooked patty, cheese, and pickles. On the underside of the top bun, spread another condiment like ketchup and place it on the burger. You can add as many or as few of the condiments and add-ons (like lettuce and tomatoes) as you like! Serve immediately.

LET'S EAT

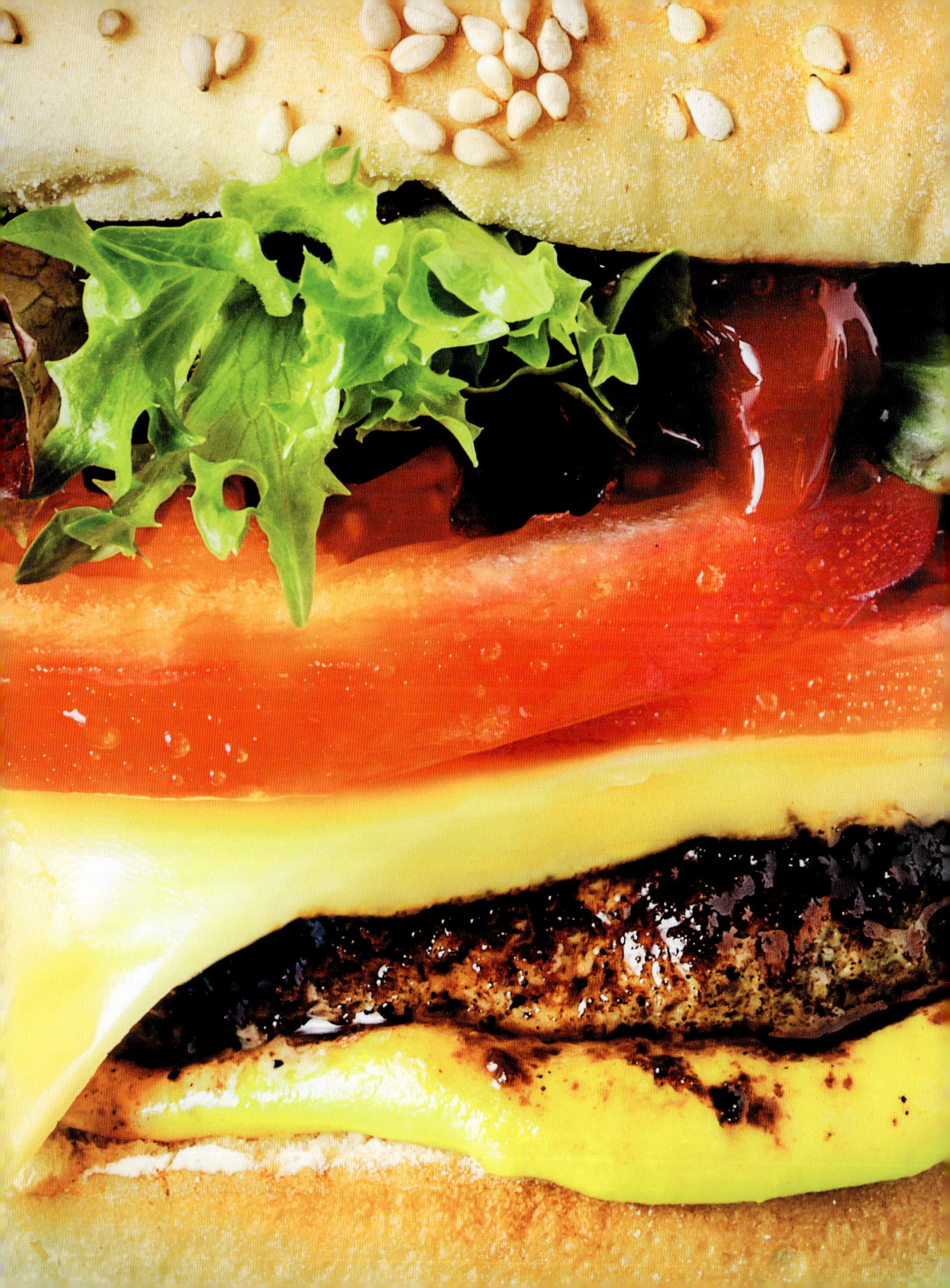

STICKY TERIYAKI BAKED SALMON

This salmon is the perfect main alongside Honey-Roasted Carrots (page 115), Sesame Roasted Broccoli (page 118), and some steamed sticky rice (page 42). Or add it as the main protein in a bowl of Spring Roll Salad (page 112).

SERVES 4

- ¼ cup (60 mL) soy sauce, tamari, or coconut aminos
- ¼ cup (60 mL) sesame oil
- ¼ cup (60 mL) lemon juice (2 lemons)
- ¼ cup (60 mL) maple syrup
- 4 salmon fillets

In a shallow dish large enough to hold all your ingredients without crowding, mix together the soy sauce, sesame oil, lemon juice, and maple syrup. Add the salmon fillets and turn to coat. Cover with plastic wrap and refrigerate for 30–60 minutes.

Preheat the oven to 400°F (200°C). **Line** a **baking sheet** with **parchment paper**.

Remove the salmon from the fridge and place the fillets in a single layer on the prepared **baking sheet**. Place the baking sheet in the top third of the oven. Bake for 10 minutes and then turn the broiler on medium to high heat and let it cook for another 3–4 minutes. Keep a CLOSE EYE on the salmon! You want it to get sticky and crispy, but it can burn very quickly if you're not careful.

Turn off the oven!

Using **oven mitts**, carefully remove the pan from the oven and serve immediately.

Mix It Up!

The salmon in this recipe can be swapped out for chicken breasts. Just add 5–7 minutes to your cooking time or bake until a **meat thermometer** reads 165°F (74°C) when inserted into the breast.

Chloë Says

This is ooey-gooey sticky perfection!

EASY PEASY TACO TUESDAY

Tacos are such a crowd pleaser because everyone gets to dress their dinner up with their own favorite toppings. If you want to shortcut this recipe, you can use the meat from a Roast Chicken (page 45) and simply mix it with a 15 oz (430 mL) jar of your favorite salsa in a **pot** on the stove.

SERVES 4-6

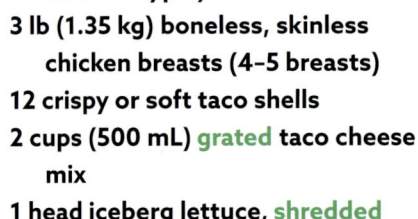

- 1 (15 oz/430 mL) jar salsa (your favorite type!)
- 3 lb (1.35 kg) boneless, skinless chicken breasts (4-5 breasts)
- 12 crispy or soft taco shells
- 2 cups (500 mL) **grated** taco cheese mix
- 1 head iceberg lettuce, **shredded**
- 1 recipe Guacamole (page 104)
- Toppings (see Try These Toppings!)

Pour half of the salsa into your **slow cooker** and then place the chicken breasts in a single layer on top. Pour the remaining salsa over the chicken, put the lid on, and cook on high for 3-4 hours or on low for 6-7 hours. The chicken is done when it is cooked all the way through and easy to pull apart with two forks.

Take the chicken out and use the forks to **shred** the meat. Put the chicken back in the slow cooker and stir it into the sauce.

Lay the shells out on a plate alongside a platter of the chicken, a **bowl** of **grated** taco cheese mix, a bowl of **shredded** lettuce, some guacamole, and whatever other toppings you'd like, and let people create their own perfect tacos.

Try These Toppings!

- Black olives
- Pickled jalapeños
- Extra salsa
- Chopped green onions

134   LET'S EAT

Félix Says

*Taco Tuesday?
Taco EVERYday!*

CRISPY SESAME CHICKEN

Using an **air fryer** for this recipe makes cleanup easier and cuts the cooking time considerably—and the chicken turns out even crispier. If you don't have an **air fryer**, an oven will do. Just make sure you bake it until it has a nice crunchy crust.

SERVES 4

3 lb (1.35 kg) boneless, skinless chicken breast (about 4 breasts)
3 whole eggs
2 egg yolks
2 Tbsp (30 mL) Worcestershire sauce
3 cups (750 mL) Italian bread crumbs or panko
2 cups (500 mL) sesame seeds
2 tsp (10 mL) sea salt
2 tsp (10 mL) freshly ground black pepper
Olive oil or avocado oil cooking spray (if cooking in the oven)
2/3 cup (165 mL) Dijon mustard
3 Tbsp (45 mL) liquid honey

Place a large **baking sheet** by your workstation. Working on a clean **cutting board**, cut each chicken breast into four evenly sized pieces. Wrap a piece of chicken in a large piece of **parchment paper** and pound the breast until it's ¼ inch (0.6 cm) thick. You can use a meat **mallet**, **rolling pin**, or even a small **pot** for this. Transfer the flattened chicken to the baking sheet. Repeat with the remaining chicken. Clean up the cutting board and wipe down your work surface.

In a shallow **bowl** large enough to hold a piece of the chicken, **whisk** together the eggs, egg yolks, and Worcestershire sauce. In a similar size of shallow bowl, combine the bread crumbs, sesame seeds, salt, and pepper.

Working with one piece of chicken at a time, use one hand to drag the chicken through the egg mixture. Let any excess drip off. Place it in the bread crumbs and, using your other hand, cover and coat the chicken. Place it back on the tray and repeat this process for the rest of the chicken.

If you're using an **air fryer**, heat it to 375°F (190°C).

Arrange the chicken in the **air fryer** basket in a single layer. You may have to work in batches, depending on the size of your air fryer. Cook until golden brown, 6–8 minutes, or until crunchy.

LET'S EAT

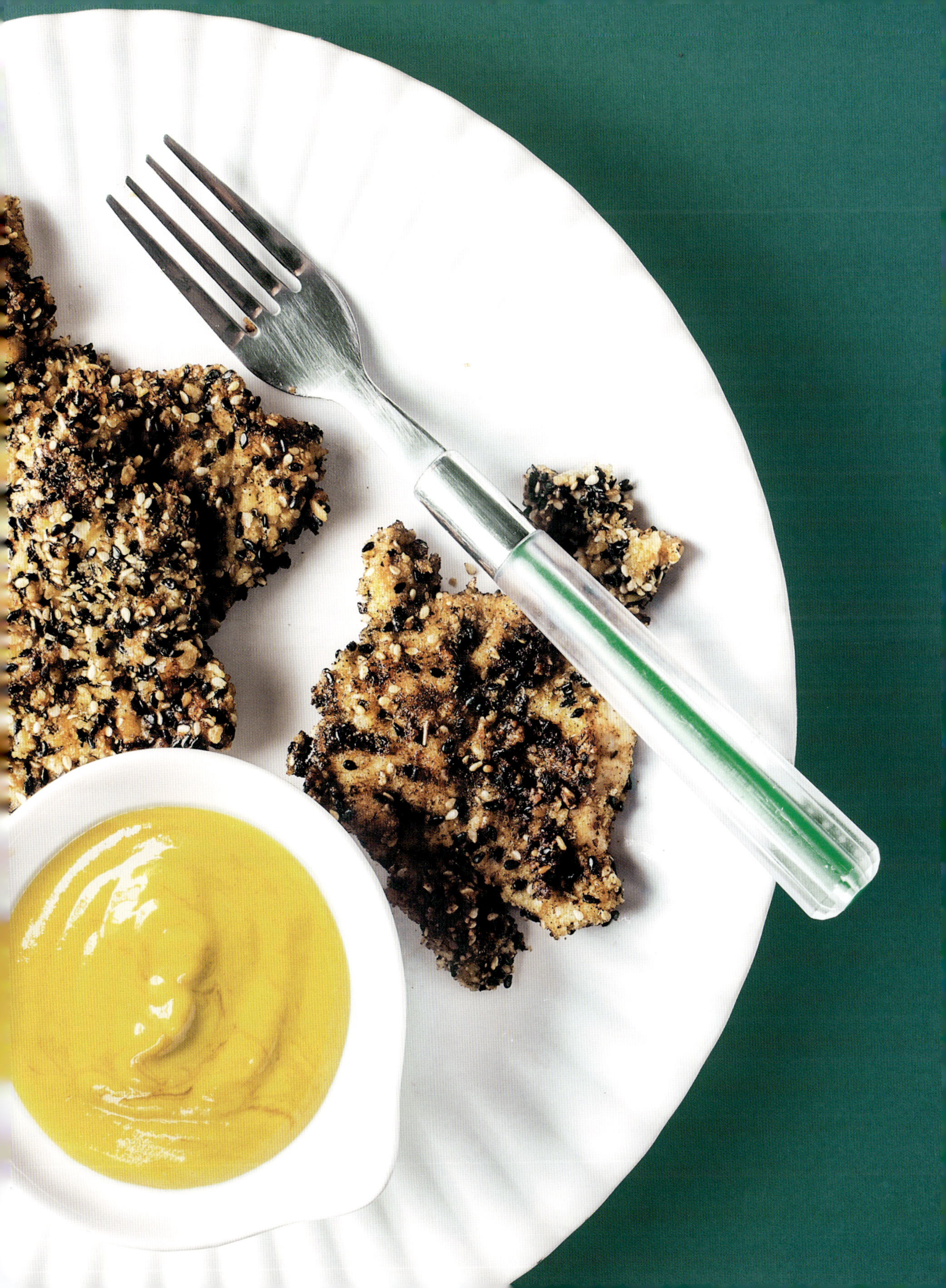

Place the cooked chicken on a clean tray or plate. Repeat with the remaining chicken if necessary.

If you're using the oven, preheat it to 425°F (220°C). **Line** a large **baking sheet** with **parchment paper**. Lay the chicken on the baking sheet in a single layer. Spray the coated chicken with the cooking spray and bake for 10 minutes. Flip the chicken over and cook until crispy and cooked through, 10–12 minutes.

While the chicken is cooking, **whisk** together the Dijon and honey in a small **bowl** to make honey Dijon sauce and serve alongside the chicken.

Remove the chicken from the **air fryer** or oven and serve immediately with honey Dijon sauce.

PIZZA YOUR WAY

Any bread, whether it's toast, naan, bannock, or pita, makes an excellent vehicle for quick and easy pizza. To take it to the next level, try your hand at making pizza dough. It's a bit time-consuming (lots of rest time but not too much hands-on time) but it's actually super easy to make.

MAKES 3 (12-INCH/30 CM) PIZZAS

1¾ cups (435 mL) warm (110°F/43°C) water, divided
2¼ tsp (11 mL) instant yeast
1 tsp (5 mL) granulated sugar
3 cups (750 mL) all-purpose flour
1 Tbsp (15 mL) fine sea salt
1½ cups (375 mL) store-bought tomato-based pizza sauce
3 cups grated pizza cheese mix
Toppings (see Try These Toppings!)

In a small bowl, place 1 cup (250 mL) of the water, the yeast, and the sugar. Stir gently. Allow to sit until thick and bubbly, 10 minutes.

In a large bowl, mix together the flour and salt. Add the bubbly yeast water and the remaining ¾ cup (185 mL) of water. Using a rubber spatula, stir gently to combine. The dough will be soft and sticky (this is why we use a rubber spatula—the dough is less likely to stick to it). Cover with a clean, dry tea towel and let rest for 10 minutes.

Using a spatula, fold the dough over several times so that you don't have any floury bits. Cover with the tea towel again and let rest in a draft-free spot until doubled in size, 45–60 minutes.

Uncover the dough. Run your hands under water. Using wet hands, scoop the dough up, turn it a quarter turn, and drop it back in the bowl. Repeat this three more times so that you turn it four times in total. Cover with the tea towel and let rest until doubled again, 30 minutes.

Preheat the oven to 450°F (230°C). Flour a baking sheet. Thoroughly grease a 12-inch (30 cm) pizza pan. Uncover and punch down the dough to deflate it. Turn out the dough onto the prepared baking sheet. Break it into three equal-sized balls (you could use a scale or just eyeball it). Cover with a tea towel and let rest for about 5 minutes.

MAKE IT THE MAIN EVENT!

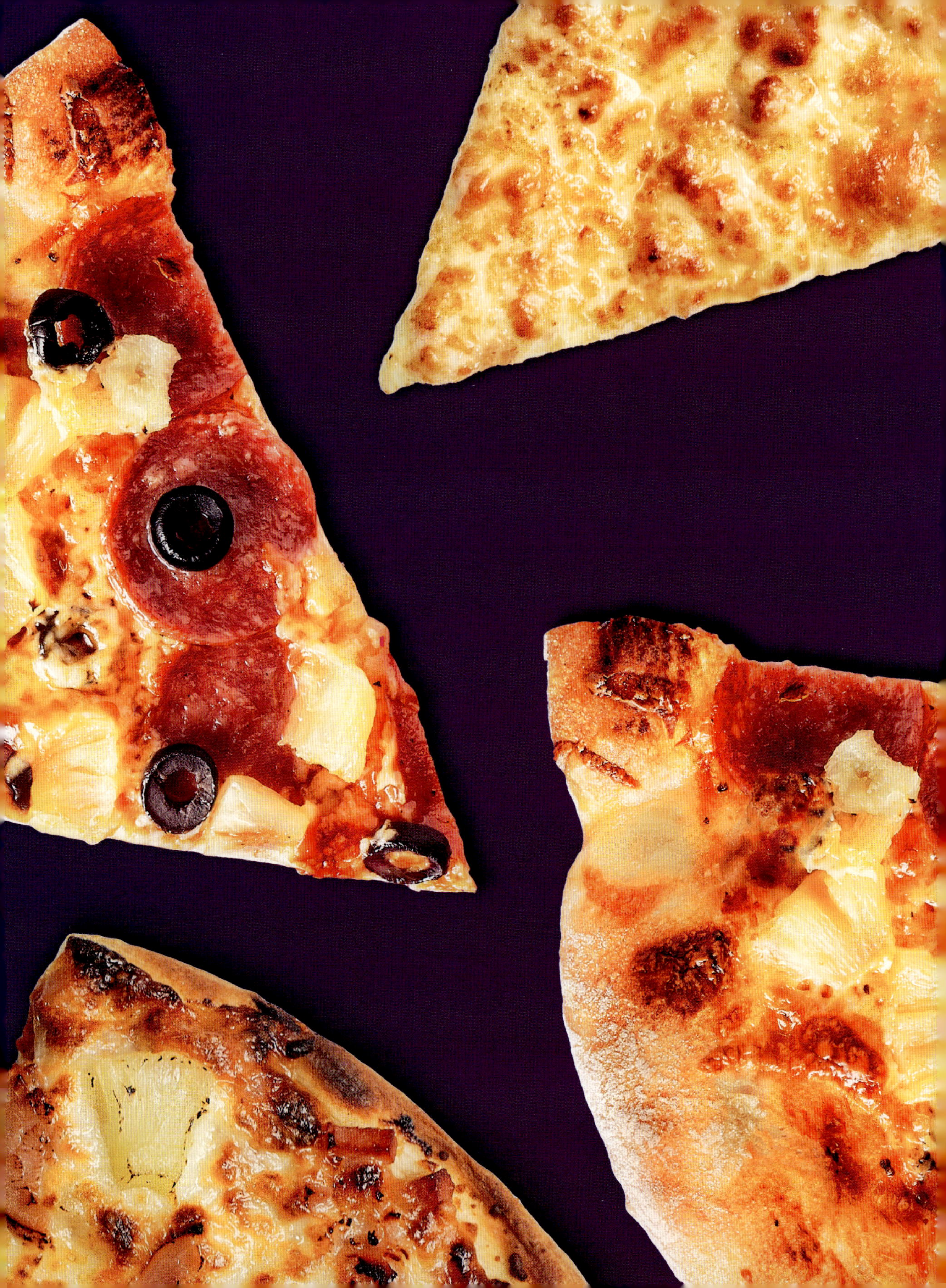

Liberally flour your work surface. Take a ball of dough (keeping the rest covered), place it in the center of the floured area, and sprinkle more flour on top. Using a **rolling pin**, gently roll out the dough to fit the pizza pan. Place it on the prepared pizza pan. Add ½ cup (125 mL) pizza sauce to the center of the pizza and spread evenly across the dough with the back of a spoon, being sure to leave a 1-inch (2.5 cm) border to the edge. Spread 1 cup (250 mL) of cheese over the tomato sauce and then top the cheese with one-third of your toppings of choice. Bake on the top rack of the oven until the cheese is golden brown, 15 minutes.

When you open the oven, a wave of heat will come out. Wait a few seconds before carefully removing the pizza from the oven with **oven mitts**. Slide the pizza onto a wooden cutting board and let rest 5 minutes. Cut into six to eight pieces and serve. Repeat for the other two pizzas.

Turn off the oven!

Try These Toppings!

PEPPERONI

1 cup (250 mL) pepperoni or salami slices

HAWAIIAN

½ cup (125 mL) ham slices cut into 1-inch (2.5 cm) squares
¼ cup (60 mL) sliced olives or capers
¼ cup (60 mL) pineapple chunks, cut into 1-inch (2.5 cm) cubes

ALL-DRESSED

1 cup (250 mL) pepperoni or salami slices
½ cup (125 mL) medium-**diced** green bell pepper
½ cup (125 mL) sliced mushrooms
½ cup (125 mL) sliced red or white onion

MEDITERRANEAN

1 cup (250 mL) feta cheese
1 cup (250 mL) washed baby spinach leaves
1 cup (250 mL) **diced** Roma tomatoes
½ cup (125 mL) chopped black olives

MAKE IT THE MAIN EVENT!

STICKY SODA POP RIBS

These are the BEST ribs and easy to make, but they do take a few hours, so give yourself some time. Serve these with Caesar Salad (page 108) and Potato Salad (page 110) for the perfect summer Saturday night meal.

SERVES 4-6

6-8 lb (2.7-3.6 kg) baby back pork ribs
2 tsp (10 mL) sea salt
1 tsp (5 mL) freshly ground black pepper
2¼ cups (560 mL) Dr. Pepper, divided
1 cup (250 mL) ketchup
½ cup (125 mL) apple cider vinegar
⅓ cup (80 mL) packed brown sugar
2 Tbsp (30 mL) garlic powder
2 Tbsp (30 mL) onion powder
1 Tbsp (15 mL) ground cumin
1 Tbsp (15 mL) Dijon mustard
2 tsp (10 mL) ground ginger

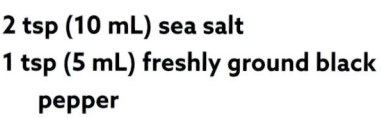

Preheat the oven to 425°F (220°C).

Lay the ribs in a 10 × 17-inch (25 × 43 cm) casserole dish, meaty side down. Make sure you can get them all in without overlapping. If they overlap, you might need to bake them in two smaller dishes. Sprinkle the salt and pepper on them.

Mix ¼ cup (60 mL) of the Dr. Pepper with the ketchup, apple cider vinegar, sugar, garlic powder, onion powder, cumin, Dijon mustard, and ground ginger in a medium **bowl**. Pour half of this sauce into a **container** and place it in the fridge. You'll need it later. Add the remaining 2 cups (500 mL) of Dr. Pepper to the sauce in the **bowl**. Stir it well and pour it over the ribs, being sure to wiggle them around so the sauce touches all parts of them.

LET'S EAT

Cover the casserole dish with **aluminum foil**, making sure that it is all wrapped up tightly. Place the ribs on the middle rack of the oven and cook for 1 hour. Lower the oven temperature to 350°F (180°C) and cook for another hour.

At this point, the meat should be almost falling off the bone. **Line** a big **cookie sheet** (at least 9 × 13-inch/23 × 33 cm) with **aluminum foil** or **parchment paper** and transfer the ribs to it, this time meaty side up. You want them in a single layer because this is where they get sticky! Discard the liquid in the casserole dish.

Switch the oven to broil. Using a **basting brush** or the back of a spoon, cover the ribs with half of the reserved sauce and place them back on the middle rack in the oven. Broil the ribs until they are crisp on the edges and the sauce is bubbling, 5 minutes. Watch them closely as they can overcook and burn quickly.

Turn off the oven!

Using **oven mitts**, remove the ribs from the oven and serve with the remaining sauce for extra dipping goodness.

Charlie Says

Try this with root beer, Coke, or cream soda—they're all good!

MAKE IT THE MAIN EVENT!

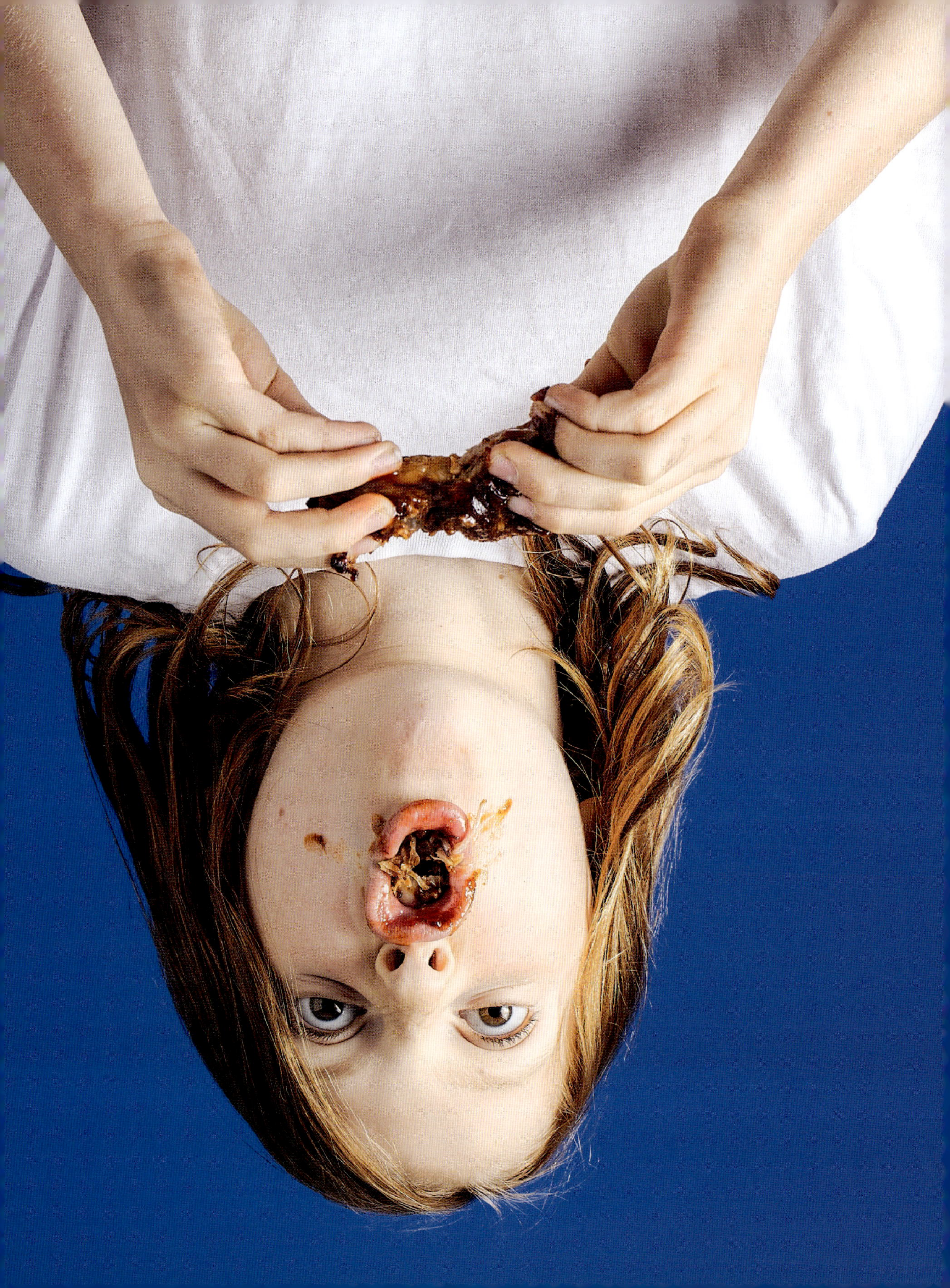

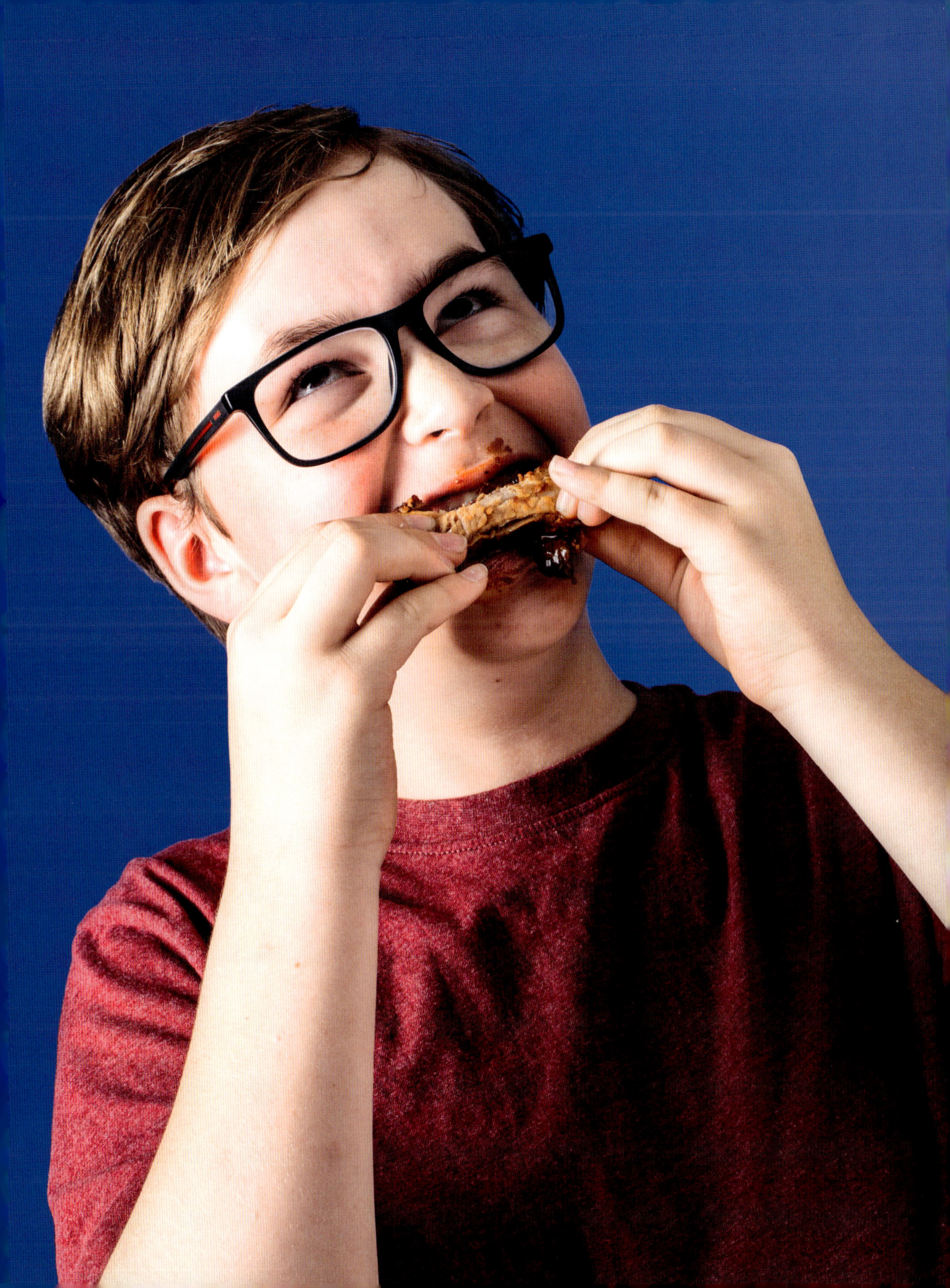

LOADED NACHOS

This one never gets old. You can literally put whatever you want on top of nachos and bake them, and they'll be perfection! Got leftover Roast Chicken (page 45) or Pajama Pants Pulled Pork (page 170)? Leftover vegetables? Throw them on! When you use tortilla chips as a base and cover them with cheese, you can't go wrong!

SERVES 4-6

- 1 (14 oz/400 g) bag of tortilla chips
- 2 cups (500 mL) shredded cheese (cheddar, Monterey Jack, and mozzarella are all good), divided
- 2 cups (500 mL) cooked meat (Pajama Pants Pulled Pork [page 170], shredded Roast Chicken [page 45], or cooked and diced bacon [see page 34] are all good)
- 1 (14 oz/398 mL) can beans (black, pinto, or kidney are all good), drained and rinsed
- ½ cup (125 mL) large-diced bell peppers
- ½ cup (125 mL) sliced olives
- 2-3 green onions, chopped
- ½ cup (125 mL) sliced cherry tomatoes

Preheat the oven to 425°F (220°C). Line a large baking sheet with parchment paper or a silicone mat.

Layer the tortilla chips on the prepared baking sheet and scatter 1 cup (250 mL) of the cheese evenly over top. Scatter the meat, beans, bell peppers, olives, green onions, and cherry tomatoes over the chips. Cover with the remaining cheese.

Bake until the cheese is bubbling and browning, 20 minutes.

Turn off the oven!

LET'S EAT

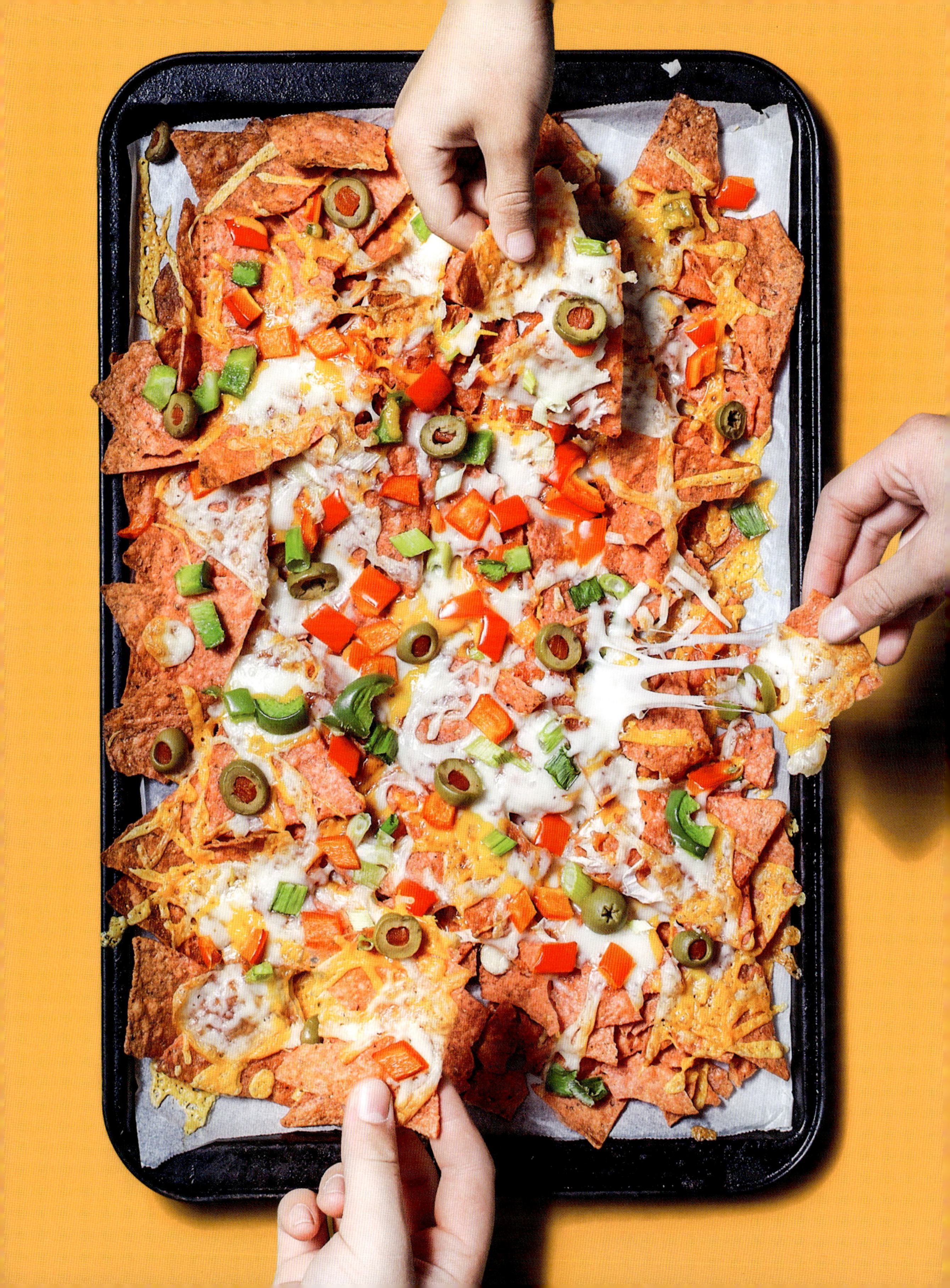

POP IT IN A POT... OR PAN!

... one-dish wonders to feed a crowd.

Chicken Noodle Soup with
   Easy Bread Rolls • 150
Sweet Potato Thai Curry • 154
Slow Cooker Baked Beans • 156
Chili con Carne • 158
Mac & Cheese • 161
Creamy Pesto Pasta • 164
Spaghetti Bolognese • 166
Pajama Pants Pulled Pork • 170
BBQ Pork Buns • 174
BBQ Sauce • 174
Chicken Pot Pie • 175
Shepherd's Pie a.k.a. Pâté Chinois • 178
Sheet Pan Dinner • 181

CHICKEN NOODLE SOUP WITH EASY BREAD ROLLS

Chicken noodle soup is the absolute best when you need a quick supper to warm you up. You can use the Roast Chicken from page 45 or grab a preroasted one from the grocery store. Either will work well.

SERVES 6

EASY BREAD ROLLS

Makes 12 rolls
1 cup (250 mL) warm water
3 Tbsp (45 mL) brown sugar
2 Tbsp (30 mL) active yeast
1 egg
⅓ cup + 1 Tbsp (95 mL) olive oil, divided
½ tsp (5 mL) sea salt
3–4 cups (750 mL–1 L) all-purpose or whole wheat flour
2 Tbsp (30 mL) milk of choice
2 Tbsp (30 mL) sesame seeds, poppy seeds, or bagel spice

Grease a 9 × 13-inch (23 × 33 cm) **baking dish** with sides at least 1½ inches (3.5 cm) high.

In a large **bowl**, combine the water, sugar, and yeast. Give it a stir and let it sit until the yeast is bubbly, about 10 minutes.

Crack the egg and place it in a small **bowl**. **Whisk** the egg with ⅓ cup (80 mL) of the oil. Add this plus the salt to the water-and-yeast mixture.

If you have a **stand mixer**, fit it with the dough hook and set the speed to the lowest setting. Add the flour 1 cup (250 mL) at a time until you have

150 LET'S EAT

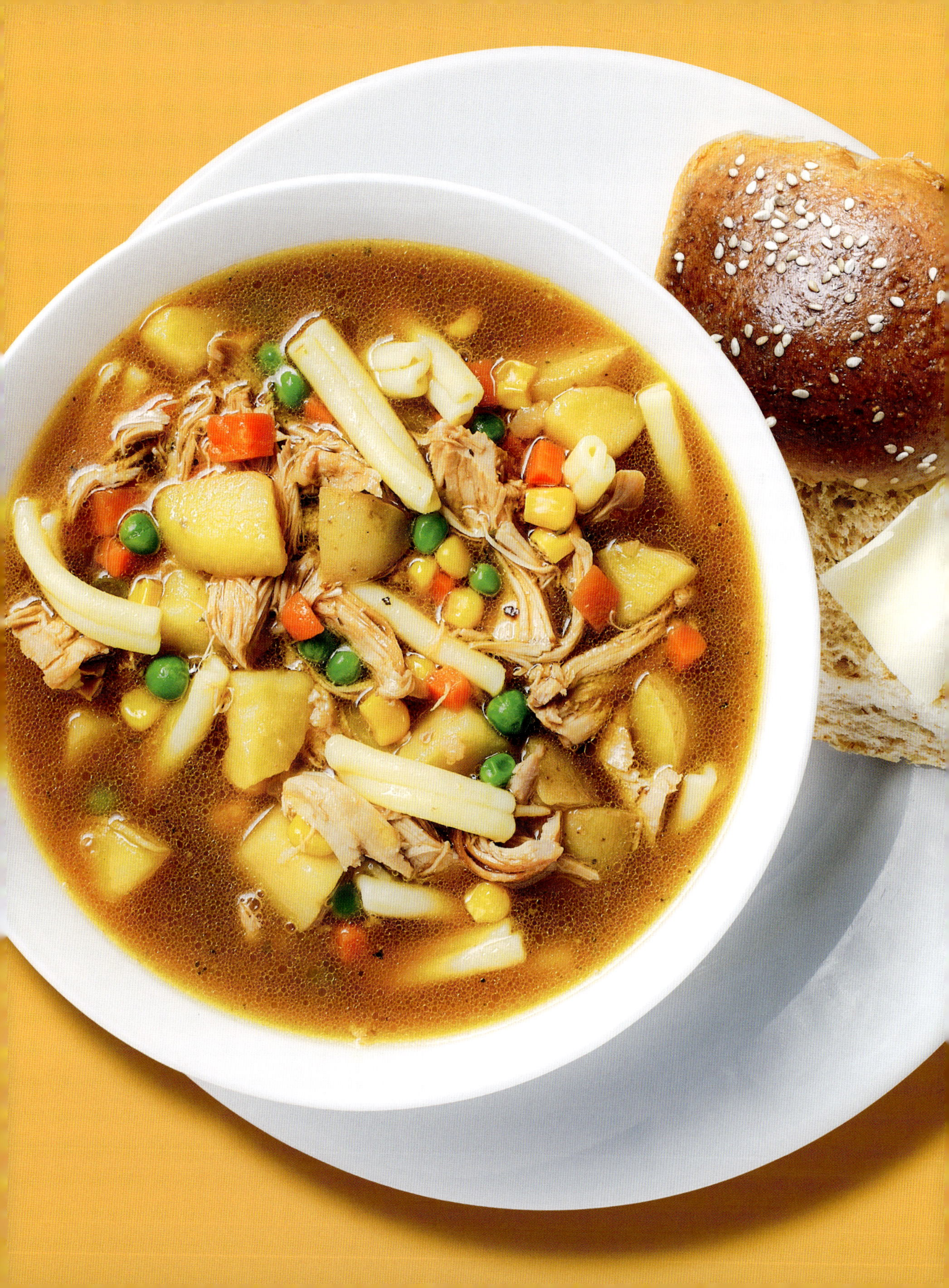

a soft dough that isn't sticky. You may not need all the flour. Up the speed to the next level and knead for another 5 minutes until the dough has become smooth and elastic.

If you're mixing by hand, use a **wooden spoon** to stir the flour into the water-and-yeast mixture 1 cup (250 mL) at a time. You may not need all the flour. Once the dough is mostly mixed together, you can take it out of the **bowl**, place it on a floured surface, and knead it with your hands for 10 more minutes. To knead, you push the ball of your hand into the dough and push forward. Take your hand up, turn the dough and fold it in half, then push into it again. Repeat for 10 minutes or until the dough is super soft and silky.

Divide the dough into 12 equal pieces and roll the pieces into balls. Place the dough balls in the prepared dish and cover it with a **cookie sheet** to keep the air out. Let the dough rise for 15–20 minutes in a warm place. The buns should start to almost double in size, but if that doesn't happen, don't worry, your room may just be cold. They will still rise in the oven.

Preheat the oven to 400°F (200°C).

Lightly brush the tops of the buns with the milk and sprinkle your topping of choice over top. Bake the buns on the middle rack of the oven until they're golden brown, about 15 minutes. Using **oven mitts**, remove the pan from the oven and place it on a **cooling rack** for 5 minutes. Turn off the heat. Remove the buns from the pan and place onto a cooling rack until ready to serve. If you're not serving immediately, once cooled, the buns will stay fresh for up to 2 days in an airtight **container** in the fridge.

CHICKEN NOODLE SOUP

1 Roast Chicken (page 45)
12 cups (3 L) chicken stock
4 cups (1 L/450 g) mixed frozen vegetables (corn, peas, carrots, and beans)
6 medium yellow potatoes, scrubbed but unpeeled, cut into 1-inch (2.5 cm) **dice**
¼ cup (60 mL) ketchup
¼ cup (60 mL) Worcestershire sauce
1 cup (250 mL) uncooked macaroni

Remove the meat from the chicken and tear it into small, bite-size pieces.

Place all of the ingredients except the macaroni in a large **pot**. Turn the stove on to high heat and bring the liquid to a **boil**. Lower the heat to medium and let **simmer**, uncovered, for 20 minutes. Add the macaroni and let simmer until the macaroni is fully cooked, 20 minutes. Serve with the rolls.

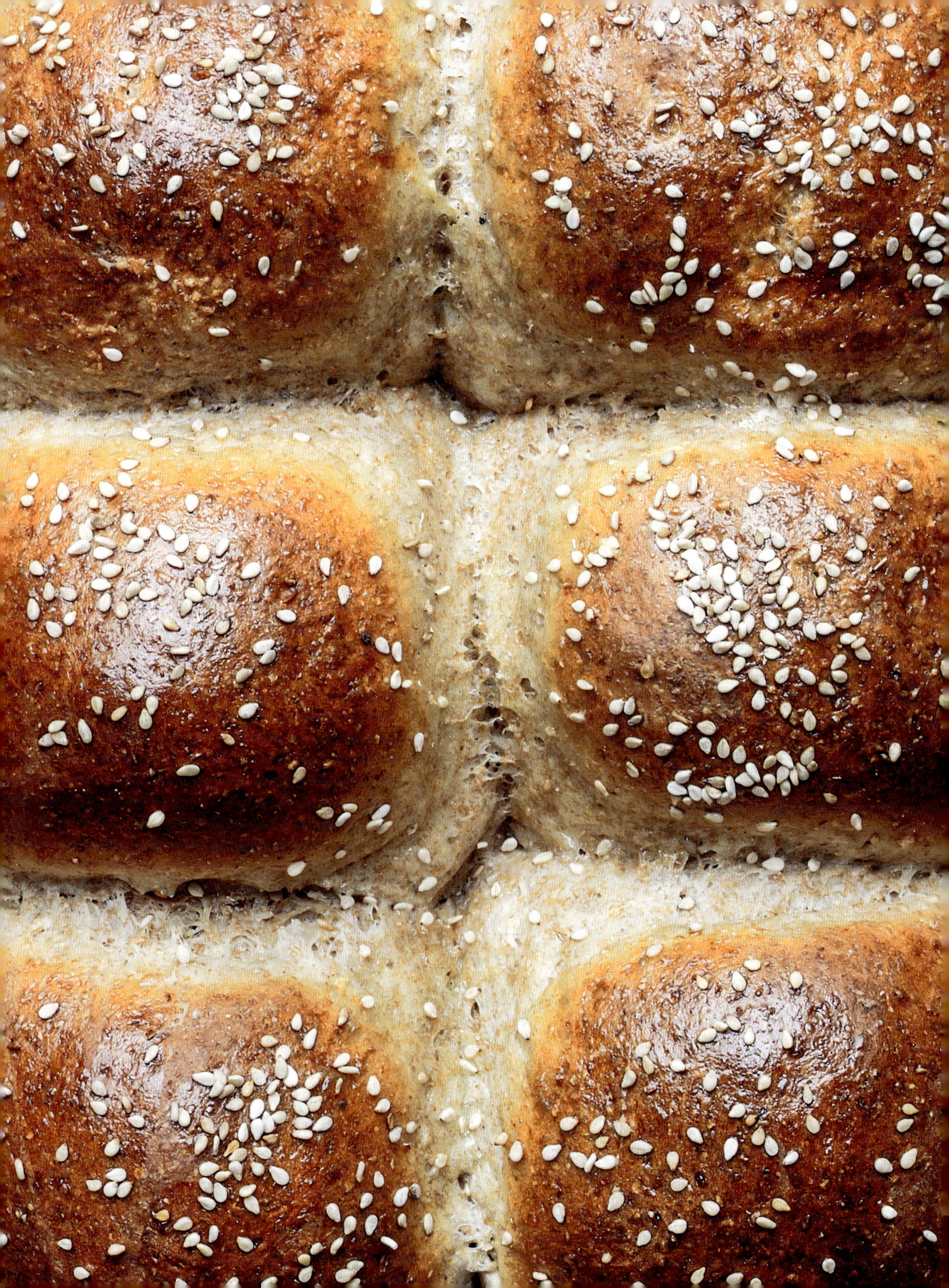

SWEET POTATO THAI CURRY

Although this recipe calls for sweet potatoes, curry is an ideal dish for vegetables like cauliflower, potatoes, or peas, and proteins like chickpeas, tofu, shrimp, or chicken. Basically, anything covered in curry sauce is YUM! Try different Thai curry pastes: there are green, yellow, and red varieties, and each has a different flavor, but be sure to check out their spice levels on the packaging for mild or spicy kinds. Not a fan of coconut milk or have an allergy? Use the equivalent amount of vegetable stock instead.

SERVES 4

- ¼ cup (60 mL) olive oil
- 4 sweet potatoes, peeled and cut into medium dice
- 2 small onions, cut into medium dice
- ¼ cup (60 mL) curry paste (like Thai Kitchen)
- 2 Tbsp (30 mL) brown sugar
- 2 (each 14 oz/400 mL) cans coconut milk
- 2 cups (500 mL) stock of choice (beef, chicken, fish, and vegetable all work well)
- 4 tsp (20 mL) fish sauce
- 2 cups (500 mL) cherry tomatoes, washed and halved
- 2 cups (500 mL) baby spinach, washed

In a large Dutch oven or soup pot, warm the olive oil over medium heat and cook the sweet potatoes and onions, stirring occasionally, until they're starting to brown.

Add the curry paste and stir it into the sweet potatoes and onions. Cook, stirring occasionally, for a few minutes to cook off the curry paste. Add the sugar, coconut milk, stock, and fish sauce and stir to combine.

Cover the pot with a lid and turn the heat down to low. Cook until the potatoes are al dente, about 10 minutes.

Stir in the tomatoes, cover, and cook another 5 minutes. Stir in the spinach and cook for another minute until the spinach has wilted.

Turn off the heat!

Serve with rice (page 42), mashed potatoes (page 36), or store-bought naan.

LET'S EAT

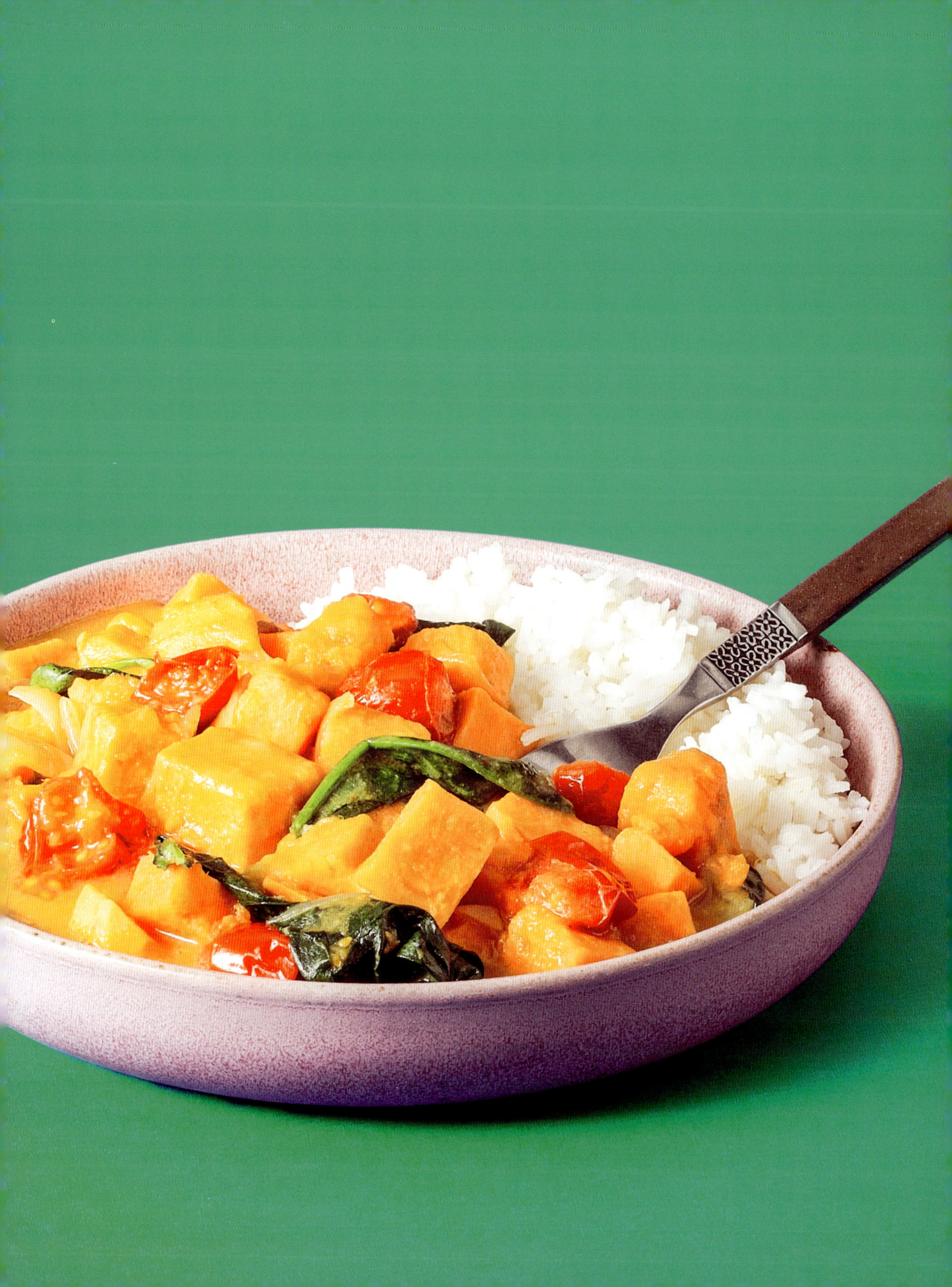

SLOW COOKER BAKED BEANS

You can eat this sweet and tangy boost of protein morning, noon, and night! Eat them on toast with a Caesar Salad (page 108), with Loaded Nachos (page 146), or with Sticky Soda Pop Ribs (page 142). This recipe can be made vegan by omitting the bacon and using vegan Worcestershire sauce.

SERVES 6-8

- 6-8 cooked bacon strips, chopped (see page 34)
- 2 (each 14 oz/398 mL) cans beans, drained and rinsed (pinto, navy, and kidney all work well)
- ½ cup (125 mL) ketchup
- ⅓ cup (80 mL) BBQ Sauce (page 174)
- ¼ cup (60 mL) dark brown sugar
- ¼ cup (60 mL) molasses
- 1 Tbsp (15 mL) Worcestershire sauce
- 2 tsp (10 mL) mustard powder
- 1 tsp (5 mL) garlic powder
- 1 tsp (5 mL) onion powder

Place everything in your **slow cooker** and mix well. Cook on low for 6 hours or on high for 3.

The beans can be stored in an airtight **container** in the fridge for up to 1 week and in the freezer for up to 3 months. Freeze them in small portions for a quick thaw.

Félix Says

I love these baked beans. They remind me of camping (*does a happy dance*).

LET'S EAT

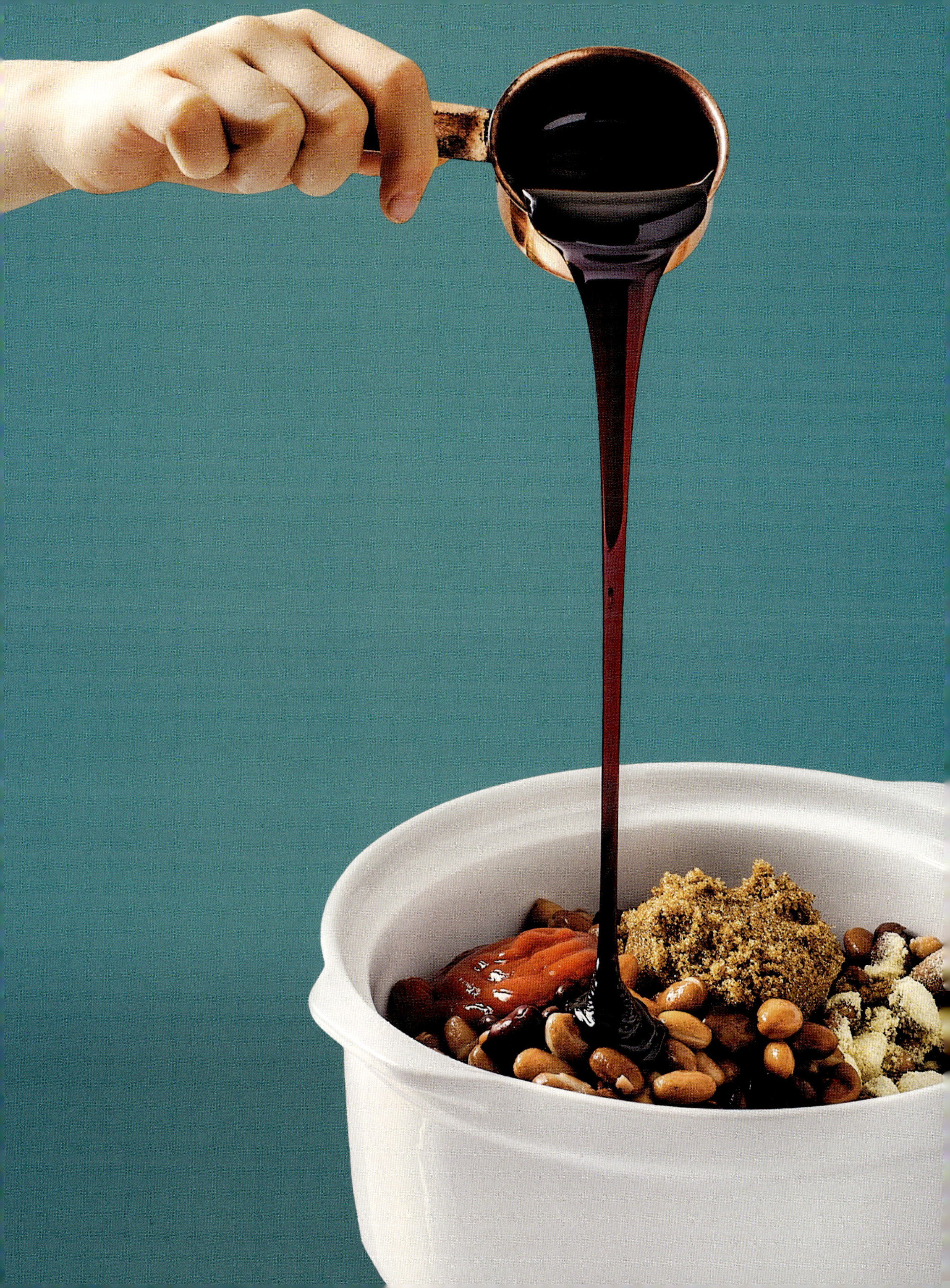

CHILI CON CARNE

Con carne means "with meat," but you can make this recipe vegetarian with a ground beef alternative. As for the chili being spicy, we leave that up to you! This will make a milder version, but if you want to turn up the heat, just add a bit more of the chipotle chili spice. To turn down the heat, eliminate it altogether. You can make this on the stove top or pop it in the slow cooker in the morning so it's ready for dinner.

SERVES 6-8

- 2 Tbsp (30 mL) olive oil
- 1½ lb (675 g) lean ground beef or veggie ground alternative, or 3 cups (750 mL) Spaghetti Bolognese sauce (page 166)
- 1 medium onion, medium-diced
- 1 (1 oz/28 g) package taco seasoning
- 1 tsp (5 mL) cocoa powder
- 1 tsp (5 mL) garlic powder
- ½ tsp (2.5 mL) chipotle pepper spice (optional)
- 2 (each 28 oz/796 mL) cans diced tomatoes, preferably fire-roasted
- 2 (each 19 oz/540 mL) cans black beans, drained and rinsed
- 2 (each 19 oz/540 mL) cans kidney beans, drained and rinsed
- 1 (14 oz/398 mL) can baked beans in tomato sauce or 1 cup (250 mL) Slow Cooker Baked Beans (page 156)
- 2 cups (500 mL) frozen corn kernels
- 2–3 cups (500–750 mL) grated cheddar cheese, for serving
- 1 recipe Guacamole (page 104), for serving
- 1 bag of tortilla chips, for serving

LET'S EAT

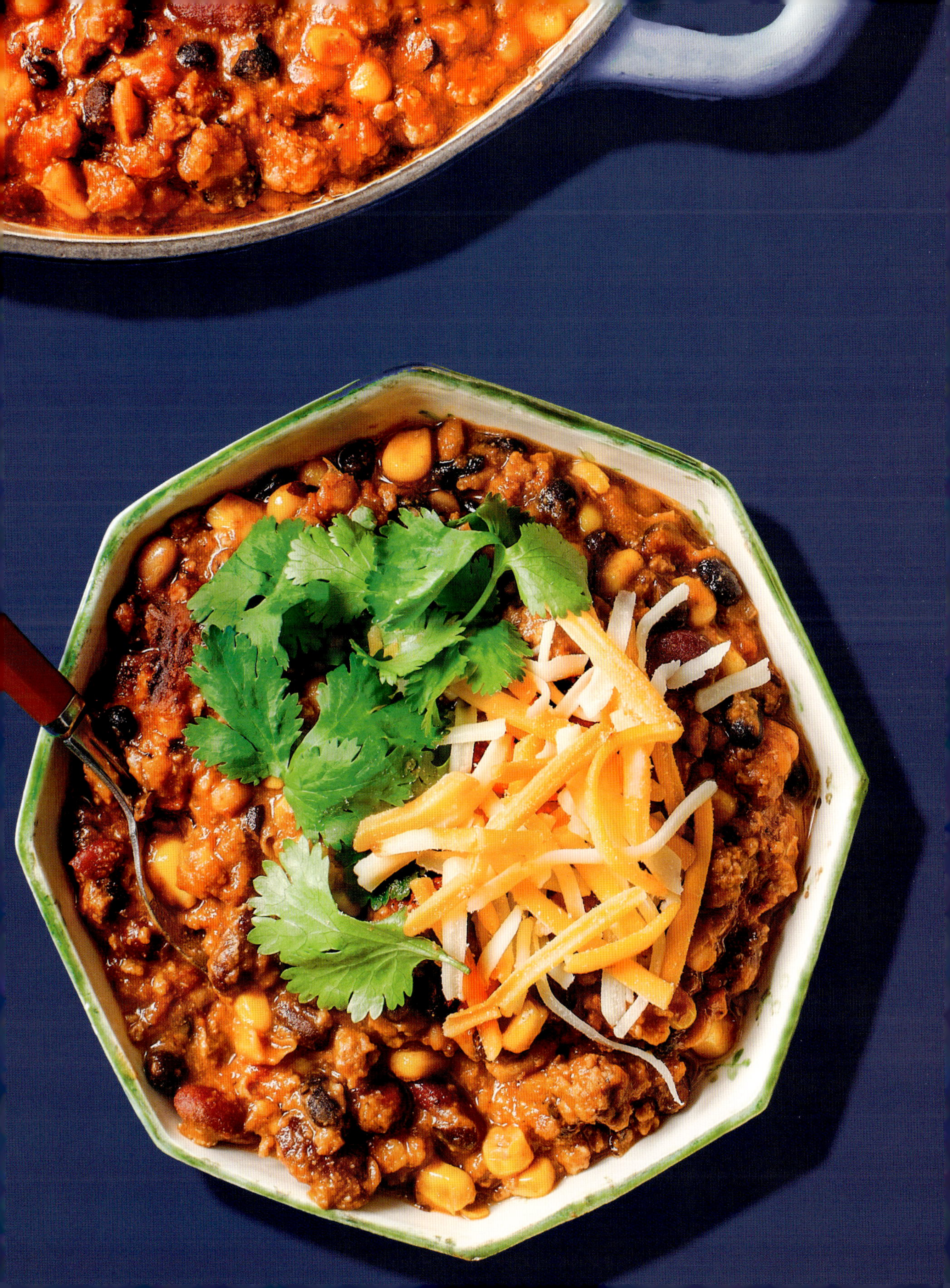

To make this on the stove top, warm the oil over medium-high heat in a large **Dutch oven** or deep **pot** and then add the ground beef. Move the beef around often, breaking it up with a long **wooden spoon**, and cook until it is all browned. (If you're using spaghetti Bolognese sauce, you can just warm it up in the pot.)

Add the onions to the meat and cook until the onions start to soften and become see-through, 4–5 minutes. Add the taco seasoning, cocoa powder, garlic powder, and chipotle pepper spice (if using) to the meat and cook for another 2 minutes. Add the tomatoes with their juice, all the beans, and the corn. Stir everything together and then turn the heat down to low.

Let the chili cook for 45–60 minutes, making sure to stir it every 10 minutes or so—you don't want the bottom to burn! The chili is ready when it has thickened slightly and all of the ingredients look like they have come together.

Turn off the heat!

To make this in the **slow cooker**, cook off the meat and spices as you would if you were cooking this on the stove top. Add them to your slow cooker along with the other ingredients. Cook on low for 6–7 hours.

Serve the chili with **grated** cheese, guacamole, and tortilla chips!

Charlie Says

Put the chili on top of your hot dog and whaddya know?!
CHILI DOG!

MAC & CHEESE

Chloë and Félix love to use the large, spiraled macaroni called cavatappi for this, but any of your favorite short pastas will do. This recipe is great straight out of the **pot**, but it also works really well as a casserole because the **roux** (butter and flour mixture) keeps the cheese creamy and rich as it bakes along with the pasta.

SERVES 4-6

- 1 lb (450 g) uncooked macaroni
- 3 Tbsp (45 mL) all-purpose flour
- ¼ tsp (1 mL) smoked paprika
- ¼ tsp (1 mL) onion powder
- 2 Tbsp (30 mL) unsalted butter
- 2 cups (500 mL) warm (hand-hot) chicken, beef, or vegetable stock
- 1 cup (250 mL) warm (hand-hot) milk
- 2 cups (500 mL) **shredded** cheese (cheddar, Asiago, and mozzarella all work well)
- ½ cup (125 mL) panko crumbs
- 1 tsp (5 mL) dried oregano
- 2 Tbsp (30 mL) olive oil
- ¼ cup (60 mL) **grated** Parmesan cheese

Bring a large **pot** of salted water to a **boil** over high heat and cook the pasta according to the package instructions. Once it's cooked, turn off the heat and drain the pasta through a **sieve**. Return the cooked pasta to the large pot.

Preheat the oven to 375°F (190°C).

Sprinkle the flour in a medium **pot** and cook, stirring frequently, on medium-low heat for a few minutes until it browns. Add the paprika and onion powder. Stir for 30 seconds to toast the spices, then add the butter. This is your **roux**. Stir and cook another 30 seconds. Slowly **whisk** in the warm stock, being careful of the steam—it's hot! Add the warm milk and **shredded** cheese and turn the heat up to medium. Cook, stirring occasionally, until thickened and bubbly, about 5-6 minutes.

Pour the thickened liquid over the pasta in the other **pot** and stir well to combine. Pour the mixture into a 9 × 13-inch (23 × 33 cm) **baking dish**. You don't need to grease it first.

In a small **bowl**, combine the panko crumbs, oregano, olive oil, and Parmesan. Sprinkle the mixture over the pasta and sauce.

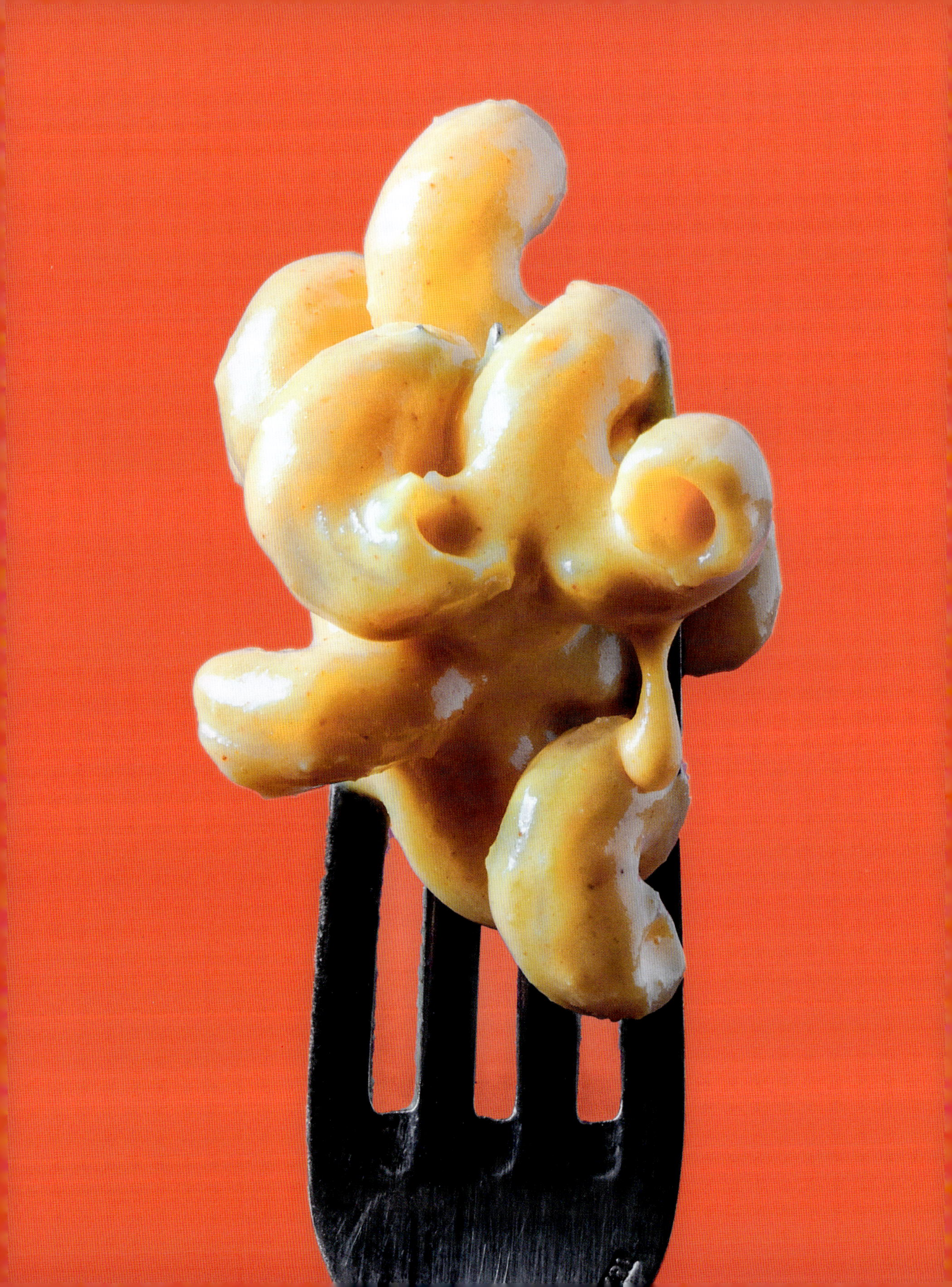

Bake until golden brown on top and bubbling on the sides, 45 minutes. Using **oven mitts**, remove from the oven and let stand for 10 minutes before serving.

Turn off the oven!

Take It to the Next Level!

Turn this into a casserole by adding your favorite veggies and protein. Stir in 2–3 cups (500–750 mL) of a mix of cooked vegetables and protein into the pasta along with the cheese sauce. Roast Chicken (page 45) and Pajama Pants Pulled Pork (page 170) work well.

Make It Vegan!

Replace the butter with a nondairy equivalent, switch out the stock and milk with vegetable stock, and use your favorite vegan cheese in place of the Parmesan.

POP IT IN A POT . . . OR PAN!

CREAMY PESTO PASTA

This is a one-pot pasta supper that is easy to mix up in no time at all. You can also make it and then pack it into a covered casserole dish to freeze until needed.

SERVES 6-8

- 2 lb (900 g) penne, rigatoni, or fusilli
- 1 cup (250 mL) heavy cream (36%) or oat milk
- ½ cup (125 mL) pesto sauce
- ½ cup (125 mL) chicken or vegetable stock
- 1 tsp (5 mL) sea salt
- 1 tsp (5 mL) freshly ground black pepper
- 4 cups (1 L) grated Parmesan cheese
- 4 cups (1 L) extras (see Add Some Extras!)

In a large pot of water, cook the pasta according to the package instructions. When the pasta has finished cooking, scoop 1 cup (250 mL) of the pasta water out, set the measuring cup aside, and then drain the pasta in a sieve placed over a bowl.

Leave the pasta in the sieve.

Place the reserved pasta water in the pot you used to cook the pasta. Add the cream, pesto, stock, salt, and pepper to it. Place on the stove and heat on medium, stirring occasionally until almost boiling. Add the pasta back into the pot and mix everything together. Stir in the Parmesan and serve immediately.

If you want to freeze this to eat another time, transfer the pasta to a 9 × 13-inch (23 × 33 cm) casserole dish, let cool completely, cover tightly, and freeze until needed. When you're ready to reheat, place the dish of frozen pasta in the oven and set the oven to 350°F (180°C). Bake until the cheese on top is nice and golden and the pasta is bubbling inside, about 45 minutes from the time you put it in the oven.

Add Some Extras!

- Roast Chicken (page 45), cut in large dice
- Sliced cherry tomatoes
- Spinach
- Feta, crumbled
- Fresh basil
- Sesame Roasted Broccoli (page 118), cut in bite-size pieces

LET'S EAT

Félix Says

If you have to eat something green, make it pesto pasta.

SPAGHETTI BOLOGNESE

This is the classic spaghetti and meat sauce that almost everyone loves. You can double the sauce recipe and freeze the extra in a large freezer bag or airtight **container** for up to 3 months—if you can wait that long to eat Bolognese again!

SERVES 4-6

- ¼ cup (60 mL) olive oil
- 1 lb (450 g) lean ground beef mince, or vegetarian alternative
- ½ lb (225 g) ground pork, or vegetarian alternative
- 2 medium yellow onions, **grated**
- 2 cloves garlic, **minced**
- 1 large carrot, **grated**
- 1 stick celery, **grated**
- 1 Tbsp (15 mL) dried basil
- 1 Tbsp (15 mL) dried oregano
- 1 Tbsp (15 mL) dried thyme
- 2 cans (each 28 oz/796 mL) diced tomatoes
- 2 cups (500 mL) water
- 1 Tbsp (15 mL) balsamic vinegar
- 1 Tbsp (15 mL) tomato paste
- 2 tsp (10 mL) sea salt
- 1 lb (450 g) dried spaghetti
- **Grated** Parmesan cheese

Mise en place is important whenever you cook, but it's super important to have everything ready for this recipe because ingredients get added quickly while you're stirring and you won't have time to stop and chop, so make sure all of your veggies are **grated** and **minced**, your herbs are measured, and your cans are open and ready to go.

Place a large, heavy-bottomed **pot** on the stove over medium-high heat and add the oil, making sure it covers the bottom of the pot evenly. Add the beef and pork to the pot and cook for 7–10 minutes, stirring and breaking up the meat with a **wooden spoon** as you go. The meat should be cooked through and beginning to turn brown before you move on. Make sure to wear an **oven mitt** as the meat can splatter a bit.

Add all of the vegetables and dried herbs and cook, stirring, for another 5 minutes. The vegetables should begin to look a bit cooked and the herbs should start smelling good! Turn down the heat to medium-low and continue to cook until the vegetables are soft,

LET'S EAT

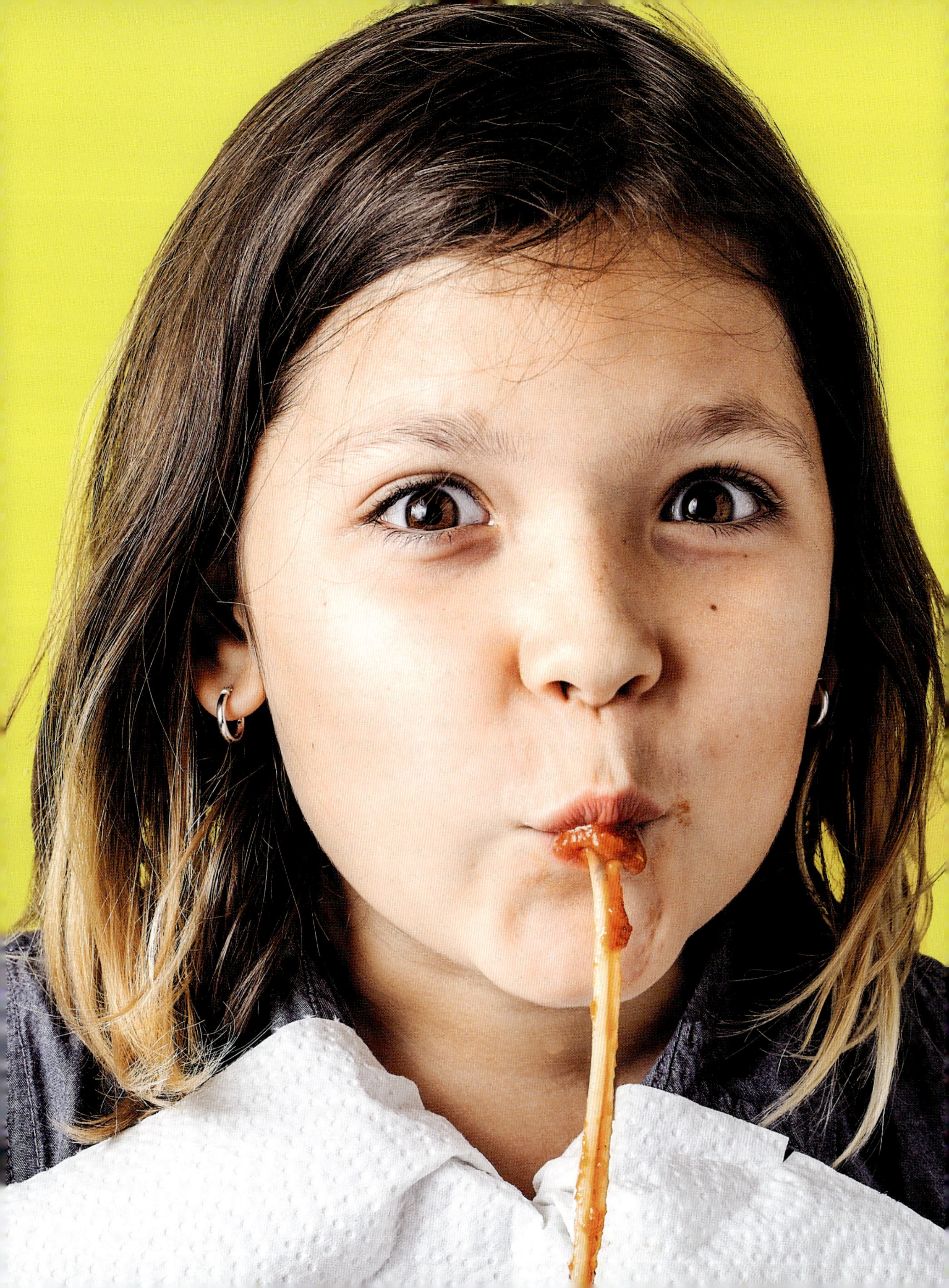

about 10 minutes, stirring as you go. Add the canned tomatoes with their juice, the water, balsamic vinegar, and tomato paste to the **pot**. Stir to combine all of the ingredients and turn down the temperature to low.

Place a lid on the **pot** and let the sauce **simmer** for 2–3 hours, stirring every 15 minutes or so. Start to look for the sauce being done at the 2½-hour mark. You'll know it's done when all the vegetables are broken down, the sauce has thickened nicely, and the color is a deep, rich red.

When you're ready to eat, bring a large **pot** of water to a **boil** over high heat and season well with sea salt. Cook the pasta according to the package instructions (see page 39) and be sure to turn off the stove when you're done. Divide the spaghetti among four plates and top with sauce and **grated** Parmesan.

Take It to the Next Level!

To make an easy lasagna, just get a 1 lb (454 g) package of no-cook lasagna pasta sheets and a 15 oz (425 g) container of ricotta cheese. Layer a 9 × 13-inch (23 × 33 cm) **baking dish** as follows: a thin layer of meat sauce, noodles, more meat sauce, noodles, the container of ricotta cheese, noodles, meat sauce, noodles, thin layer of meat sauce, 1 cup (250 mL) **grated** Parmesan cheese and 1 cup (250 mL) grated mozzarella. Bake at 375°F (190°C) until the noodles are soft, the sauce is bubbling, and the cheese on top is golden and crispy, 50–60 minutes.

Chloë Says

Serve this with some good bread so you get every drop of the sauce!

LET'S EAT

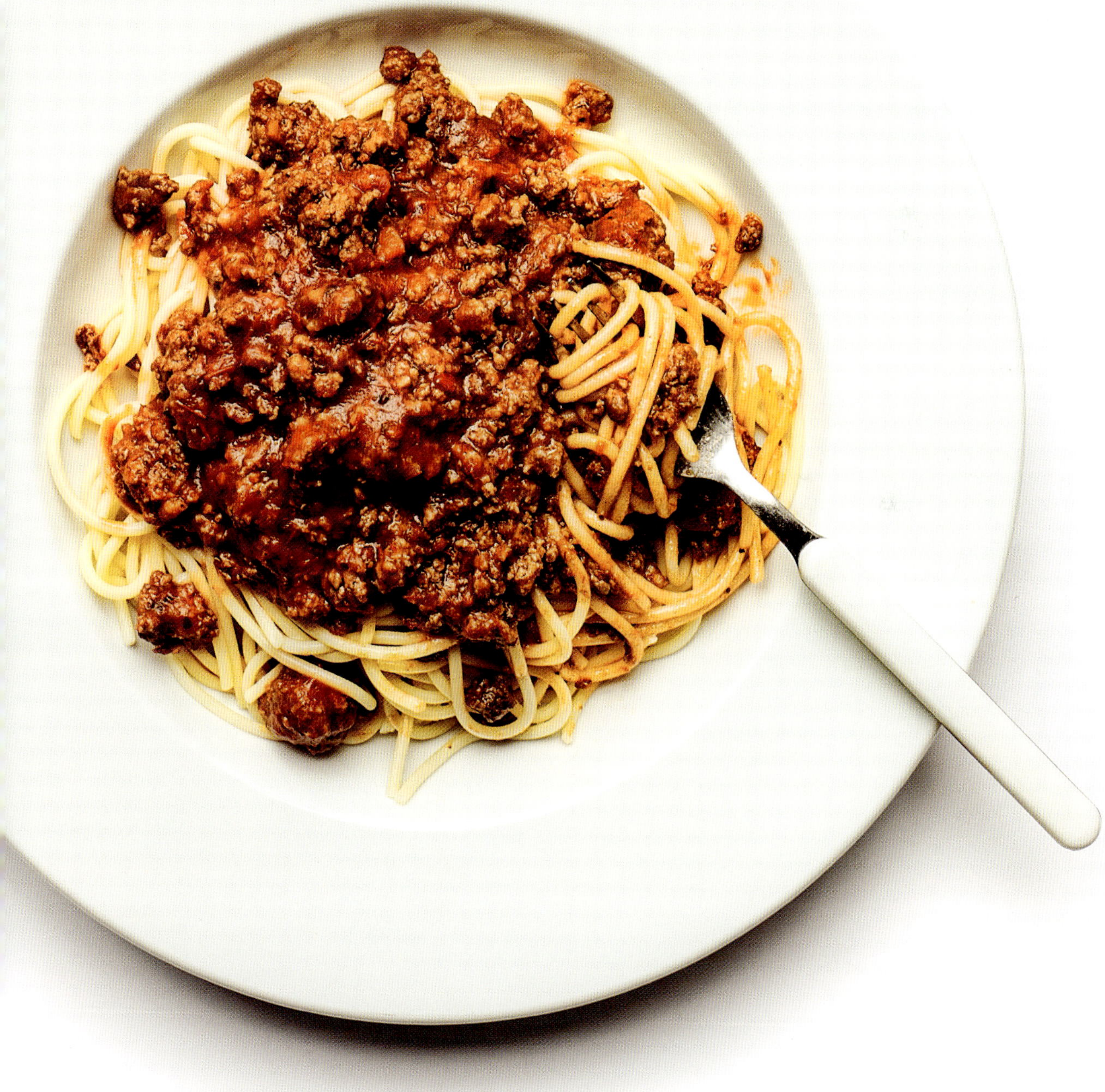

PAJAMA PANTS PULLED PORK

We call this Pajama Pants Pulled Pork because it's super easy to throw together when you get out of bed. Plop it all in the **slow cooker**, forget about it for the next 6-8 hours, and the perfect supper is ready for you when it's time to eat. (Note: If you don't have a slow cooker, you can also make this in a **Dutch oven**.)

SERVES 6-8

- 1 Tbsp (15 mL) onion powder
- 1 Tbsp (15 mL) garlic powder
- 2 tsp (10 mL) ground cumin
- 2 tsp (10 mL) dried or ground thyme
- 2 tsp (10 mL) sea salt
- 1 tsp (5 mL) ground black pepper
- 1 (4½-5 lb/2-2.25 kg) boneless pork shoulder (also known as pork butt)
- 3 Tbsp (45 mL) olive oil
- ¼ cup (60 mL) apple juice
- ¼ cup (60 mL) apple cider vinegar
- 1 Tbsp (15 mL) Worcestershire sauce
- 1 cup (250 mL) BBQ Sauce (page 174) (optional)

In a small **mixing bowl**, mix the onion powder, garlic powder, cumin, thyme, salt, and pepper together to make a "rub." This will be your seasoning for the meat.

Cut the meat into 4 pieces and then coat all sides of each piece with the rub. Use your hands so all of the meat is really covered. Save any of the rub that doesn't stick and go wash your hands.

Charlie Says

Pulled pork on EVERYTHING.

To cook in a slow cooker:

This next step can be splattery with the oil, so be sure to wear **oven mitts**. Heat a large **frying pan** over medium-high heat and add the oil. Place the meat in the frying pan and let it sit for 2–3 minutes—a good, dark brown crust will form on the sides touching the pan to **sear** the meat. Turn all of the pieces of meat over onto their sides and repeat this until all of the pieces are completely seared on all sides. Remove the meat from the pan.

Turn off the heat!

Place the pork in the **slow cooker** and add the apple juice, apple cider vinegar, Worcestershire sauce, and any remaining rub. Mix to combine everything. Cover the slow cooker and cook on low for 6–8 hours or high for 4–6. At 6 hours (if you're cooking on low heat) or 4 hours (if you're cooking on high), check to see if the pork can be easily torn apart with a fork. Once you can do this, remove the lid from the slow cooker and cook for 1 more hour.

To cook in a Dutch oven:

Preheat the oven to 300°F (150°C).

Follow the instructions above to **sear** the meat in the **Dutch oven**. Add the apple juice, apple cider vinegar, Worcestershire sauce, and any remaining rub. Mix to combine everything. Cover the Dutch oven with its lid and then cook the pork in the oven for 4 hours. Check the pork at the 3-hour mark and if it needs more cooking, return it to the oven for another 30 minutes or until the pork is "pullable." Once you can pull the pork apart with two forks, remove the lid and let the meat cook until it's nice and crispy around the edges, 45 minutes to 1 hour. Turn off the heat.

To finish the pork:

When the pork is finished cooking, remove it from the **slow cooker** or **Dutch oven**, being sure to save the cooking liquid inside the pot, and place it on a large **cutting board**. Use two forks to **shred** the meat. You can do this by pulling at the meat in opposite directions, hence "pulled" pork. Once the meat is completely shredded, add it back to the pot and stir to mix it into the cooking liquids. If you're using BBQ sauce, mix it in now.

Serve as is, on buns, or on top of Avocado Toast (page 74), Loaded Nachos (page 146), or even Sunday Waffles (page 82).

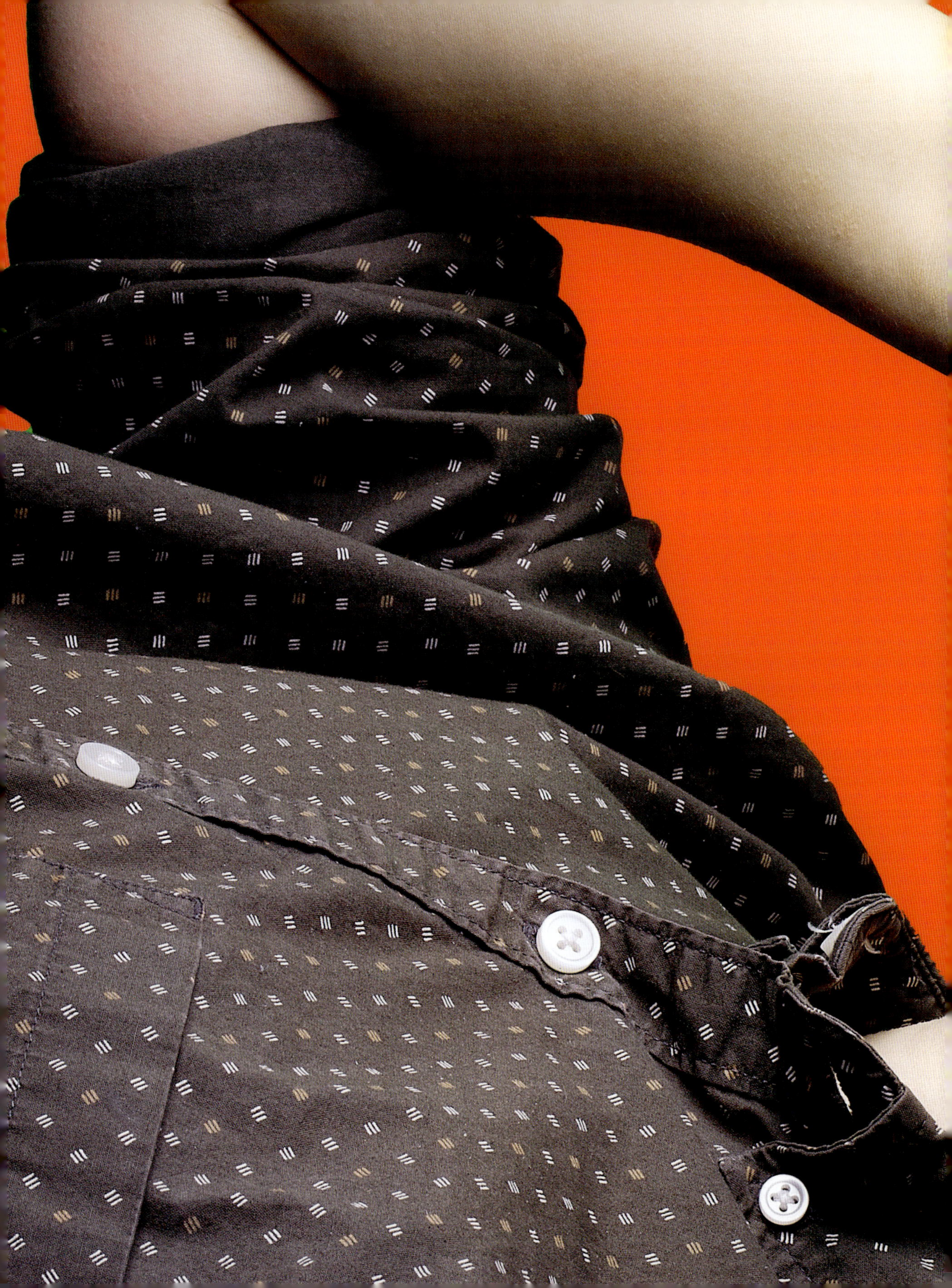

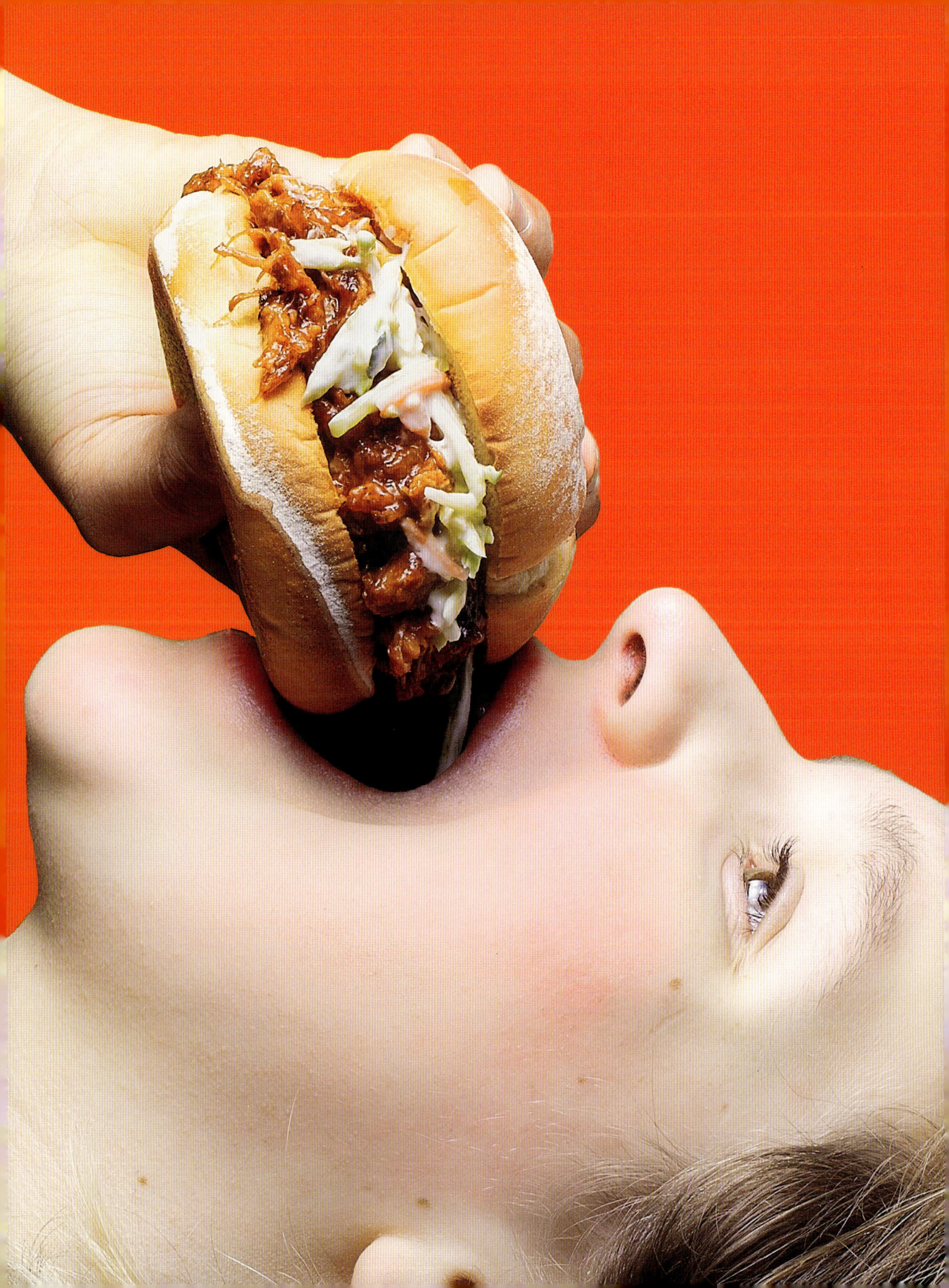

BBQ Pork Buns

SERVES 6

This is Charlie's favorite way to eat pulled pork! It's a quick and easy supper when you have Pajama Pants Pulled Pork (page 170) on hand. Serve this with Caesar Salad (page 108) or Carrot and Apple Salad (page 106).

- 1 recipe Pajama Pants Pulled Pork (page 170)
- 1 cup (250 mL) BBQ Sauce (see recipe below)
- 1 (1 lb/450 g) package shredded slaw salad mix
- ¼ cup (60 mL) apple cider vinegar
- 1 Tbsp (15 mL) granulated sugar
- ½ cup (125 mL) plain Greek yogurt
- 1 tsp (5 mL) sea salt
- 1 recipe Easy Bread Rolls (page 150) or store-bought buns

Preheat the oven to 350°F (180°C).

Shred the pork into a bowl and mix it with the BBQ sauce. Place it in an ovenproof dish large enough to hold everything without it spilling over the sides, and pop it in the oven until warmed through, about 20 minutes.

Place the slaw mix, apple cider vinegar, and sugar in a mixing bowl. Stir together and let sit uncovered at room temperature for 15–20 minutes. The slaw mix will soften as it sits. Add the yogurt and salt and mix all of the ingredients together.

Slice the buns in half the sandwich way and place a good scoop of pork inside. Top with slaw and serve immediately.

BBQ Sauce

MAKES 3 CUPS

- 2 cups (500 mL) ketchup
- ½ cup (125 mL) apple cider vinegar
- ¼ cup (60 mL) packed brown sugar
- 2 Tbsp (30 mL) maple syrup
- 1 Tbsp (15 mL) Worcestershire sauce or coconut aminos
- 1 Tbsp (15 mL) Dijon mustard
- 1 Tbsp (15 mL) lemon juice
- 1 tsp (5 mL) ground cumin
- 1 tsp (5 mL) hot sauce of choice (optional)

Combine the ingredients in a small pot over medium-high heat. Bring to a boil and turn immediately down to low. Simmer for 5 minutes, stirring often with a wooden spoon. Be careful—the mix may bubble and will be hot! Let cool before serving.

CHICKEN POT PIE

Pot pies make a great family meal and are easy to make in a short amount of time. Once you have all the ingredients on hand, you can have this dish in the oven in under 20 minutes and on the table within the hour.

SERVES 4-6

- 2 Tbsp (30 mL) olive oil
- 1 small white onion, cut into small **dice**
- 3 stalks celery, cut into small **dice**
- 2 cloves garlic, **minced**
- 6 Tbsp (90 mL) unsalted butter
- 1 tsp (5 mL) dried thyme
- 1 tsp (5 mL) dried sage
- ½ cup (125 mL) all-purpose flour
- 3 cups (750 mL) chicken stock
- ½ cup (125 mL) milk
- Meat from one full Roast Chicken (page 45) (about 3 cups/750 mL), cut into bite-size pieces
- 2 cups (500 mL) frozen vegetable mix (carrots, peas, corn, and beans)
- 1 tsp (5 mL) sea salt
- ½ tsp (2.5 mL) freshly ground black pepper
- 1 sheet frozen puff pastry, thawed
- 1 egg
- 1 Tbsp (15 mL) water

Place a large **pot** on the stove over medium heat and add the oil. Add the onions, celery, and garlic to the pot and cook, stirring constantly with a **wooden spoon**, until the celery and onion start to soften, 4-5 minutes. Add the butter, thyme, and sage and cook, stirring constantly again, until the butter is fully melted.

Add the flour. Use a **whisk** to mix it in and then continue to cook until the mixture starts to turn a golden color, 2-3 minutes. Add the stock ½ cup (125 mL) at a time and **whisk** quickly to mix all of the mixture smoothly together. Whisk in the milk and cook until your mixture starts to thicken, 3-4 minutes. As soon as the mixture starts to thicken, remove the **pot** from the heat and stir in the chicken, frozen vegetables, salt, and pepper.

Turn off the stove!

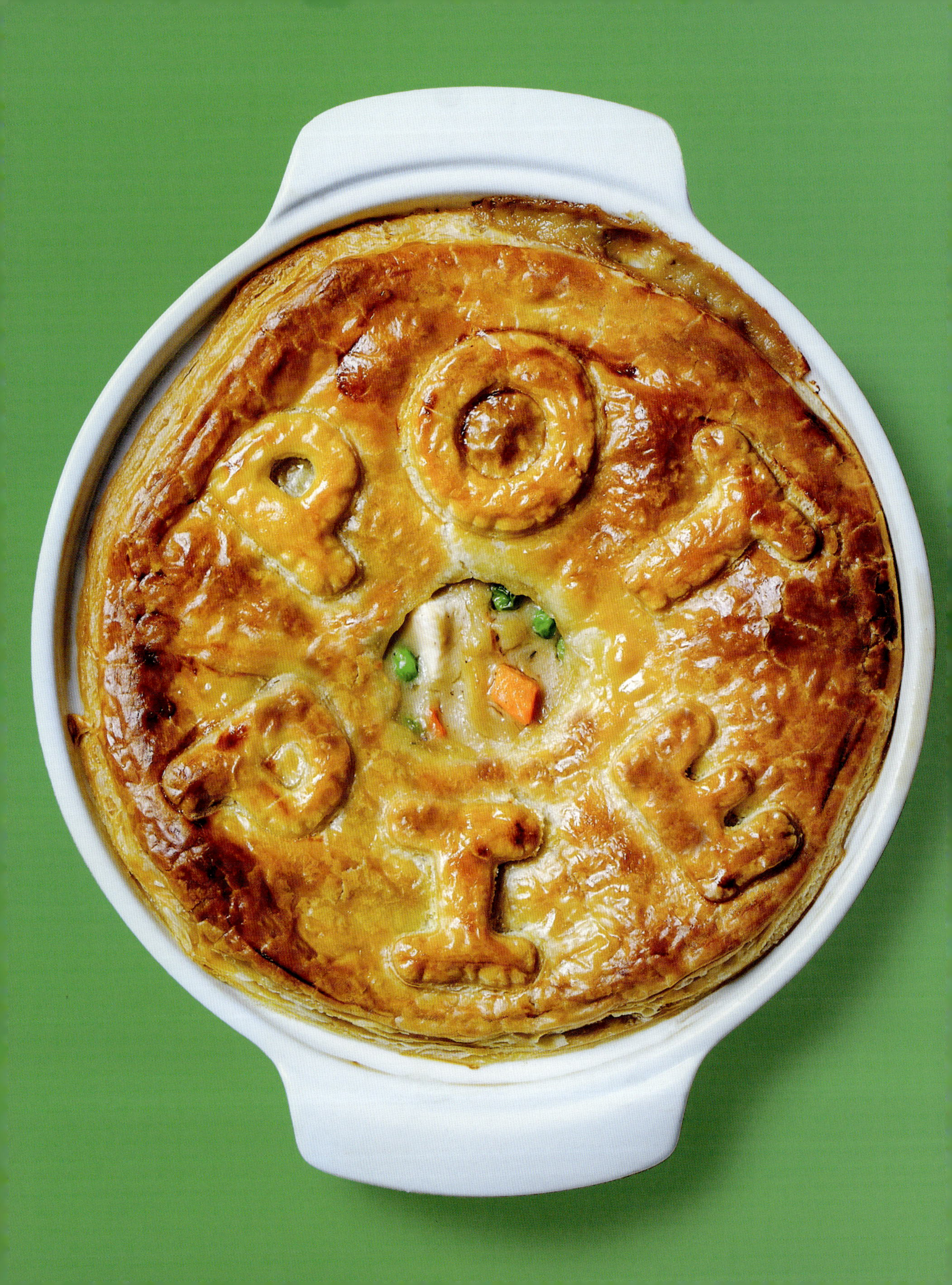
POT PIE

Preheat the oven to 400°F (200°C).

Scoop the mixture into an ungreased 9 × 13-inch (23 × 33 cm) **baking dish** with sides at least 2 inches (5 cm) high. Place the puff pastry sheet on top of the filling. Or use cookie cutters to cut out fun shapes and place them on top of the filling. Use a fork to lightly beat the egg and water together to make an egg wash, and then use a **pastry brush** to brush the top of the pastry with the egg wash. Place the dish on the middle rack in the oven and bake until the pastry is puffed and golden and the filling is bubbly, 25–30 minutes.

Using **oven mitts**, remove the pan from the oven and let the pastries sit for at least 10 minutes before serving.

Turn off the oven!

Mix It Up!

PULLED PORK & APPLE PIE

Wash and **grate** (no need to peel or core) 1 Granny Smith apple and add it with the onions and garlic. Use 3 cups (750 mL) Pajama Pants Pulled Pork (page 170) instead of the chicken.

SWEET POTATO & CORN PIE

Replace the chicken with 3 cups (750 mL) peeled and cubed (1 inch/ 2.5 cm) sweet potatoes, swap the frozen vegetable mix for just corn, and, to keep it vegetarian, use vegetable stock instead of chicken stock.

SHEPHERD'S PIE AKA PÂTÉ CHINOIS

This classic French casserole is the perfect comfort food for chilly winter nights. Using creamed corn allows the vegetable starches to blend with the beef juices, making a delicious gravy as it bakes.

SERVES 6-8

- 3 large Russet potatoes, peeled and cut into 2-inch (5 cm) chunks
- 3 Tbsp (45 mL) unsalted butter, cubed
- ¼ cup (60 mL) milk or whipping cream
- ¼ tsp (1 mL) sea salt
- ¼ tsp (1 mL) freshly ground black pepper
- 1 lb (450 g) ground beef (or a mix of pork, chicken, and turkey)
- 2 tsp (10 mL) onion powder
- 2 tsp (10 mL) garlic powder
- 2 tsp (10 mL) dried oregano
- 2 tsp (10 mL) smoked paprika, plus more for garnish (optional)
- 1 (14 oz/398 mL) can corn niblets, drained, or 1½ cups (375 mL) frozen corn niblets
- 1 (14 oz/398 mL) can creamed corn

Fill a large **pot** with water. Add the potatoes, cover, and place over high heat until **boiling**. Turn down the heat to medium-high and slightly uncover the pot. Cook until the potatoes are fork-tender (can be easily pierced with a fork), about 10 minutes. Carefully drain the potatoes into a **sieve**.

Turn off the heat!

Working over top of your original potato pot, use a fork or spoon to place a scoop of potatoes into a **potato ricer** and press down on the lever. Repeat this until all the potatoes are mashed. If you don't have a ricer, use a **potato masher** to mash the potatoes. Add the butter and the milk to the potatoes and stir until combined. Add the salt and pepper and mix to combine.

Preheat the oven to 400°F (200°C).

178   LET'S EAT

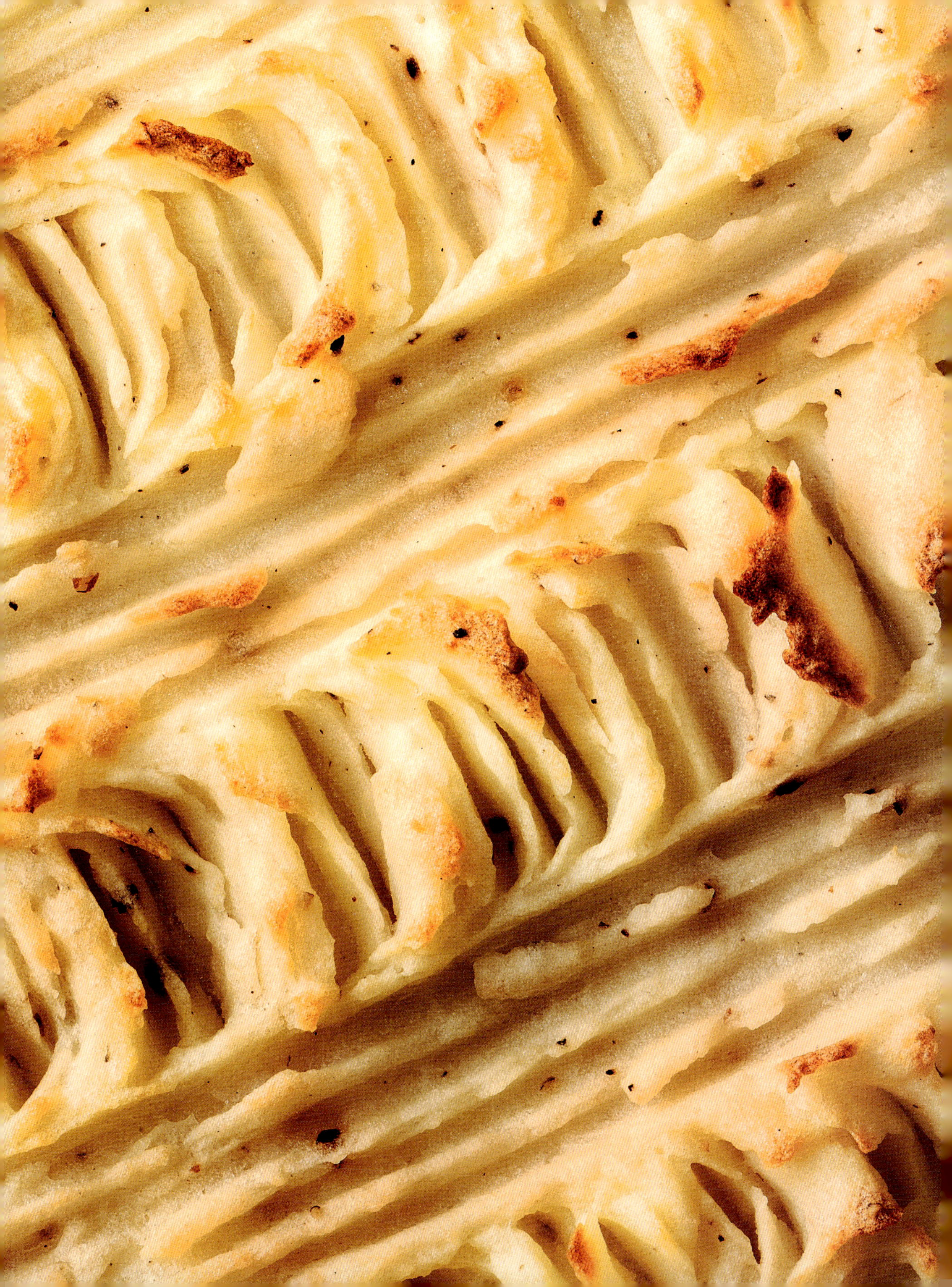

Heat a large **frying pan** over medium-high heat. Add the meat and brown it. Add the onion powder, garlic powder, oregano, and paprika and stir well. Turn off the heat and set the pan aside (set it on a pot holder or cool part of the stove top). If there is a lot of liquid in the pan, you can use a **sieve** to drain the excess.

Transfer the meat to an ungreased 9 × 9-inch (23 × 23 cm) **baking dish**. Add the corn niblets and spread them out in an even layer. Repeat with the creamed corn. Finally, add the mashed potatoes. Using a fork or the back of a spoon, smooth out the top and push the mashed potatoes right to the edges of the dish to seal in the other layers. You can make wavy patterns with the fork or a swooping pattern with the spoon if you like.

Sprinkle a bit of paprika on top (if using) and bake until the sides are bubbling and the top is golden brown, 45 minutes. Using **oven mitts**, remove the dish from the oven and let it rest on the counter for at least 5 minutes before serving.

Turn off the oven!

The casserole can be frozen before baking in an airtight glass **container** for up to 3 months. To bake, let it thaw completely. Preheat the oven to 375°F (190°C), and then bake until the top is crispy and the dish is bubbling, about 45–55 minutes.

SHEET PAN DINNER

The expression "sheet pan dinner" basically means that all the ingredients for your entire meal get cooked in one pan at the same time. Feel free to swap the chicken out for pork loin or chops if that's what you have in the fridge, and any combination of vegetables will work.

SERVES 6

- ¼ cup (60 mL) olive oil
- 2 Tbsp (30 mL) freshly squeezed lemon juice (1 lemon)
- 2 tsp (10 mL) liquid honey
- 3 garlic cloves, minced
- 2 tsp (10 mL) chopped fresh rosemary leaves
- 1 tsp (5 mL) sea salt
- 6 bone-in, skin-on chicken thighs
- 6 bone-in, skin-on chicken drumsticks
- 6 English-style sausages
- 1 lb (450 g) Yukon Gold or new unpeeled potatoes, cut into 1–2-inch (2.5–5 cm pieces)
- 1 red bell pepper, cut into bite-size pieces
- 1 broccoli crown, chopped into bite-size florets
- 1 organic lemon, cut into 6 wedges

In a large mixing bowl, whisk together the oil, lemon juice, honey, garlic, rosemary, and salt. Add the chicken, sausages, potatoes, red peppers, broccoli florets, and lemon wedges. Using a pair of tongs, toss the ingredients, making sure all the pieces are covered with the dressing. Cover the bowl and put it in the fridge for at least 30 minutes and up to overnight.

When you're ready to cook, preheat the oven to 400°F (200°C).

Line a large baking sheet with parchment paper. Use one that has sides at least ½ inch (1.25 cm) high. Arrange the ingredients in a single layer in the baking sheet. Scrape out any remaining marinade from the bowl and pour it over the chicken and vegetables. Place the tray on the middle rack in the oven. Bake until a meat thermometer inserted into the chicken reads at least 165°F (74°C) and the potatoes are tender, 50–60 minutes. Using oven mitts, remove from the oven and turn off the heat. Divide the food on the tray evenly among six plates.

POP IT IN A POT . . . OR PAN!

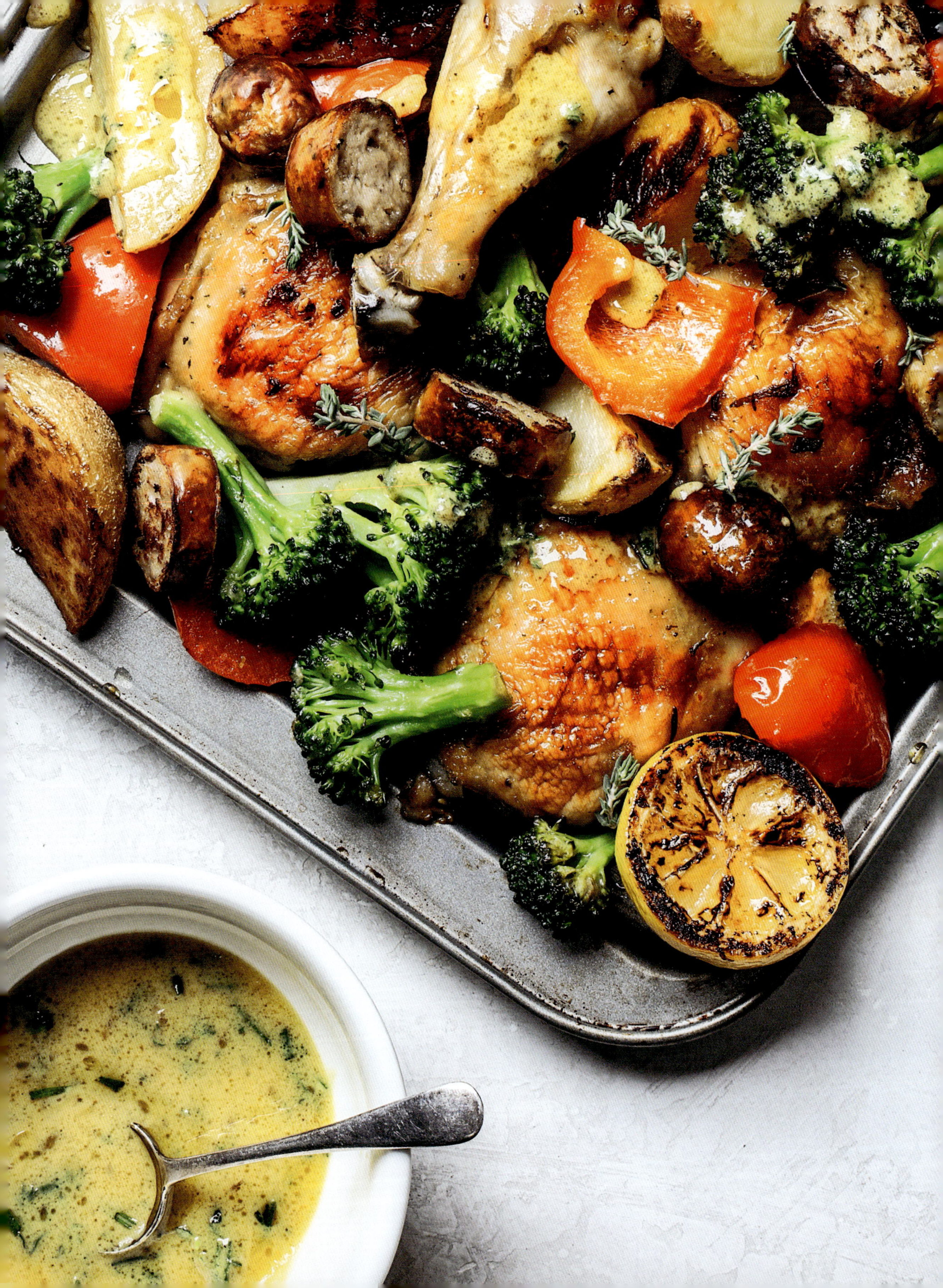

Mix It Up!

SWEET & SPICY

Replace the honey with 1 Tbsp (15 mL) maple syrup and swap the rosemary for 2 tsp (10 mL) sriracha sauce.

HONEY MUSTARD

Double the honey and replace 1 Tbsp (15 mL) of the lemon juice with 1 Tbsp (15 mL) Dijon mustard. Replace the rosemary with thyme.

TERIYAKI

Replace the honey with 1 Tbsp (15 mL) brown sugar, replace the lemon juice with 2 Tbsp (30 mL) tamari or coconut aminos, and replace the rosemary with 1 tsp (5 mL) ground ginger.

DON'T FORGET DESSERT!

. . . as if you would.

All-in Oat Cookies • 186
Super Snappy Sugar Cookies • 189
Gingerbread Cookies • 192
Doughnuts • 195
Brownies • 198
Best Ever Banana Bread • 200
Pound Cake • 203
Fruit Pie • 206
One-Pot Pumpkin Pie • 210
Fruit Sorbet • 212
Milkshakes • 214
Popsicles • 216
Fudge • 218
Birthday Cake • 220
Homemade Hot Chocolate Mix • 223

ALL-IN OAT COOKIES

These cookies are so versatile! You can add almost anything to them, making them super customizable. Add some cinnamon and raisins for classic oatmeal raisin cookies or throw in some M&M's for a chocolatey party-packed punch of color.

MAKES ABOUT 24 COOKIES

- 1 cup (250 mL) unsalted butter
- ¾ cup (185 mL) granulated sugar
- ¾ cup (185 mL) lightly packed brown sugar
- 2 eggs
- 2 cups (500 mL) all-purpose flour
- 2 tsp (10 mL) baking soda
- 2 tsp (10 mL) sea salt
- 3 cups (750 mL) old-fashioned rolled oats
- 2 cups (500 mL) extras (see Add These Extras!)

Preheat the oven to 325°F (160°C). **Line a baking sheet** with **parchment paper**.

Using a **stand mixer** fitted with a paddle attachment, **cream** together the butter and both sugars, about 3 minutes. Crack the eggs and add them one at a time, beating until fully incorporated after you add each egg.

Add the flour, baking soda, and salt, and mix well on low speed so that the flour does not fly out of the mixer! Add the oats and extras. Mix well.

Using a 1-inch (2.5 cm) **ice-cream scoop** or a tablespoon, scoop the dough onto the prepared **baking sheet**, spacing each scoop 2 inches (5 cm) apart. Flatten slightly with the back of a spoon.

Bake until starting to go golden brown, 12–15 minutes. When the cookies are done, using **oven mitts**, remove the tray from the oven and place it on a **cooling rack**. Let the cookies cool for a few minutes on the tray and then place them directly on the cooling rack.

Turn off the oven!

LET'S EAT

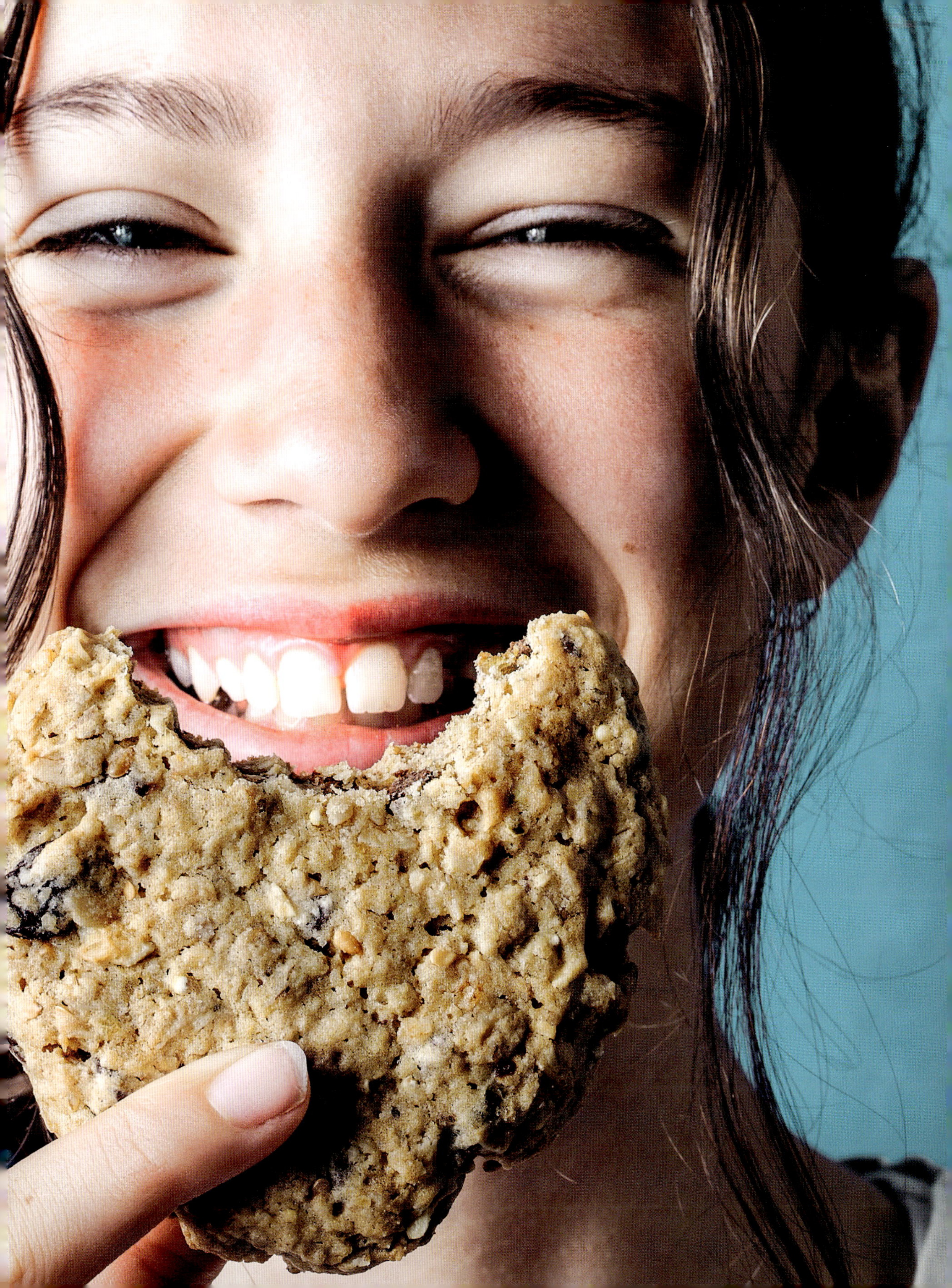

These will keep in an airtight **container** for a week. If you want to freeze them, scoop the balls of dough onto the prepared baking tray and freeze, uncovered, for 3 hours. When they are frozen, transfer to a freezer-safe bag or container and store in the freezer for up to 3 months. Allow to thaw at room temperature for about 30 minutes before baking.

Add These Extras!

- Caramel chips
- Chocolate chips (milk or semisweet)
- Chopped dried apricots
- Chopped nuts
- Cinnamon and raisins
- Cranberries and white chocolate chips
- Dried blueberries
- Dried cherries
- M&M's
- Pumpkin seeds
- Sunflower seeds
- Unsweetened coconut flakes

SUPER SNAPPY SUGAR COOKIES

The rice flour in these classic cookies gives them an extra SNAP that is sooooo satisfying. Celebrate a holiday by cutting out seasonal shapes and decorating with Royal Icing (page 192) or make a batch for easy lunch box snacks. Either way, these will become a fast favorite.

MAKES 36 COOKIES

- 1 cup (250 mL) unsalted butter
- 1 cup (250 mL) granulated sugar
- 1 egg
- 1 tsp (5 mL) vanilla extract
- 2 cups (500 mL) all-purpose flour
- 1 cup (250 mL) rice flour
- 1 tsp (5 mL) baking powder
- ½ tsp (2.5 mL) fine sea salt
- 1 recipe Royal Icing (page 192), for decorating

Preheat the oven to 350°F (180°C).

Using a **stand mixer** fitted with the paddle attachment, **cream** the butter and sugar until the mixture looks light and fluffy and is a light yellow color. This will take about 3 minutes at medium-high speed. Crack the egg and add it to the **bowl**. Add the vanilla and mix to combine well.

In a separate **bowl**, mix together both flours, the baking powder, and salt. Add the dry mixture 1 cup (250 mL) at a time to the butter mixture and mix on low speed until the dough comes together into a ball. If you find after a minute or two of mixing that it's too dry, add 1 tsp (5 mL) of water and continue to mix. The dough should be pulling away from the sides of the **mixer** and beginning to form a ball in the center.

Divide the dough in half. Get two large pieces of **parchment paper**—each about 18 inches (45 cm) long—and place half of the dough in between the parchment pieces. Use a **rolling pin** to roll the dough between the paper until it's about ¼ inch (0.6 cm) thick. Remove the top piece of parchment

DON'T FORGET DESSERT!

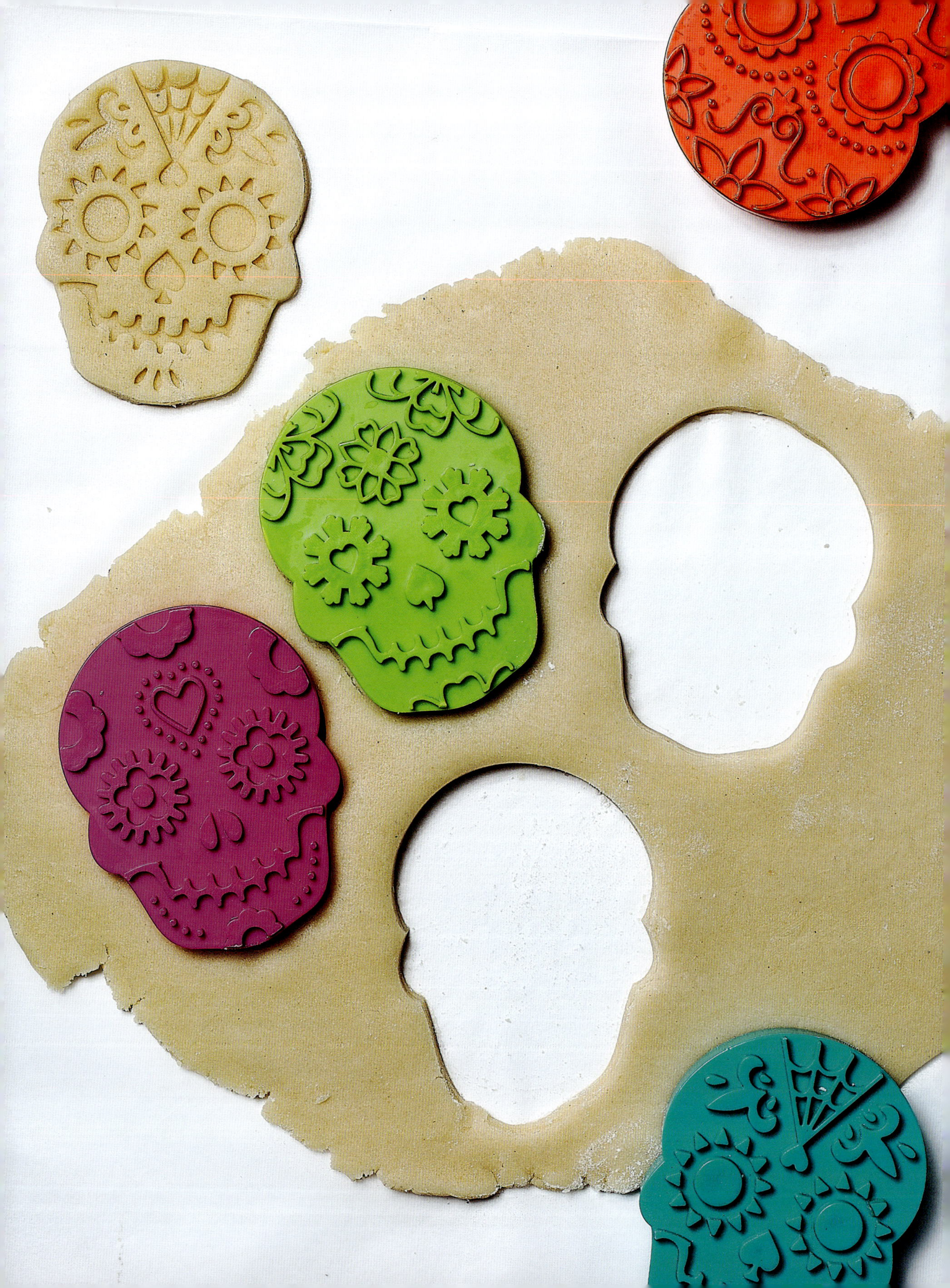

and then use your favorite cookie cutters to cut out the dough, removing the extra pieces of dough between your cookies as you go. When you're done, you should have a piece of parchment covered in cookies ready for the oven. Slip the parchment with the cookies onto a **cookie sheet** and bake on the center rack of the oven until the edges of the cookies just start to turn slightly golden, 8–10 minutes.

When the cookies are done, using **oven mitts**, remove the cookie sheet from the oven, slide the **parchment paper** onto a **cooling rack**, and let the cookies cool until they're firm enough to move. Repeat with the rest of the dough until it is all used up.

Turn off the oven!

Alice Says

These are sooooo good, even without icing. Put ½ tsp of pumpkin spice in at Halloween for a fall-flavored treat.

GINGERBREAD COOKIES

This recipe makes a lot of cookies, but the individual balls of dough can be frozen so they're on hand whenever you get a craving for perfect, crispy gingerbread.

MAKES 48 COOKIES

Cookies
- ⅔ cup (165 mL) unsalted butter, room temperature
- ¾ cup (185 mL) packed brown sugar
- 1 large egg
- ⅔ cup (165 mL) fancy-grade molasses
- 1 tsp (5 mL) vanilla extract
- 3½ cups (875 mL) all-purpose flour
- 1 tsp (5 mL) baking soda
- ½ tsp (2.5 mL) fine sea salt
- 1½ Tbsp (23 mL) ground ginger
- 1 Tbsp (15 mL) ground cinnamon
- 1 tsp (5 mL) ground allspice
- 1 tsp (5 mL) ground cloves
- ½ tsp (2.5 mL) freshly ground black pepper (optional)
- Candies of choice to decorate (Smarties, sprinkles, Jelly Tots, and M&M's all work well)

Royal Icing
- 4 cups (1 L) icing sugar
- ¼ cup (60 mL) meringue powder
- 6 Tbsp (90 mL) hand-hot water
- 1 tsp (5 mL) vanilla extract

Using a **stand mixer** fitted with the paddle attachment, beat the butter and sugar on medium-high speed until whipped and fluffy, about 3 minutes. Crack the egg and add it along with the molasses and vanilla to the butter mixture. Beat for another 3 minutes so that everything is well combined.

In another large **mixing bowl, whisk** together the flour, baking soda, salt, ginger, cinnamon, allspice, cloves, and pepper (if using).

With your **stand mixer** set to low speed, add the flour mixture to the unsalted butter mixture 1 cup (250 mL) at a time until everything is fully combined. The mixture will be sticky and that's ok.

Take the dough out of the **stand mixer** and divide it into four equal pieces. Use your hands to press each piece into a squashed sort of ball and wrap each one tightly with plastic wrap. Press down on the wrapped balls to form

192   LET'S EAT

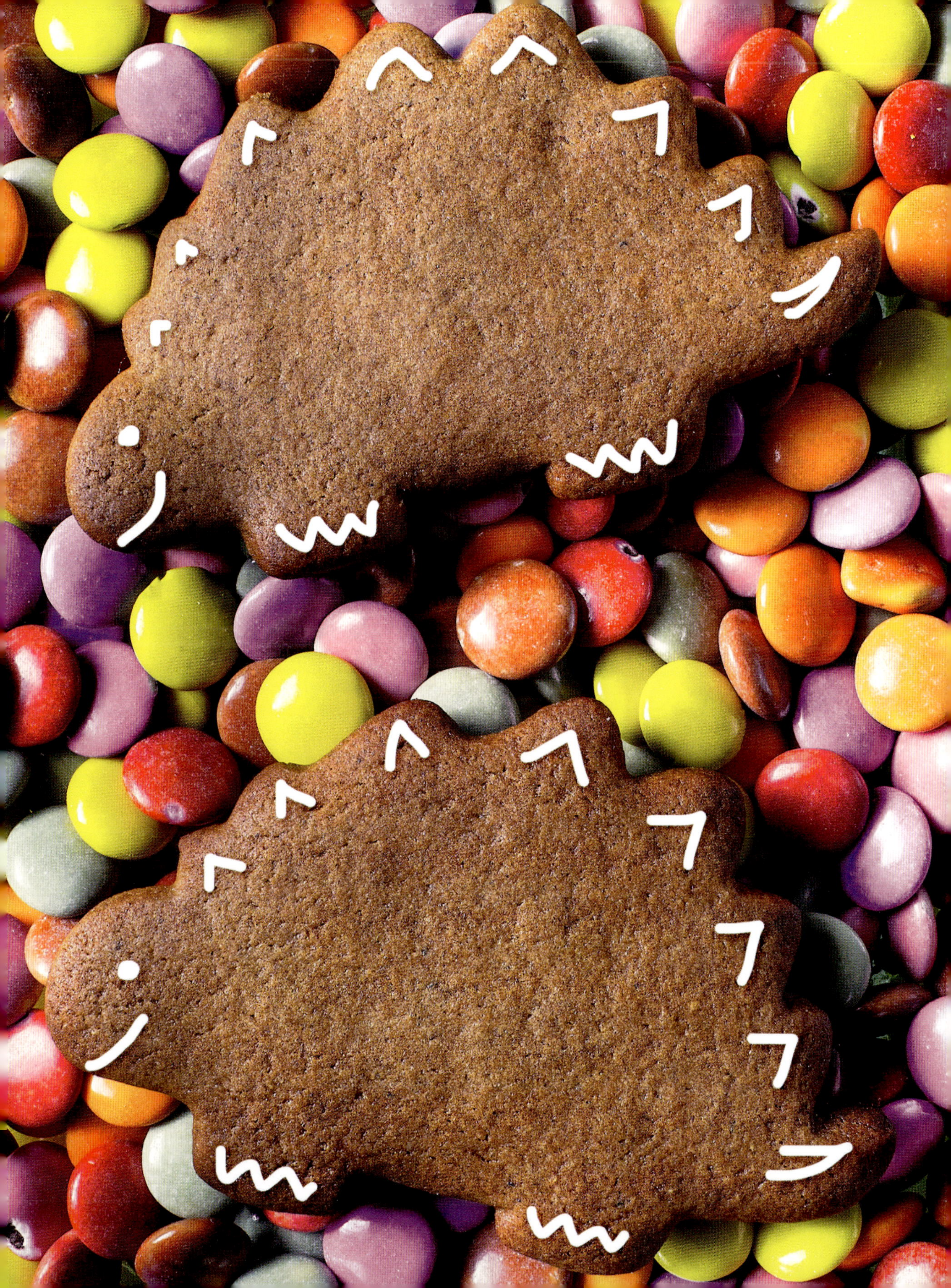

disks about 2 inches (5 cm) thick and place these in the fridge for at least 3 hours. We leave ours overnight. Note: At this point you can easily freeze the dough. Double wrap any balls you don't want to use right away and place them in the freezer for up to 3 months.

When you're ready to make cookies, take one disk out of the fridge and unwrap it. Preheat the oven to 350°F (180°C). Cut four pieces of **cookie sheet**-sized **parchment paper**.

Lay one of the pieces of **parchment** out on the counter and place a cookie dough disk in the center of it. Cover this disk with another piece of parchment and use your **rolling pin** to roll the dough out between the parchment sheets until it's about ¼ inch (0.6 cm) thick. The dough may seem really stiff at first, but it will start to soften up as you go.

Once the dough is rolled out, remove the top piece of **parchment**, and use your cookie cutters to cut out the shapes you want, being sure to leave at least 1 inch (2.5 cm) between each shape. Do NOT pick the cookie shapes up! When you've cut as many pieces as you can, just remove the dough between the pieces, gather that extra dough into a new ball, and slide the piece of parchment with the cookie shapes on it onto a **baking sheet**.

Place the **cookie sheet** on the center rack in the oven and bake until the tops of the cookies look dry, about 8–11 minutes. Longer baking makes for crispier cookies. When the cookies are done, turn off the heat and, using **oven mitts**, remove the cookie sheet from the oven, place it on a **cooling rack**, and let the cookies cool on the cookie sheet for at least 5 minutes. After 5 minutes, transfer the cookies to the cooling rack to cool completely. If you're going to decorate them with royal icing, place the cookies in the fridge for 30 minutes to an hour to chill first so that the icing **sets** properly.

Repeat until all of the dough is used up. Note: You can reuse the **parchment paper** sheet that you already baked on. I give it a wipe and make sure that there aren't any dark burnt spots on it.

To make the icing, place the icing sugar and meringue powder in a **stand mixer** fitted with the **whisk** attachment and mix on low speed for a few seconds to combine. With the mixer running on low, slowly add the water and vanilla until the mixture is wet through. Turn the speed to medium-high and beat until the icing is thick and stiff. When you pull the whisk out of the icing, the icing should stay up in **stiff peaks**. Spoon the icing into an **icing bag**, cut the tip off, and decorate the gingerbread with icing and candies.

The cookies will stay fresh in an airtight **container** for up to 1 week.

LET'S EAT

DOUGHNUTS

These baked doughnuts will soon become a go-to treat when you feel a sweet craving coming on. Get creative with the glaze colors and sprinkles to let your inner artist shine.

MAKES 12 DOUGHNUTS

- 1⅓ cups (330 mL) milk, warmed to 100°F (38°C), divided
- ¼ cup (60 mL) granulated sugar
- 2 tsp (10 mL) active yeast
- 2 large eggs, room temperature
- 2 Tbsp (30 mL) unsalted butter, melted and slightly cooled
- 2 ½ cups (625 mL) all-purpose flour, plus more for sprinkling
- 1 tsp (5 mL) ground nutmeg or cinnamon
- ½ tsp (2.5 mL) fine sea salt
- 1 cup (250 mL) sprinkles
- 1½ cups (375 mL) icing sugar
- 2 Tbsp (30 mL) 35% whipping cream
- 1 tsp (5 mL) vanilla extract
- 2–3 drops gel food coloring

In a small bowl, mix together ⅓ cup (80 mL) of the milk, the sugar, and the yeast. Let stand for 5–10 minutes or until the yeast forms a foam on the top.

Crack the eggs. In a stand mixer fitted with the paddle attachment, mix the eggs, remaining 1 cup (250 mL) of milk, and butter on medium speed until combined. Add the flour, the nutmeg, the salt, and the foamy yeast mixture and mix on low speed until just combined. The dough will be sticky. That's ok! Do not overmix or add too much flour as the dough will become too hard.

Cover with a clean, dry tea towel and let rest in a warm, draft-free spot until doubled in size, about 1 hour.

Line a large baking sheet with parchment paper or a silicone mat.

Turn the dough out onto a floured surface. Lightly sprinkle the top with flour and use a rolling pin to roll it out to about ½ inch (1.25 cm) thickness. Using a doughnut cutter, a cookie cutter, or a glass about 3 inches (7.5 cm) in diameter, cut out circles. Using a smaller circle like a piping tip, cut out a center hole. Transfer the doughnuts and the doughnut holes to the prepared tray. Cover with the tea towel again and let stand another 45 minutes. At this point, you can cover the doughnuts with plastic wrap and put them in the fridge overnight.

If you do this, bring them out of the fridge to sit at room temperature for 45 minutes before you bake them.

Preheat the oven to 375°F (190°C).

DON'T FORGET DESSERT!

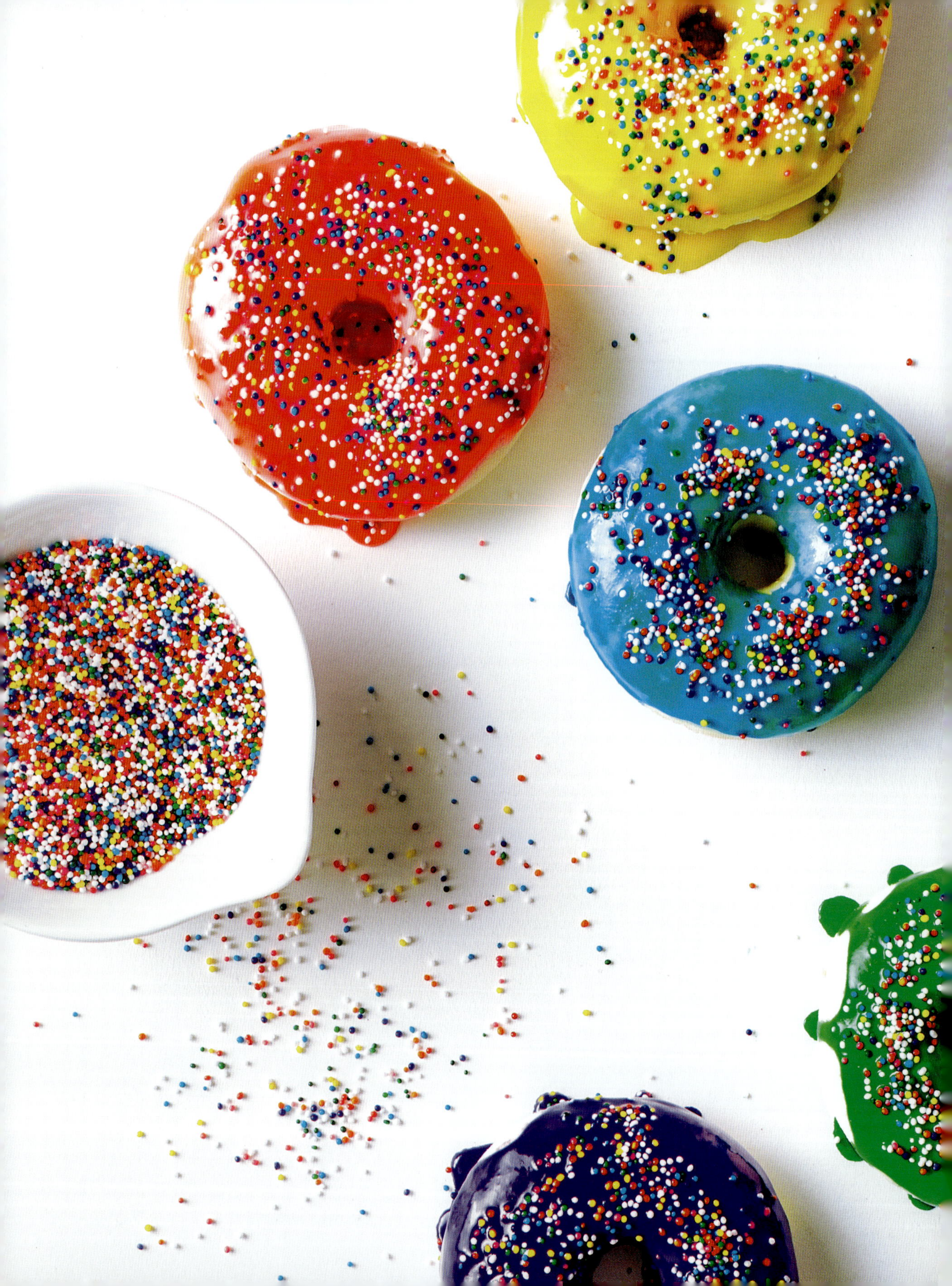

Bake the doughnuts until just starting to turn golden, 8-10 minutes. Using **oven mitts**, remove the pan from the oven and transfer the doughnuts to a **cooling rack**.

Turn off the oven!

Allow the doughnuts to cool completely before topping.

Sit a **cooling rack** over a large piece of **parchment paper**.

Place the sprinkles in a shallow **bowl**. In another bowl, combine the icing sugar, cream, vanilla, and food coloring. Dunk one side of the doughnut in the icing and then in the sprinkles. Place the iced doughnuts on the **cooling rack**, letting any excess drip onto the **parchment paper** underneath. Allow the glaze to dry for 5 minutes before serving. The doughnuts will keep in an airtight **container** for up to 5 days.

Option:

If you have an adult working with you, these doughnuts can also be deep-fried the traditional way. In a large, heavy-bottomed pot, bring 6 cups (1.5 L) of frying oil (canola or peanut) to 350°F (175°C). Working in small batches, fry for 1-2 minutes per side or just until they turn golden brown. Remove the doughnuts and doughnut holes from the oil with a slotted spoon and place on paper towel to cool before glazing.

BROWNIES

Brownies are the ultimate chocoholic treat—soft, gooey, and packed with cocoa goodness. These will freeze well in the tin they're baked in . . . if you can resist eating them all as soon as they're out of the oven.

MAKES 24 BROWNIES

¾ cup (185 mL) all-purpose flour
⅔ cup (165 mL) Dutch-process cocoa powder
½ cup (125 mL) icing sugar
½ tsp (2.5 mL) sea salt
1¼ cups (310 mL) granulated sugar
2 large eggs
½ cup (125 mL) vegetable or grapeseed oil
¾ tsp (4 mL) vanilla extract
½ cup (125 mL) chocolate chips (milk, semisweet, or white)

Preheat the oven to 325°F (160°C). Grease a 9 × 9-inch (23 × 23 cm) **baking pan**.

Over a large **bowl**, sift the flour, cocoa powder, icing sugar, and salt. **Whisk** in the sugar.

Crack the eggs. In another large **bowl**, whisk the eggs, oil, vanilla, and chocolate chips. Pour the dry ingredients over the wet and stir to combine. Pour the batter into the prepared pan and use a spoon to distribute it evenly.

Bake on the center rack of the oven until a toothpick inserted in the center of the brownies comes out with only a few crumbs stuck to it, 40–45 minutes. Using **oven mitts**, remove the pan from the oven and place it on a **cooling rack**.

Turn off the oven!

Allow the brownies to cool for at least 10 minutes before cutting into squares and serving.

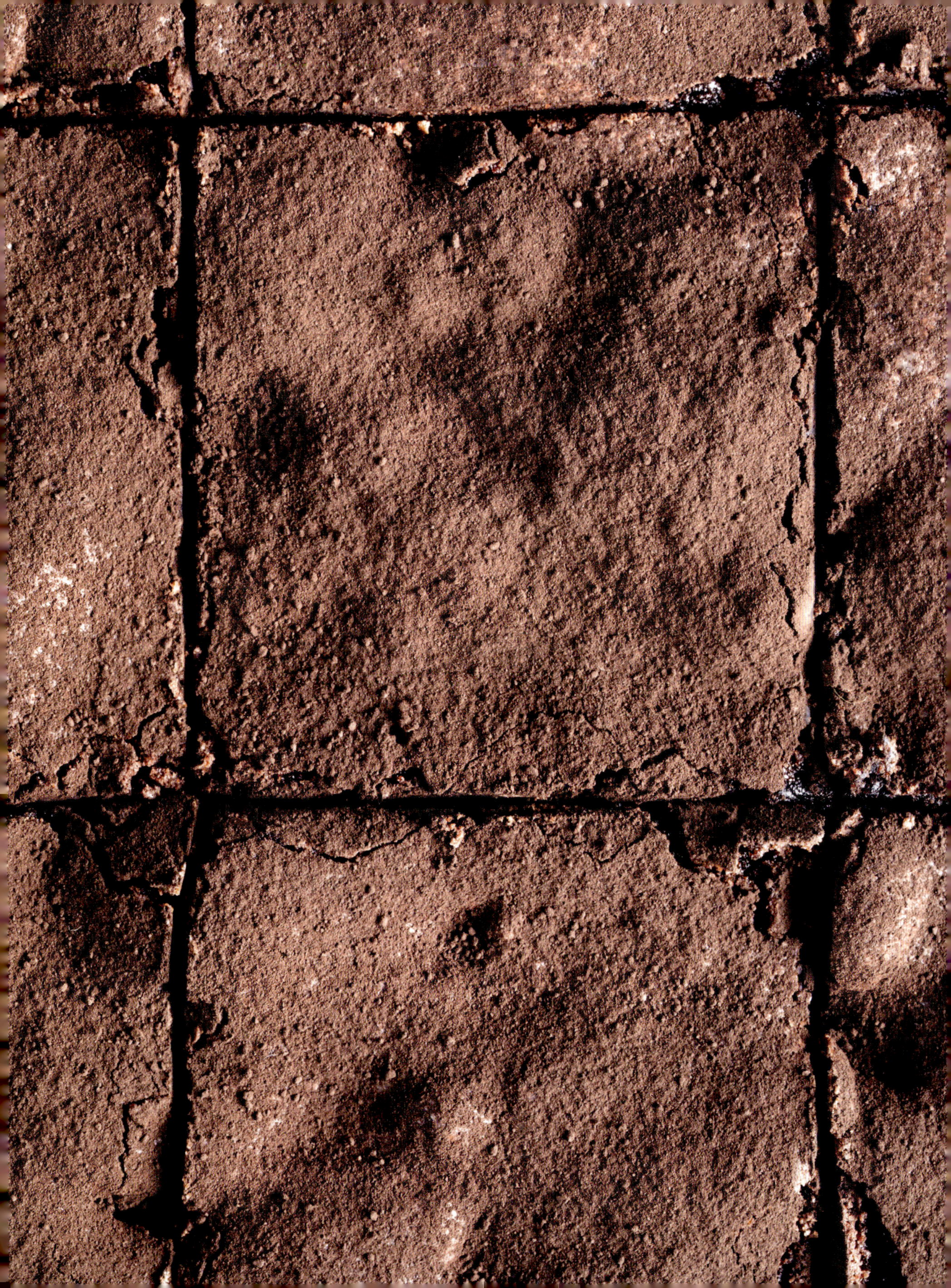

BEST EVER BANANA BREAD

Whenever you have overripe bananas, toss them into the freezer for making banana bread. When you thaw bananas, they automatically become a banana purée, perfect for blending into your baking. If you don't have buttermilk, you can use the same amount of regular milk with 1 tsp (5 mL) of apple cider vinegar.

MAKES 1 LOAF

- ½ cup (125 mL) unsalted butter, at room temperature
- ½ cup (125 mL) granulated sugar
- ½ cup (125 mL) brown sugar
- 2 large eggs
- 4 very ripe bananas, frozen and then thawed
- ½ cup (125 mL) buttermilk
- 1 tsp (5 mL) vanilla extract
- 2 cups (500 mL) all-purpose flour
- 1 tsp (5 mL) baking powder
- 1 tsp (5 mL) baking soda
- 1 tsp (5 mL) ground cinnamon
- ½ tsp (2.5 mL) fine sea salt
- Extras (see Add These Extras!)
- 1 firm banana, sliced, for topping (optional)

Preheat the oven to 375°F (190°C). **Line** a loaf pan or 9 × 9-inch (23 × 23 cm) **cake pan** with **parchment paper**.

In a **stand mixer** fitted with the paddle attachment, **cream** the butter with both sugars until light and fluffy. Crack the eggs. Add the eggs, bananas, buttermilk, and vanilla to the butter mixture. Beat on medium-high speed until all the wet ingredients are well blended, 2 minutes.

Place the flour, baking powder, baking soda, cinnamon, and salt in a large **bowl** and **whisk** together. Add these dry ingredients to the wet ingredients and mix on low speed until everything is combined. If you're using any extras, stir them in now.

Pour the batter into the loaf pan and decorate with the sliced banana (if using). Bake until a toothpick inserted into the center of the banana bread comes out clean, 45–50 minutes.

Turn off the oven!

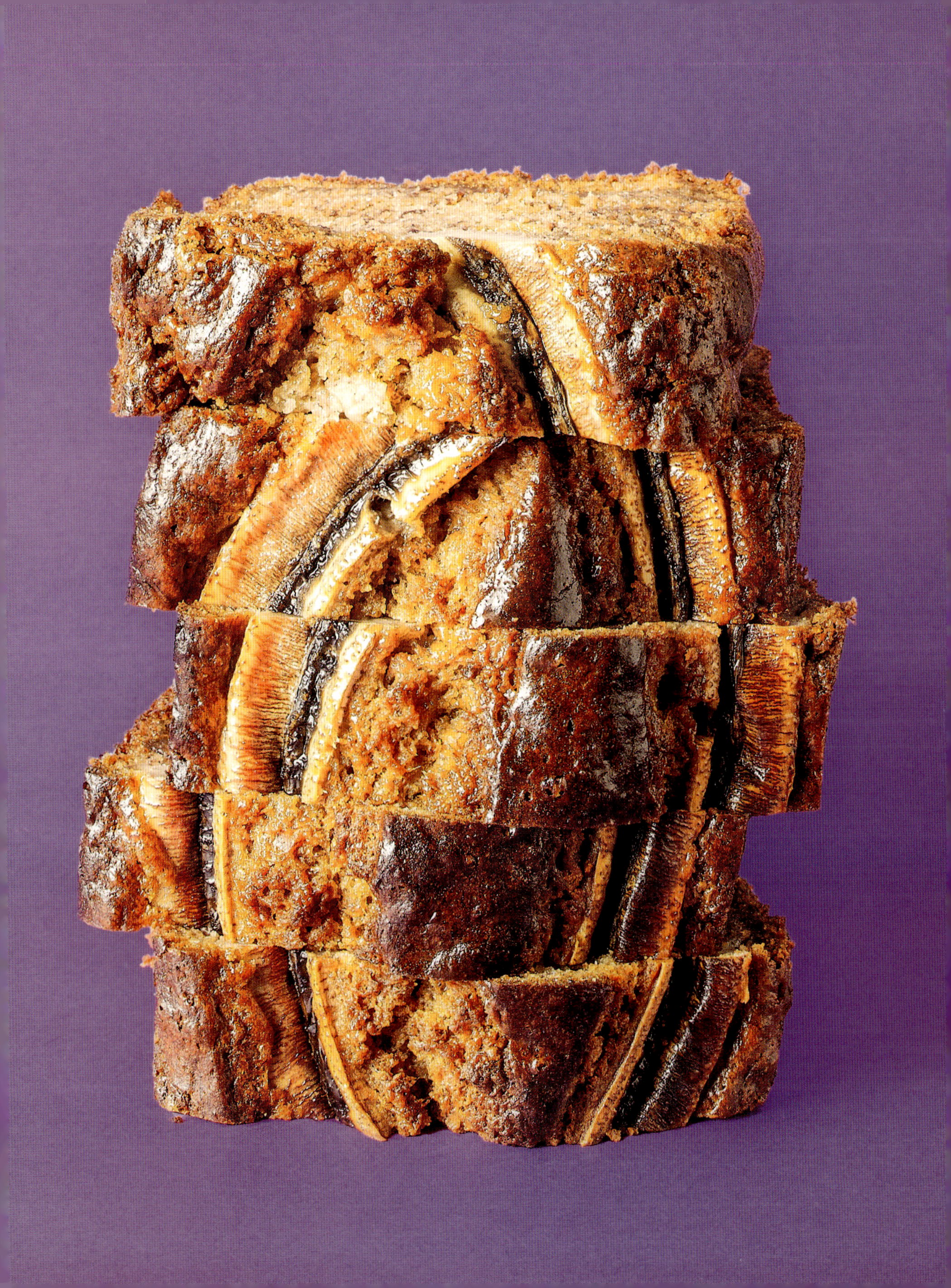

Using **oven mitts**, remove the pan from the oven and place it on a **cooling rack** for at least 30 minutes—we know it's hard—before lifting the banana bread out. It will keep in an airtight **container** on the counter for 3 days and in the fridge for up to a week.

Add These Extras!

CHOCOLATE BANANA

1 cup (250 mL) semisweet, milk, or dark chocolate chips

CARAMEL BANANA

1 cup (250 mL) caramel chips

NUTTY BANANA

1 cup (250 mL) chopped pecans or walnuts

TROPICAL BANANA

½ cup (125 mL) shredded unsweetened coconut + ½ cup (125 mL) chopped macadamia nuts

DOUBLE CHOCOLATE

¼ cup (60 mL) dark cocoa added to dry ingredients + 1 cup (250 mL) semisweet, milk, or dark chocolate chips

William Says

You can double this recipe and freeze half (wrapped in plastic wrap) for up to 6 weeks.

LET'S EAT

POUND CAKE

This cake got its name from an old-fashioned recipe that called for a pound of butter, a pound of sugar, and a pound of flour; we've evened out the proportions for a slightly lighter, less dense—but equally delicious—cake. The base recipe is easily adaptable for whatever flavors you want to create. This one doubles well so you can make an extra cake to be cooled, wrapped in plastic wrap, and frozen for up to 3 months.

MAKES 1 CAKE

- 3 large eggs, room temperature
- 1 cup (250 mL) granulated sugar
- ½ cup (125 mL) unsalted butter, melted and cooled
- ⅓ cup (80 mL) sour cream
- 1 tsp (5 mL) vanilla extract
- 1½ cups (375 mL) self-rising flour
- ⅓ cup (80 mL) icing sugar
- 1 tsp (5 mL) milk or water

Preheat the oven to 350°F (180°C). Grease and flour a 9-inch (23 cm) Bundt pan.

Crack the eggs. In a **stand mixer** fitted with the paddle attachment, mix together the eggs, sugar, butter, sour cream, and vanilla. Add the flour and mix on low speed until combined.

Bake on the center rack of the oven until a toothpick inserted into the cake comes out clean, 50–60 minutes.

Turn off the oven!

Place the pan on a **cooling rack** and let the cake cool in the pan for 10 minutes before turning it out onto the cooling rack to cool completely.

Mix together the icing sugar and milk and decorate the cake.

DON'T FORGET DESSERT!

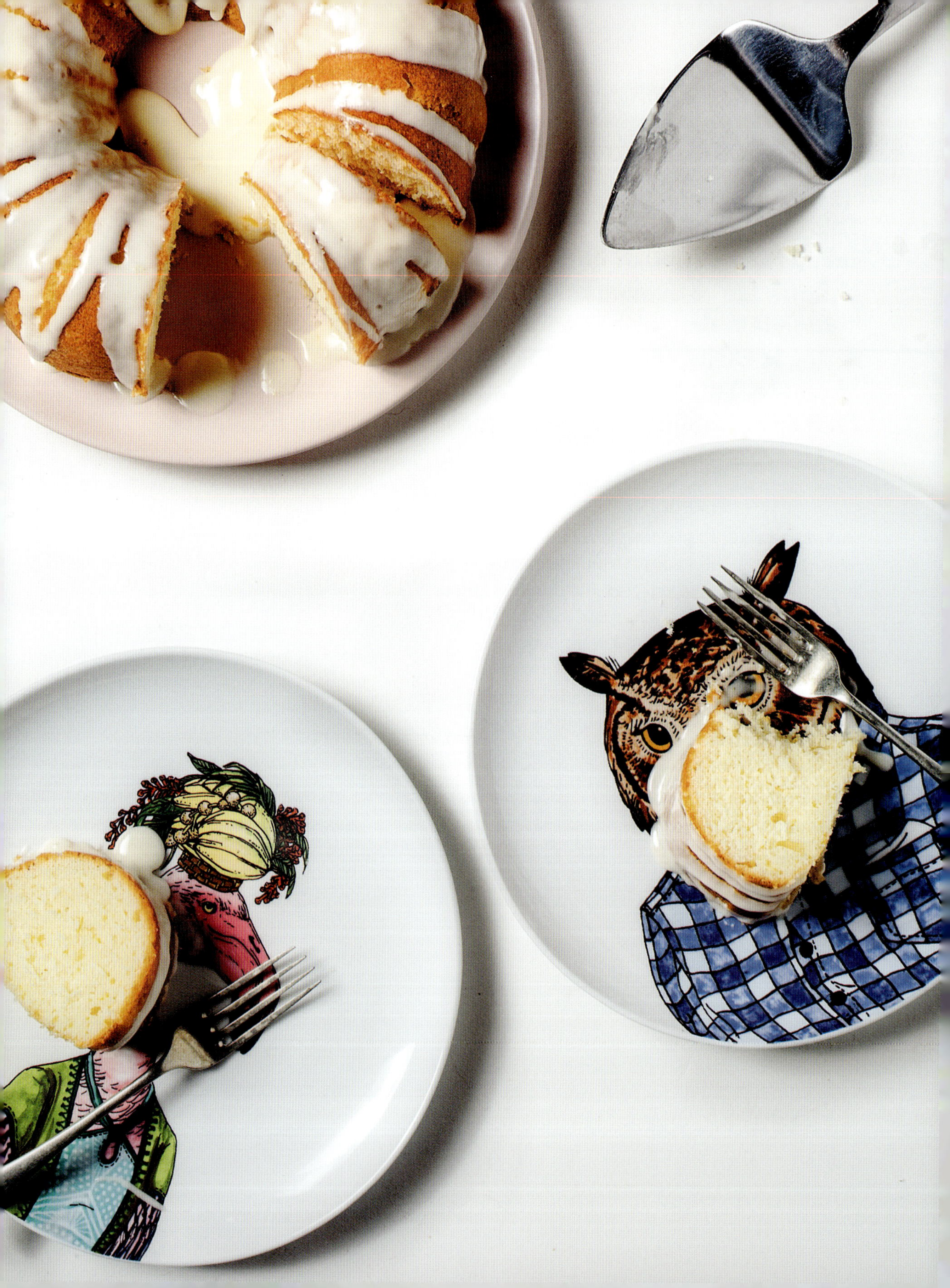

Switch Up the Flavor!

COCONUT

Add ½ cup (125 mL) shredded unsweetened coconut to the wet ingredients. Toast ¼ cup (60 mL) coconut by placing the coconut in a dry **frying pan** over medium heat and cooking until it starts to turn a light golden brown. Scatter the toasted coconut over the glazed cake.

LEMON POPPY SEED

Add ¼ cup (60 mL) freshly squeezed lemon juice (2 lemons) and 2 Tbsp (30 mL) poppy seeds to the wet ingredients. Add 1 tsp (5 mL) lemon juice to the glaze.

LEMON BLUEBERRY

Add ¼ cup (60 mL) freshly squeezed lemon juice (2 lemons) and 1 cup (250 mL) fresh or frozen blueberries to the wet ingredients. Add 1 tsp (5 mL) lemon juice to the glaze.

CHOCOLATE

Add ¼ cup (60 mL) dark, unsweetened cocoa to the wet ingredients and stir in 1 cup (250 mL) of semisweet chocolate chips after the flour. Add 2 tsp (10 mL) cocoa to the glaze.

CINNAMON CAPPUCCINO

Add 2 Tbsp (30 mL) espresso powder and 2 tsp (10 mL) ground cinnamon with the dry ingredients. Add 1 tsp (5 mL) ground cinnamon to the glaze.

FRUIT PIE

Pies are almost more popular in our house than cake, so we tend to make them constantly throughout the year with whatever fruit happens to be in season. The pie crust recipe I've given you here is easy to master, but if you're in a pinch or want to whip up a pie quickly, a store-bought version will work well too. Most store-bought crusts are sold in packs of two, so just put the fruit into one pie crust and then place the other one over top.

MAKES 1 (9-INCH/23 CM) PIE

Pie crust
- 2½ cups (625 mL) all-purpose flour
- 1½ tsp (7.5 mL) granulated sugar
- ½ tsp (2.5 mL) sea salt
- 1 cup (250 mL) SUPER-COLD unsalted butter, cut into 1-inch (2.5 cm) chunks
- ½ cup (125 mL) ice water (keep the ice cubes in to keep the water really cold), **divided**
- 1 egg
- 1 Tbsp (15 mL) water

Filling
- 5 cups (1.25 L) fruit (see Favorite Fillings!)
- 1 tsp (5 mL) lemon zest
- 2 Tbsp (30 mL) freshly squeezed lemon juice (1 lemon)
- 1 tsp (5 mL) vanilla extract
- ½ cup (125 mL) granulated sugar
- 3 Tbsp (45 mL) all-purpose flour
- 2 Tbsp (30 mL) cornstarch
- ½ tsp (2.5 mL) ground cinnamon
- ½ tsp (2.5 mL) sea salt
- 2 Tbsp (30 mL) coarse golden sugar, for topping (optional)

For the crust, place the flour, sugar, and salt in a **food processor** fitted with the steel blade and use the pulse option a couple of times to combine everything. Add the butter and pulse until the mixture has a coarse, sand-like texture with small, pea-sized chunks of butter visible throughout.

Add 7 Tbsp (105 mL) of the ice water and pulse just until the dough starts to form small balls. Press a piece of dough between your fingertips. If the dough sticks together, you have added enough water. If not, add more ice water 1 tsp (5 mL) at a time. Be careful not to add too much water or the dough will be sticky and difficult to roll out.

LET'S EAT

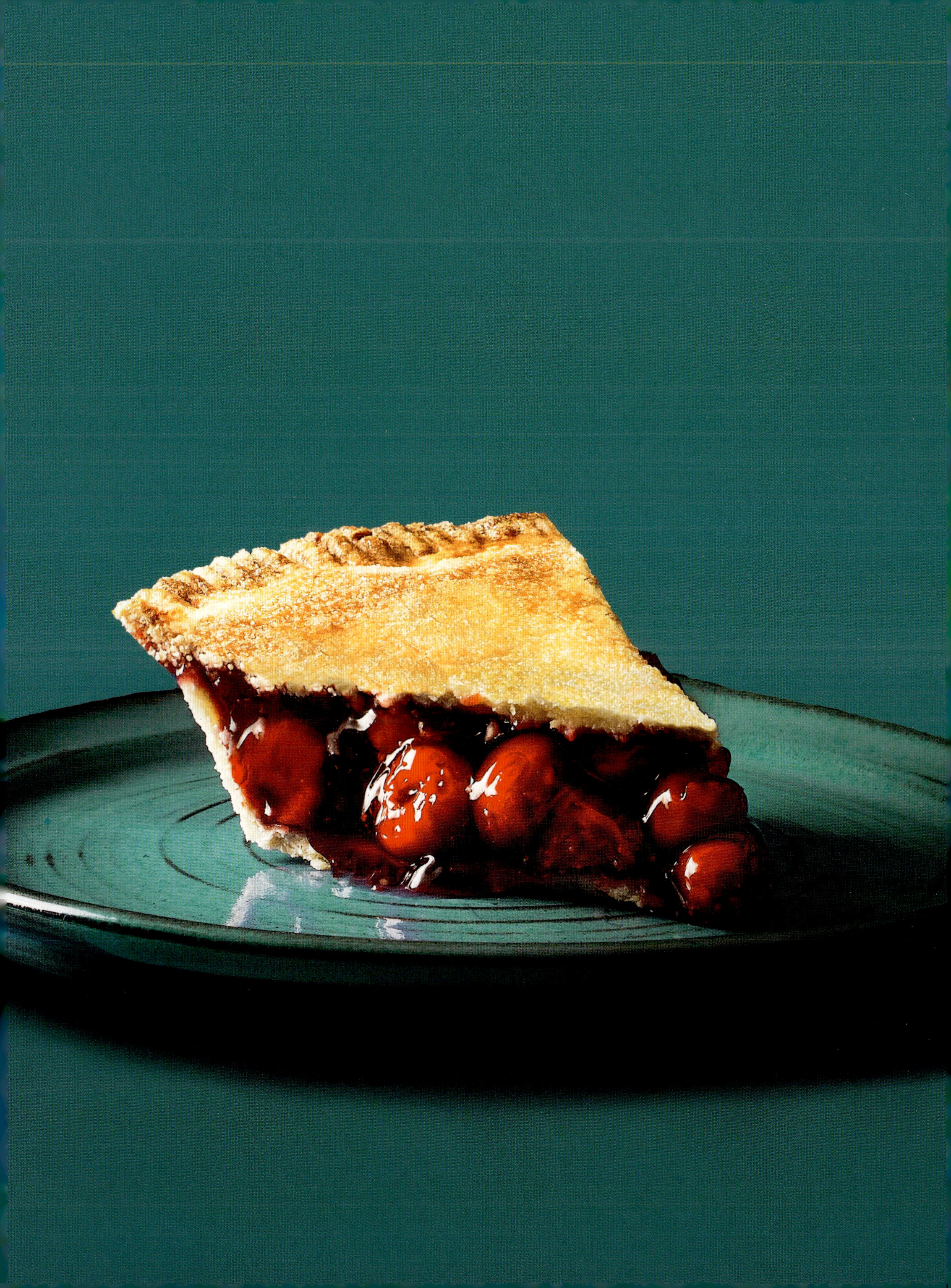

Dump the dough out onto a clean countertop and use your hands to form it into a ball. Split the dough in half and flatten each half to form two 1-inch-thick (2.5 cm) disks. Cover each of the disks with plastic kitchen wrap and place in the fridge for at least 1 hour before using.

When you're ready to make the pie, sprinkle some flour onto your counter so that the pie crust dough doesn't stick. Take one of the disks from the fridge and use a **rolling pin** to roll the dough out into a circle with a diameter of about 12–13 inches (30–33 cm). To keep the circle shape, it helps to push outward from the center of the dough in each direction. When you're done rolling, fold the dough in half and then in half again. It should look like a large pie wedge. Place the dough in a 9-inch (23 cm) pie plate with the point in the middle and then carefully unfold the dough to fill the plate. Use your fingers to gently push the dough down into the pie plate. Place in the fridge until you're ready to add the filling.

To make the filling, place the fruit, lemon zest, lemon juice, vanilla, and sugar in a large **mixing bowl** and stir with a **wooden spoon** to combine. Let the mixture sit for 15 minutes until the fruit starts to macerate—that means the sugar will cause the fruit to release some of its juice and the juice will become your sauce. Add the flour, cornstarch, cinnamon, and salt to the fruit and stir it all again to combine.

Preheat the oven to 375°F (190°C).

Roll out the second dough disk until it has a diameter of about 12 inches (30 cm). Fold it in half, then in half again and set aside.

Pour the fruit filling into the bottom pie crust. Place the folded pie dough wedge onto the top of the pie with the point in the middle and carefully unfold the dough. Use a pair of kitchen scissors to trim the two pie crusts around the pie plate and then use a fork to go around the edge and press the top and bottom crusts together. Use a sharp **knife** to cut a couple of vents in the top of the crust. If you're feeling fancy, you can make a design but just a few lines will do the trick.

Crack the egg. Use a fork to beat the egg and 1 Tbsp (15 mL) water together, and brush this mixture across the top of the pie with a **pastry brush**. Sprinkle the top of the pie with golden sugar (if using) and place the pie on a **baking sheet**. Put the baking sheet with the pie on it into the oven on the middle rack and bake until the top is nicely golden brown, 45–50 minutes.

Turn off the oven!

Using **oven mitts**, remove the pie from the oven, place the pie dish on a **cooling rack**, and let sit for at least 20–30 minutes before serving.

Favorite Fillings!

Cut larger fruits into 1-inch (2.5 cm) pieces. You can use either frozen or fresh fruits and berries.

- Apples
- Apples and blackberries
- Peaches
- Pears
- Strawberries
- Rhubarb
- Strawberries and rhubarb
- Blueberries
- Blackberries and cherries
- A mix of blueberries, blackberries, strawberries, and raspberries to make bumbleberry

Charlie Says

Pie and ice cream are best friends.

DON'T FORGET DESSERT!

ONE-POT PUMPKIN PIE

This pie could not be easier—or more delicious! You just dump all the ingredients into one big bowl, give it a stir, and get baking! If you want to try your hand at homemade pie crust, grab the recipe on page 206, but store-bought frozen versions work perfectly as well.

MAKES 1 (9-INCH/23 CM) PIE

3 large eggs
1 (14 oz/398 mL) can puréed pumpkin
1 (10 oz/300 mL) can condensed milk
½ cup (125 mL) brown sugar
2 Tbsp (30 mL) pumpkin spice
1 Tbsp (15 mL) all-purpose flour
½ tsp (2.5 mL) fine sea salt
½ tsp (2.5 mL) freshly ground black pepper
1 (9-inch/23 cm) deep dish pie crust shell (store-bought or recipe on page 206)

Preheat the oven to 375°F (190°C).

Crack the eggs. Place the eggs and all of the other ingredients except the pie crust in a **stand mixer** fitted with the **whisk** attachment. **Whisk** together on medium speed until the mixture is well blended. (If you're using a hand whisk, place the ingredients in a large **mixing bowl** and whisk for a minute or two to combine everything.)

Place the pie crust on a cookie sheet and pour the pumpkin mixture into the shell, leaving at least ½ inch (1.25 cm) of space for the filling to rise. Bake until the center of the pie is no longer wobbly, 45–55 minutes.

Turn off the oven!

Using **oven mitts**, remove the pie from the oven, place the pie plate on a **cooling rack** and let the pie cool for at least 1 hour before eating. Serve with whipped cream or ice cream.

The pie will keep, uncovered, in the fridge for up to 1 week.

William Says

Make two. One is never enough!

FRUIT SORBET

Sorbet is one of the easiest and most allergy-friendly—not to mention YUMMY—frozen desserts. Experiment by adding different fruits together: mangoes, bananas, raspberries, and strawberries all work well. You can swap out the sugar here for ¼ cup (60 mL) of maple syrup if you enjoy a slightly tarter fruity flavor.

SERVES 6-8

- 2 cups (500 mL) frozen raspberries
- 1 cup (250 mL) granulated sugar
- 5½ cups (1.38 L) frozen mango chunks
- 2-3 Tbsp (30-45 mL) lime juice (2 limes)

In a small **pot** over medium-high heat, cook the raspberries and sugar, stirring occasionally, until bubbly and the raspberries have broken down, about 5 minutes. Set a **sieve** over a **bowl**.

Remove the **pot** from the heat and pour the raspberries into the sieve to catch the seeds. Discard the seeds and let the liquid cool to room temperature. You can pop it in the fridge or freezer to help it cool quicker.

In a **food processor** fitted with the steel blade, blend the mango and lime juice until creamy, about 5 minutes. You will have to stop the machine and push down the sides to help it along.

Once the mango is smooth, transfer 2 cups (500 mL) of it to the **bowl** with the raspberry liquid and mix well. Transfer the remaining mango to a loaf tin or other freezer-safe **container**. Add the raspberry mixture and use a spoon to swirl the two flavors together.

Place in the freezer for 2 hours to firm up. If it's too hard coming out of the freezer, let stand at room temperature for ten minutes before serving.

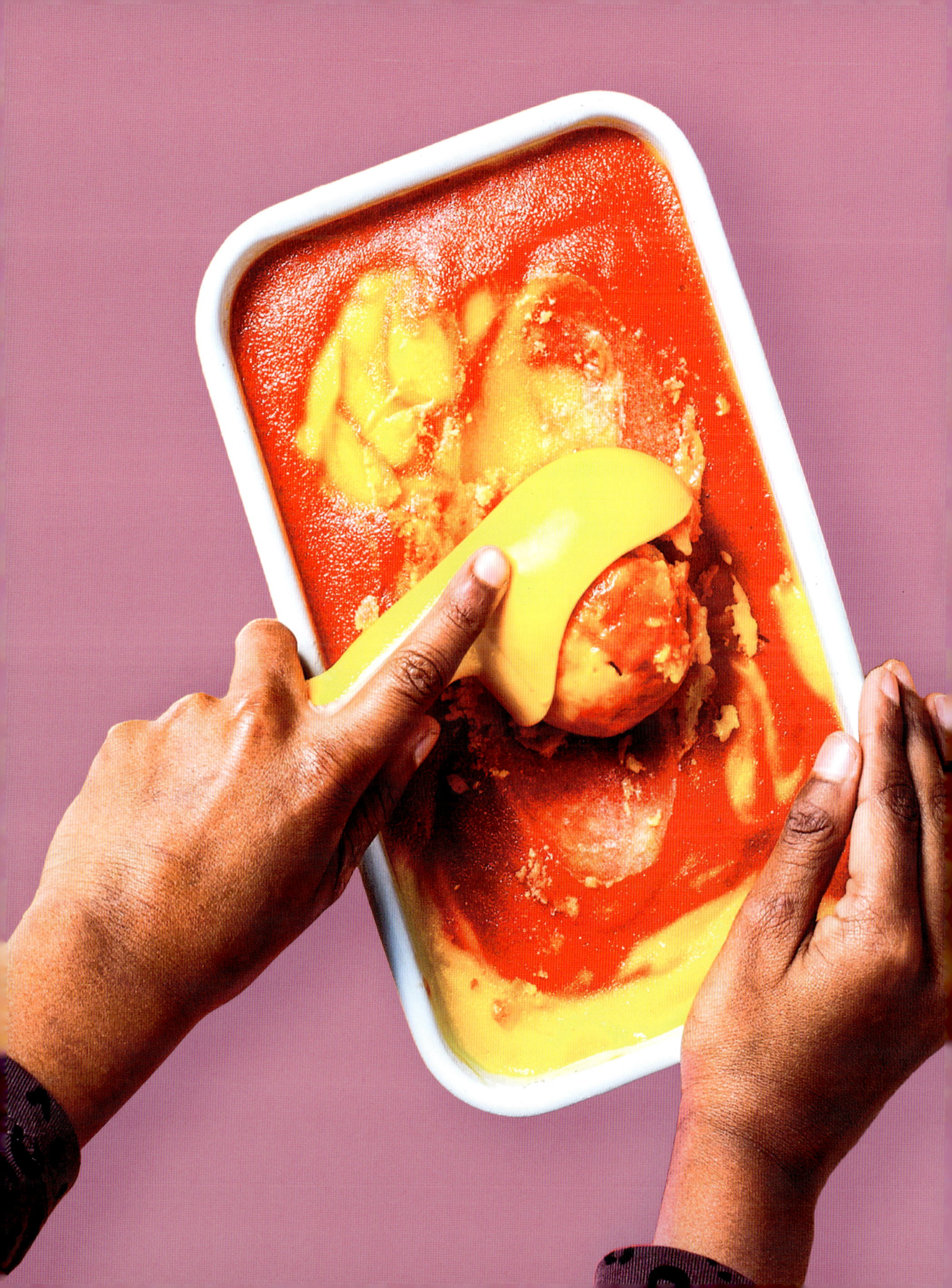

MILKSHAKES

The options for milkshake flavors are only as limited as your imagination! Any ice cream plus milk and a little time in a **blender** shakes into the perfect frozen concoction. Throw in some extras for an even more delicious treat. Feel free to use fresh or frozen fruits!

SERVES 2

1 cup (250 mL) ice cream of choice
¼ cup (60 mL) milk of choice (cow, oat, coconut, soy, and almond all work well)
Pinch of sea salt

Combine all the ingredients in a **blender** and blend for 1 full minute.

Shake It Up!

CHOCOLATE

Chocolate ice cream and ¼ cup (60 mL) chocolate sauce

PB&J

Vanilla ice cream, 1 Tbsp (15mL) nut butter, and 1 Tbsp (15mL) strawberry jam

PEACH MELBA

Vanilla ice cream, ¼ cup (60 mL) fresh or frozen raspberries, ¼ cup (60 mL) peaches

NEAPOLITAN

Vanilla ice cream, ½ cup (125 mL) fresh or frozen strawberries, 2 Tbsp (30 mL) chocolate sauce

STRAWBERRY SHORTCAKE

½ cup (125 mL) strawberry ice cream and 10 Nilla Wafers cookies

LET'S EAT

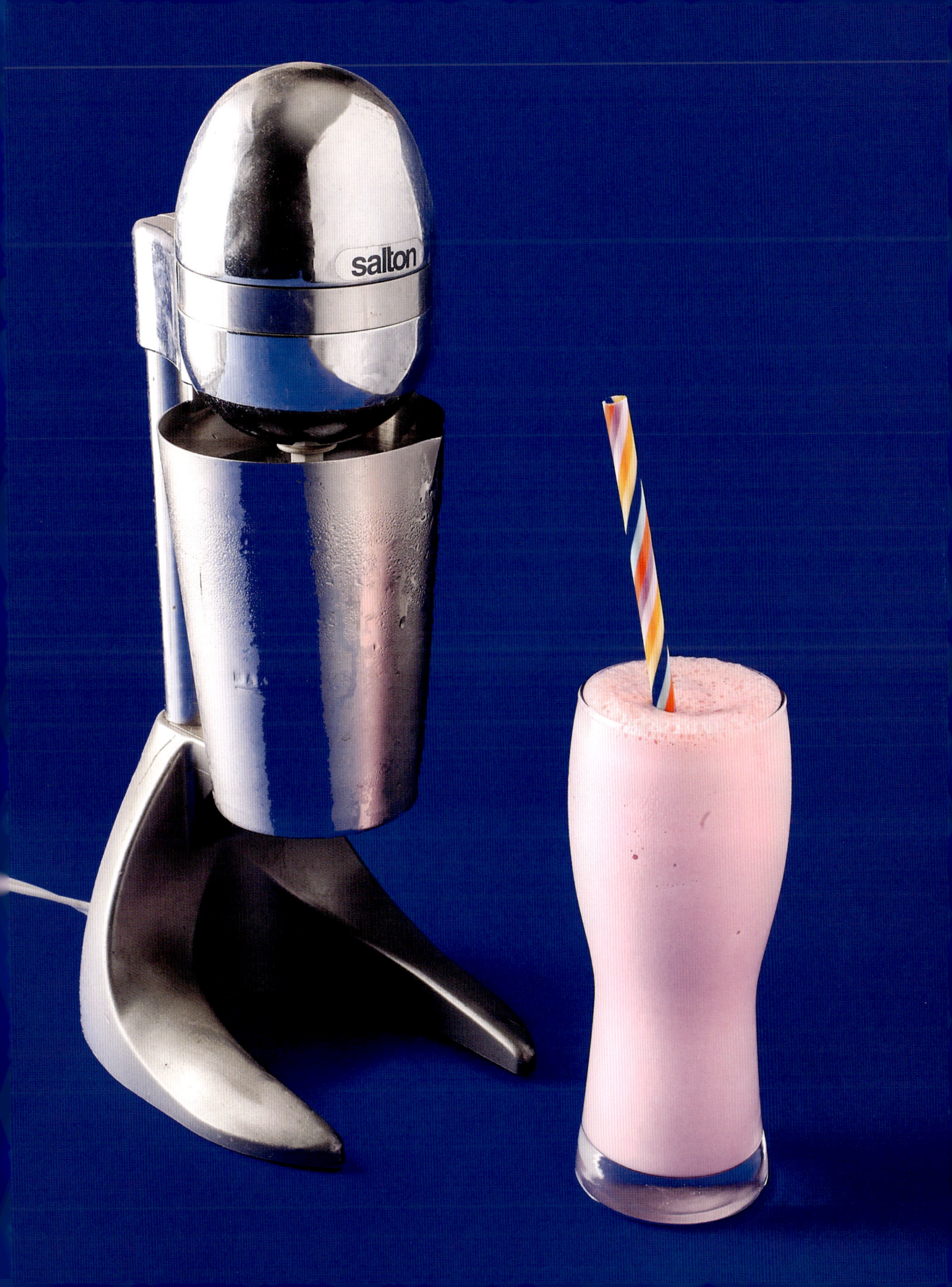
salton

POPSICLES

Popsicles are essentially any liquids frozen into a mold with a stick to hang on to, so the possibilities for flavors are endless. Let your creativity play and see which ones are your favorite!

MAKES 8 POPSICLES

½ cup (125 mL) fruits of choice, sliced or cut into small pieces
2 cups (500 mL) juice of choice

Divide the fruit among 8 popsicle molds and top with the juice. Freeze for 6–8 hours or overnight.

Mix It Up!

THE JUICY

Use three juices like cherry, wild berry, and orange. Pour one flavor of juice into the mold and freeze for 2 hours. Repeat with a second flavor of juice. Repeat with the third flavor of juice. You will get a fun, colorful popsicle.

THE HALF 'N' HALF

1 cup (250 mL) lemonade and 1 cup (250 mL) iced tea—combine the two flavors and freeze.

THE YOGURT

2 cups (500 mL) yogurt of choice and ½ cup (125 mL) jam—stir until just combined, leaving swirls visible.

THE FRUIT SALAD

2 cups (500 mL) orange juice and ½ cup (125 mL) cut fruits such as sliced grapes, raspberries, and blueberries—add the fruits and top with orange juice.

THE CREAMSICLE

1 cup (250 mL) orange juice and 1 cup (250 mL) vanilla yogurt.

THE FUDGESICLE

2 cups (500 mL) chocolate pudding and 8 tsp (40 mL) chocolate sprinkles. Place the sprinkles into the molds first and top with pudding.

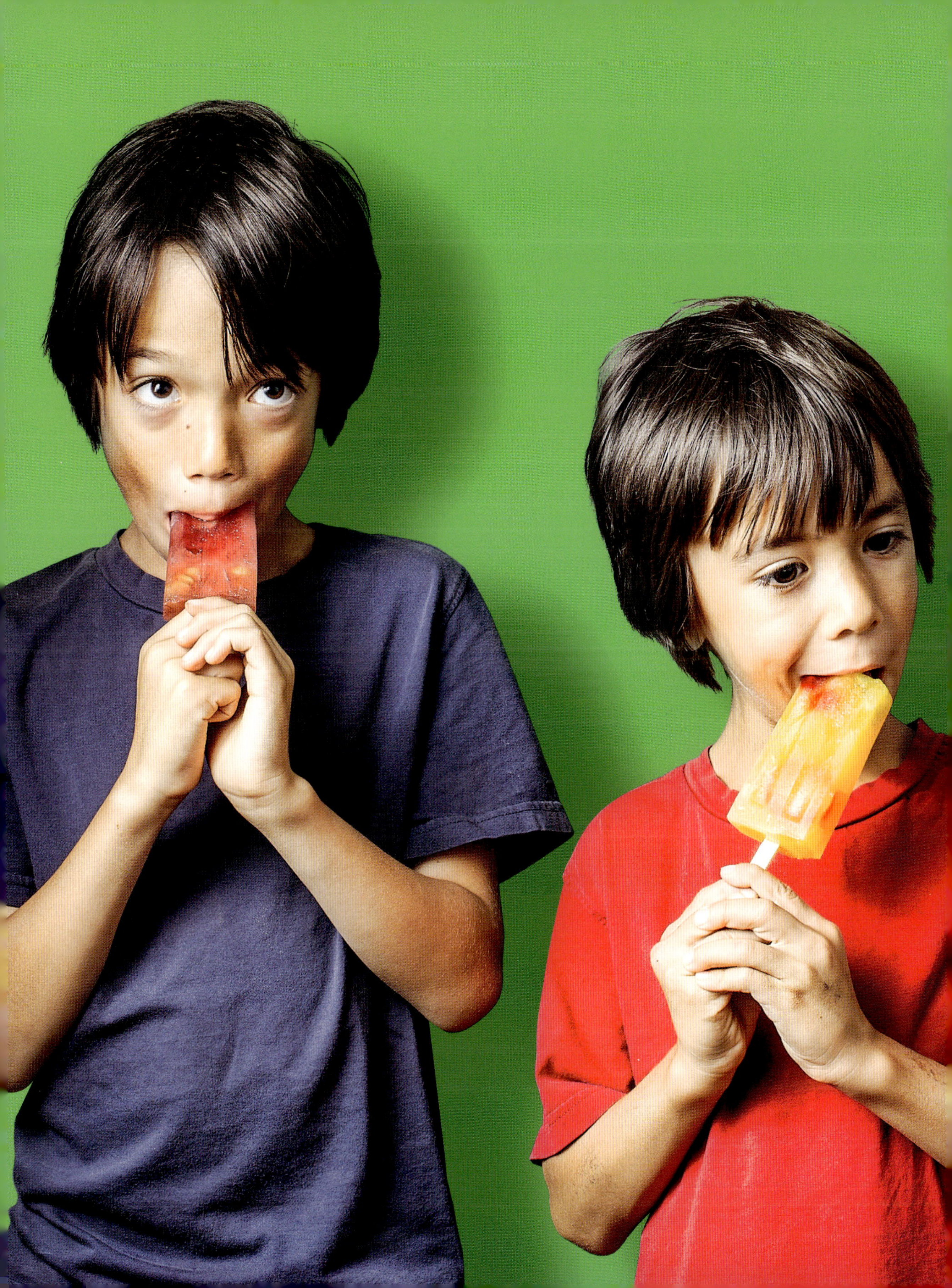

FUDGE

Food flavoring can be bought at your local food store or baking store. Match the flavor with the food gel color for a festive effect. Feeling creative? Divide the batter into two, then color and flavor each half separately. Mix the two varieties together loosely using a toothpick to create a swirly pattern.

MAKES ABOUT 16 SQUARES

- 3½ cups (875 mL) white chocolate chips
- 1 (10 oz/300 mL) can condensed milk
- ½ tsp (2.5 mL) flavor of choice (maple, vanilla, orange, almond, cotton candy, strawberry)
- 2 drops food gel coloring

Line a 9 × 9-inch (23 × 23 cm) cake pan with parchment paper.

In a microwaveable bowl, combine the chocolate chips and condensed milk and heat on high for 30 seconds. Stir and then heat for another 30 seconds. Continue like this until the chocolate has melted.

Add the food flavoring and the food gel and stir well to combine.

Pour the fudge into the prepared pan. Cover with plastic wrap and place in the fridge for 3–4 hours to set. Cut into small squares. The fudge will keep in an airtight container at room temperature for up to two weeks.

Chloë Says

Playing with the flavors is FUN!

LET'S EAT

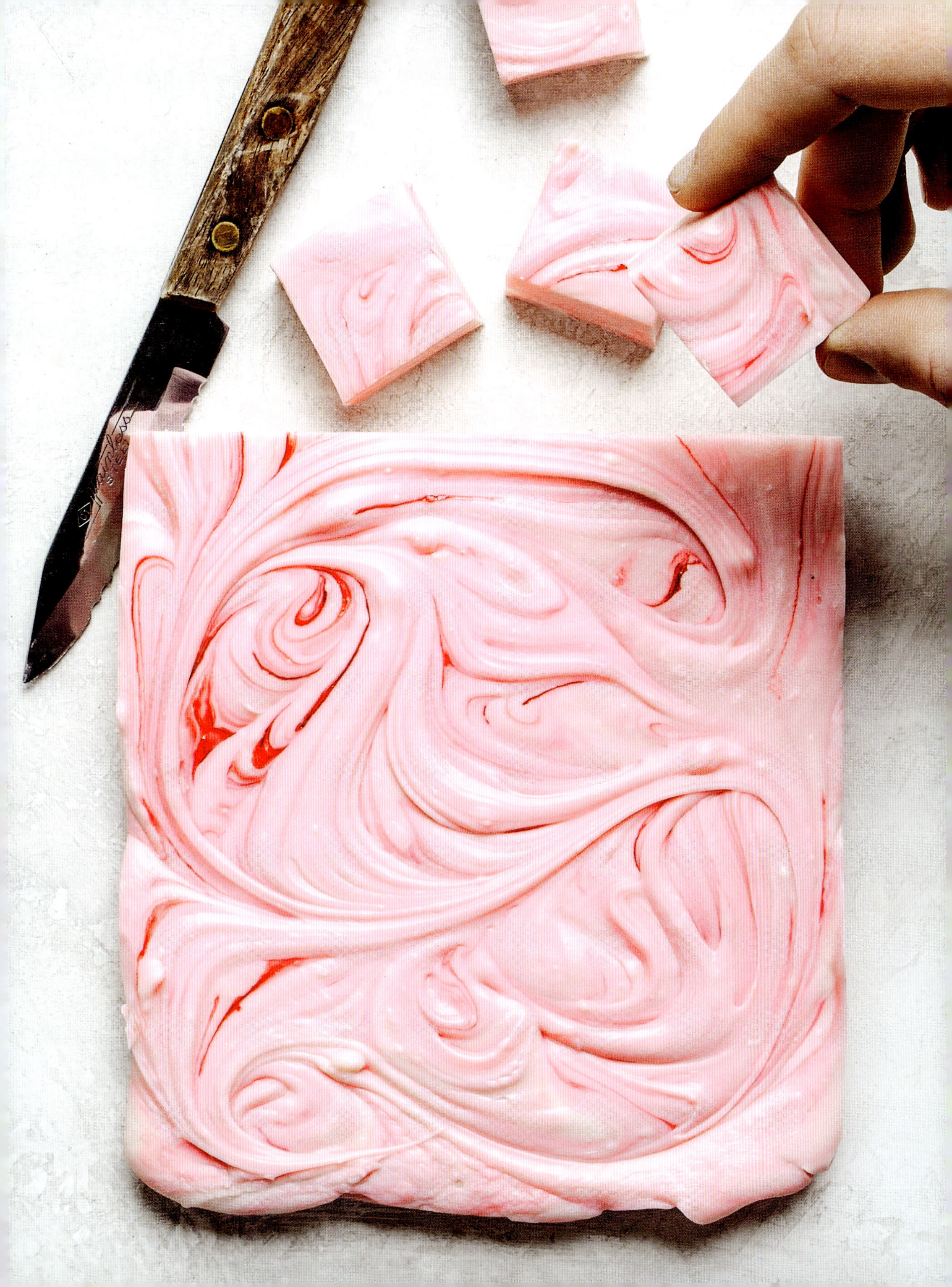

BIRTHDAY CAKE

Being able to bake someone a birthday cake is such a wonderful gift, and once you start to play with decorating, we bet you'll be hooked! Many online specialty stores sell all kinds of fun seasonal sprinkles, so play with the color of your icing and toppings to really customize your creation. Want to go small? Try cupcakes arranged on a platter instead of one big cake. The artificial vanilla here gives this recipe that quintessential "funfetti" birthday cake flavor. Don't worry if you only have regular vanilla extract—that will work just fine too!

MAKES 1 (9-INCH/23 CM) 2-LAYER CAKE

Cake
¾ cup (185 mL) unsalted butter, softened
1½ cups (375 mL) granulated sugar
2 eggs, room temperature
2 tsp (10 mL) artificial vanilla flavoring
2½ cups (625 mL) cake and pastry flour (also known as self-rising flour)
1 cup (250 mL) milk
⅓ cup (80 mL) sprinkles

Frosting
1 cup (250 mL) unsalted butter, softened
5 cups (1.25 L) icing sugar
1 Tbsp (15 mL) 35% whipping cream or milk
1 tsp (5 mL) artificial vanilla flavoring
¼ cup (60 mL) sprinkles, decorations

Preheat the oven to 325°F (160°C). Grease and flour two 9-inch (23 cm) cake pans.

To make the cake, use a **stand mixer** fitted with the paddle attachment or a large **bowl** and a **hand mixer** to **cream** together the butter and sugar, about 3 minutes.

Crack the eggs. Add the eggs to the butter mixture one at a time, beating between additions and scraping down the sides of the **bowl** until fully incorporated. Beat in the vanilla.

Add one-third of the flour and beat on low speed until incorporated. Add half of the milk and beat to incorporate. Repeat with half the remaining flour, then the remaining milk, then the remaining flour. Add the sprinkles and beat until combined. Pour half the batter into one of the prepared pans and the remaining half into the other.

LET'S EAT

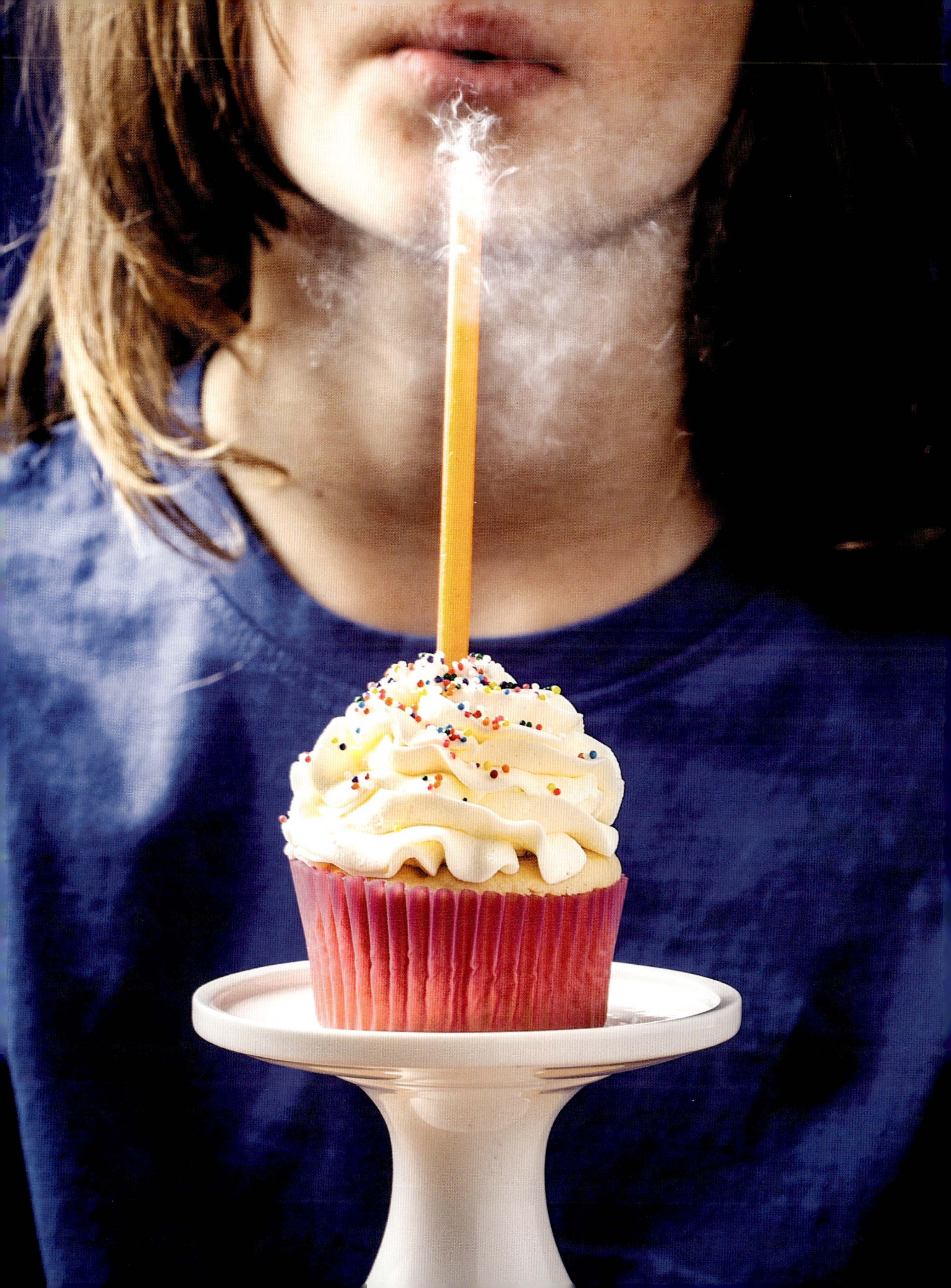

Bake in the center of the oven until a toothpick inserted in the center of a cake comes out clean, 45–50 minutes.

Turn off the oven!

Using **oven mitts**, remove the cake pans from the oven, place each one on a **cooling rack**, and let the cakes cool in the pan for 5 minutes. Run a butter **knife** along the edges of each cake and turn them out onto the cooling racks to cool completely.

To make the frosting, use a **stand mixer** fitted with the paddle attachment or an **electric hand mixer** to **cream** the butter until soft, about 1 minute. Add the icing sugar and slowly beat to incorporate. You might prefer to add the icing sugar about 1 cup (250 mL) at a time. Add the cream and vanilla and beat on high speed until smooth and fluffy, 2 minutes.

Place one cake on a plate slightly larger than the cake. You can also use a cutting board. Using an offset **spatula**, smooth a third of the frosting on the cake. Place the other cake on top and smooth the remaining frosting on the top and sides. Top with sprinkles.

Mix It Up!

CUPCAKES

If you want to make cupcakes, **line** the cups of two 12-cup **muffin pans** with paper liners. Divide the batter evenly among the cups and bake until a toothpick inserted in the center of a cupcake comes out clean, 18–20 minutes.

HOMEMADE HOT CHOCOLATE MIX

This hot chocolate mix is SO much better than the store-bought variety. It works well with any type of milk and is delicious topped with whipped cream or marshmallows!

MAKES ABOUT 40 SERVINGS

- 2 cups (500 mL) unsweetened cocoa powder
- 1½ cups (375 mL) icing sugar
- 1 Tbsp (15 mL) ground cinnamon
- 1 tsp (5 mL) fine sea salt

Place all of the ingredients in a **mixing bowl** and mix together until well blended.

Place the powder mix into an airtight jar and store until ready to use. It will stay fresh for up to 6 months.

To make hot chocolate, place 1 heaping tablespoon (20 mL) of the mix in a cup and top with 1 cup (250 mL) warm milk of choice.

Alice Says

Make sure you count out the marshmallows so everyone gets the same amount. Fair's fair!

DON'T FORGET DESSERT!

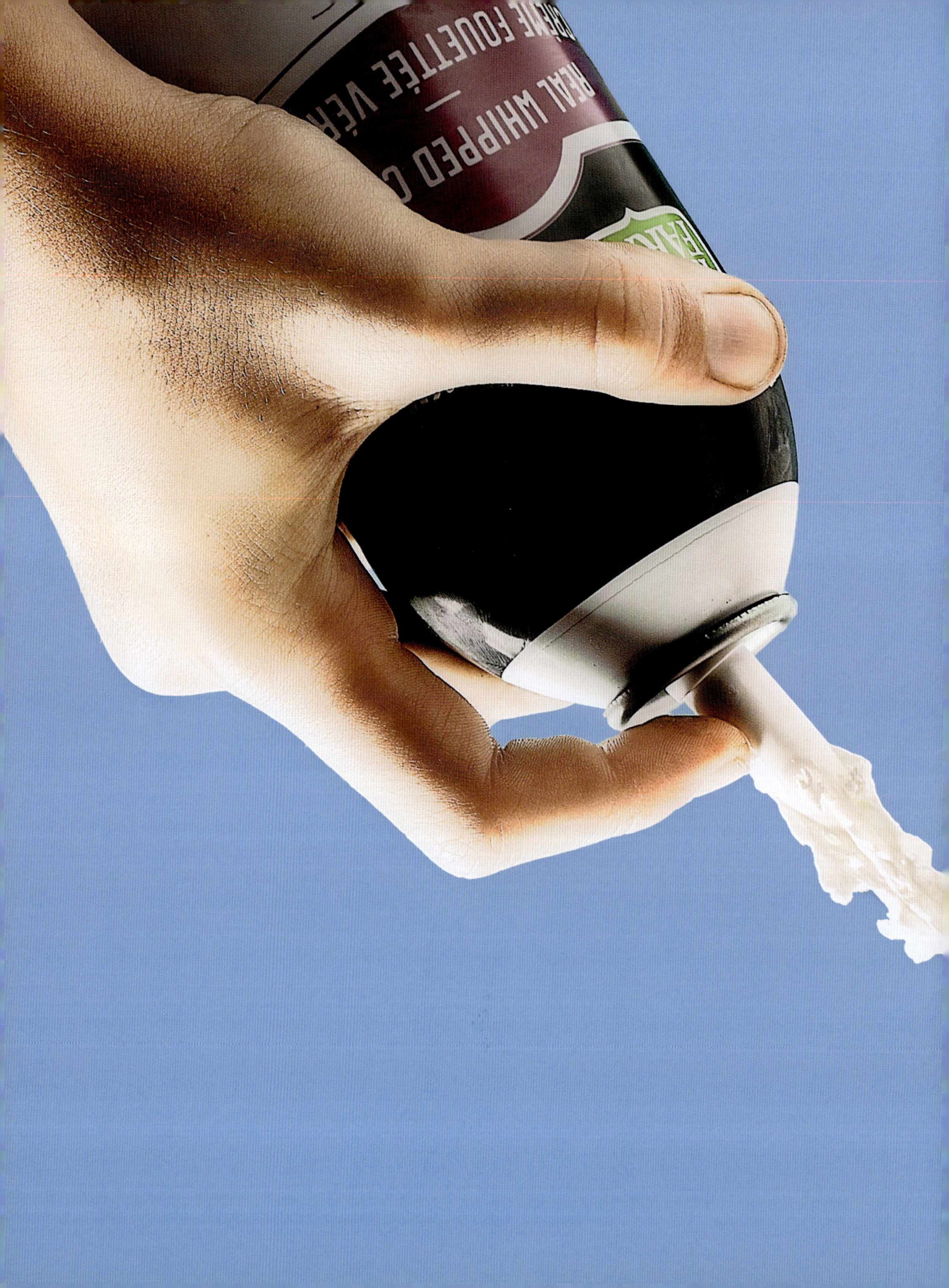
REAL WHIPPED
FOUETTÉE

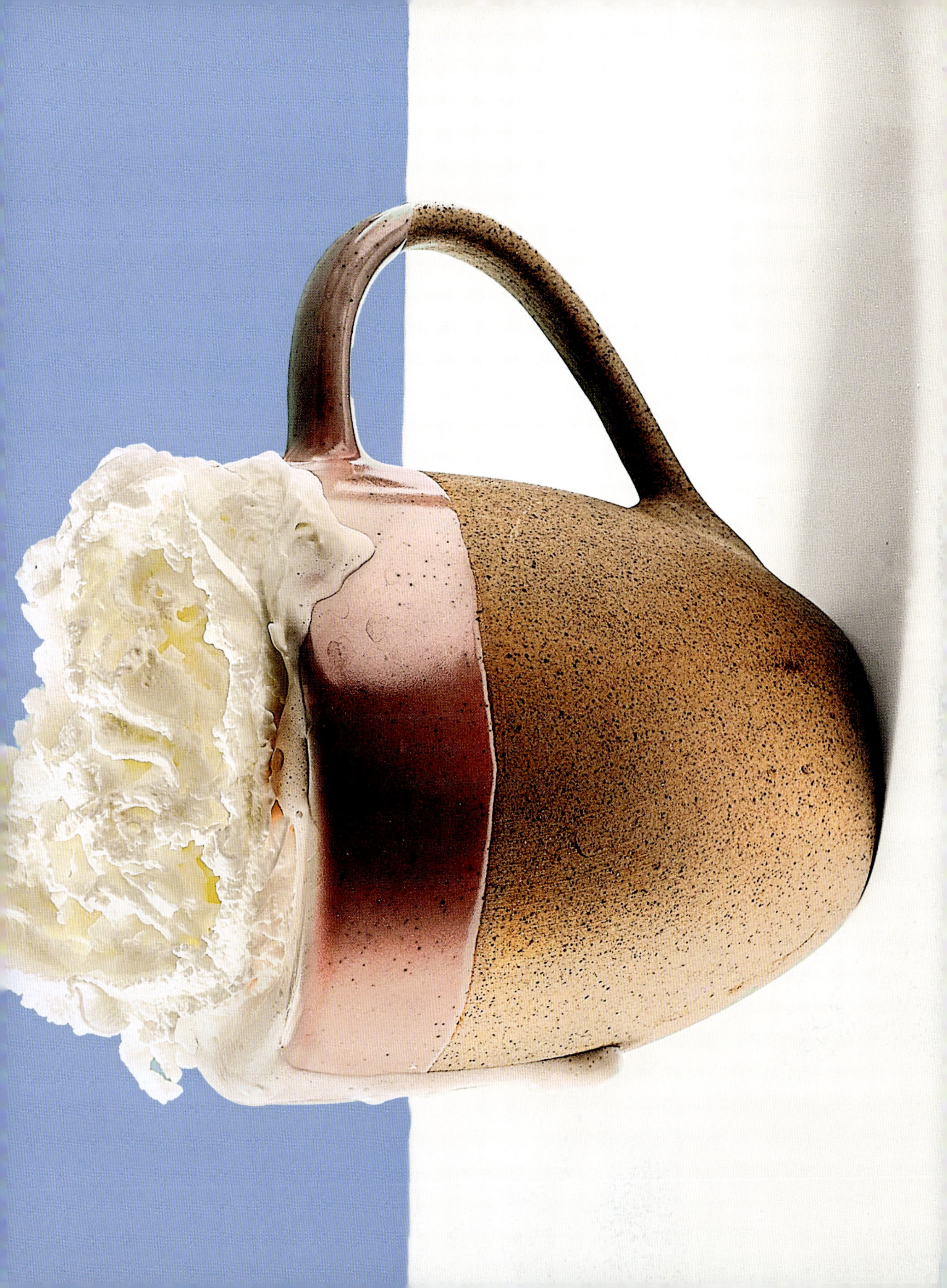

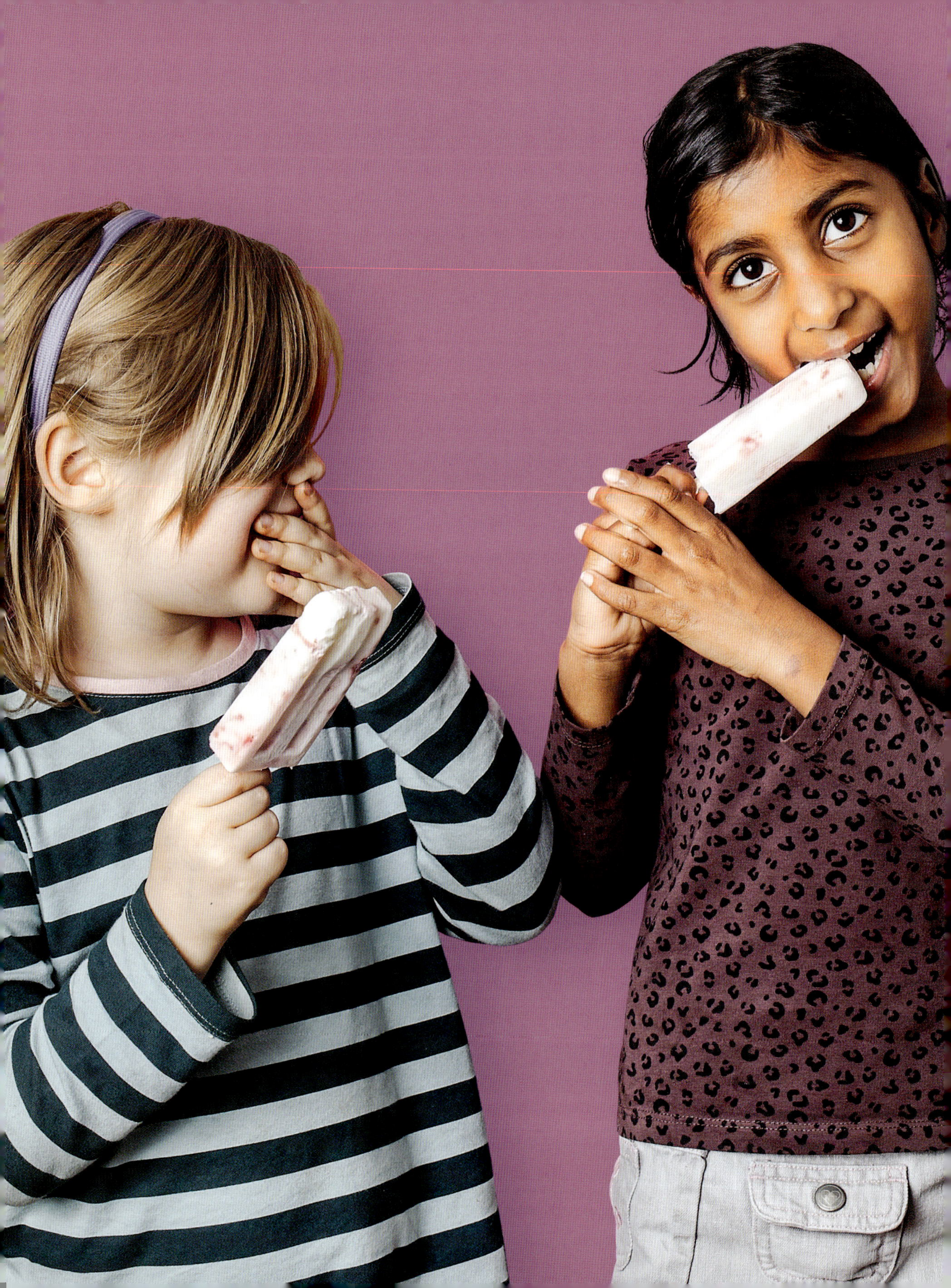

WITH THANKS!

From Aurelia:

A colossal thank you to my partner in crime Danielle! You have given me a perfect platform to create and a playground from which to translate crazy ideas to reality. I am forever grateful for the experiences we've had together.

The greatest thank you to our dream team, the incredible outgoing and incoming publishers at TouchWood Editions, Taryn Boyd and Tori Elliott, for continuously supporting our concepts, the brilliant Lesley Cameron for patiently editing, and the extraordinary Jazmin Welch for the beautiful design that completes our vision.

The deepest thank you to my family who supports my creative adventures—my husband, François, and our children, Chloë and Félix—tasting and critiquing my endeavors, encouraging me to be my best, and providing endless inspiration! I love you so much.

Lastly, mega high fives to all the kids (and their parents) who participated in creating the wacky and wonderful images for this book; we could not have done it without you!

From Danielle:

From the bottom of my heart, I would like to thank Taryn and Tori from TouchWood Editions for seeing what we saw and believing that KIDS CAN COOK! As publishers you are so incredibly supportive, and as people you are always our biggest cheerleaders. Without you none of this is possible.

To Lesley Cameron, thank you, THANK YOU, for the many hours of impeccable editing. It's not easy to meld two voices into one beautifully fashioned and coherent work. We appreciate you!

A great big squishy group hug to Alex, Elsa, Iris, Leo, Macy, Marshall, Morgan, Naraya, Nola, Patrick, Rory, Ryder, Selena, and Winston. Without all of you this book would not have been half as much fun or looked half as cool!

To James, Caitlin, William, Georgia, Charlie, and Alice, thank you SO much for always believing in me and putting up with my crazy shenanigans in our kitchen. I know it's not always easy to have the fridge filled with foods you're not allowed to touch, but your continued support has earned you all second helpings of dessert. You are always the inspiration for every dish and your critiques and tweaks to recipes have made me a better cook.

To Aurelia, what can I even say? THANK YOU for over half a decade of inside jokes, giggles, and full-on belly laughs. You make me a better photographer every single day, and I adore every second I get to work with you. Your talent is limitless, and that I get to call you my friend is one of the greatest gifts I have received in this lifetime.

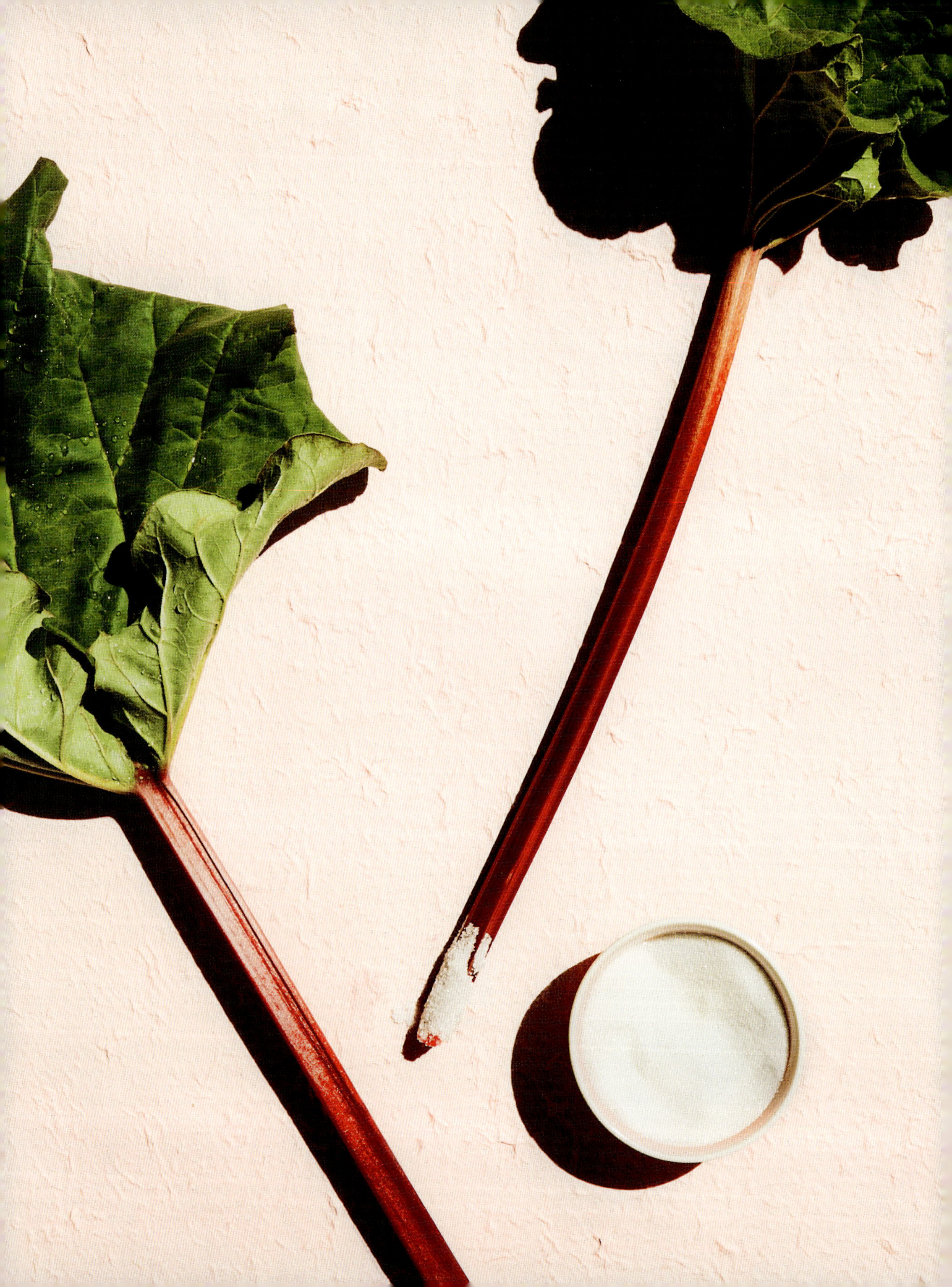

INDEX

A

air fryer, 14
allergens, about, 25–27
allspice
    Gingerbread Cookies, 192–194
almond flour
    Falafel Veggie Burgers, 127–129
almond milk
    Blueberry Spice Smoothie, 58
    Mango Madness Smoothie, 56
    Super Green Smoothie, 58
almonds. *see also* almond flour; almond milk
    Carrot and Apple Salad, 106
    Puff Pastries, 62–64
    Spring Roll Salad, 112–114
aluminum foil, 14, 20
anchovy paste
    Caesar Salad, 108
apple cider vinegar
    BBQ Pork Buns, 174
    BBQ sauce, 174
    Carrot and Apple Salad, 106
    Deviled Eggs, 122
    Herby Green Goddess Salad Dressing, 50
    Pajama Pants Pulled Pork, 170–174
    Sticky Soda Pop Ribs, 142–143
    Toasted Sesame Salad Dressing, 50
apple juice
    Pajama Pants Pulled Pork, 170–174
apples
    Apple Cinnamon Scones, 71
    Carrot and Apple Salad, 106
    Fruit Pie, 206–209
    Pineapple Cream Cheese Dip with Fruit Skewers, 98–101
    Puff Pastries, 62–64
    Pulled Pork & Apple Pie, 175–177
    Sweet or Savory Bread Pudding, 93
apricots
    All-In Oat Cookies, 186–188
    Yogurt Parfait, 86
aprons, 13
Asiago cheese
    Mac & Cheese, 161–163
    Sweet or Savory Bread Pudding, 93
avocado oil
    Crispy Sesame Chicken, 136–138
    Falafel Veggie Burgers, 127–129
    potatoes, how to mash, 36–38
avocados
    Avocado Toast, 74
    Guacamole, 104

B

bacon
    Caesar Salad, 108
    Deviled Eggs, 122
    how to cook, 34
    Loaded Nachos, 146
    Slow Cooker Baked Beans, 156
    Sweet or Savory Bread Pudding, 93
bagel spice
    Easy Bread Rolls, 150–152
baking dish, 15
baking sheet, 14, 15, 20
balsamic vinegar
    Balsamic Salad Dressing, 50
    Spaghetti Bolognese, 166–168
bananas
    Best Ever Banana Bread, 200–202
    Blueberry Spice Smoothie, 58
    Chocolate Peanut Butter Cup Smoothie, 56
    French Toast, 79–81
    Mango Madness Smoothie, 56
    Mixed Berry Smoothie, 56
    Pancakes, 76–78
    Pineapple Cream Cheese Dip with Fruit Skewers, 98–101
    Pumpkin Spice Smoothie, 58
    Super Green Smoothie, 58
    Sweet or Savory Bread Pudding, 93
basil
    Creamy Pesto Pasta, 164
    Herby Green Goddess Salad Dressing, 50
    Spaghetti Bolognese, 166–168
basting brush, 15
BBQ sauce
    Pajama Pants Pulled Pork, 170–174
    Slow Cooker Baked Beans, 156
bean sprouts
    Spring Roll Salad, 112–114
beans
    Chicken Noodle Soup with Easy Bread Rolls, 150–152
    Chicken Pot Pie, 175–177
    Chili Con Carne, 158–160
    Falafel Veggie Burgers, 127–129
    Loaded Nachos, 146
    Slow Cooker Baked Beans, 156
beef
    Best Burgers, 130
    Chili Con Carne, 158–160
    Shepherd's Pie AKA Pâté Chinois, 178–180
    Spaghetti Bolognese, 166–168
    Spring Roll Salad, 112–114
    Sweet or Savory Bread Pudding, 93
bell peppers. *see* peppers
berry juice
    The Juicy Popsicle, 216
best-before dates, 13
black beans
    Chili Con Carne, 158–160
    Loaded Nachos, 146

229

blackberries
- Fresh Berry Scones, 71
- Fruit Pie, 206–209
- Mixed Berry Smoothie, 56
- Very Berry Salad Dressing, 48

blender, 14

blueberries
- All-In Oat Cookies, 186–188
- Berry Iced Tea, 96
- Blueberry Muffins, 67
- Blueberry Spice Smoothie, 58
- Dried Fruit Scones, 71
- Fresh Berry Scones, 71
- Fruit Pie, 206–209
- Fruit Stand Popsicle, 216
- Lemon Blueberry Pound Cake, 203–205
- Pancakes, 76–78
- Puff Pastries, 62–64
- Sweet or Savory Bread Pudding, 93
- Yogurt Parfait, 86

boiling, 20

bowls, 14, 17, 19

box grater, 14, 20, 21

braising, 20

bread
- Best Ever Banana Bread, 200–202
- Caramel Best Ever Banana Bread, 200–202
- Chocolate Best Ever Banana Bread, 200–202
- Double Chocolate Best Ever Banana Bread, 200–202
- Easy Bread Rolls, 150–152
- how to make, 51–53
- Nutty Best Ever Banana Bread, 200–202
- Tropical Best Ever Banana Bread, 200–202

bread crumbs
- Coconut Shake 'N' Bake, 124–126
- Crispy Sesame Chicken, 136–138

bread pudding
- Sweet or Savory Bread Pudding, 90–93

broccoli
- Sesame-Roasted Broccoli, 118
- Sheet Pan Dinner, 181–183
- Sweet or Savory Bread Pudding, 93

bumbleberry
- Fruit Pie, 206–209

burgers
- BBQ Pork Buns, 174
- Best Burgers, 130
- Falafel Veggie Burgers, 127–129

burner safety, 13

buttermilk
- Best Ever Banana Bread, 200–202

C

cake
- Birthday Cake, 220–222
- Chocolate Pound Cake, 203–205
- Cinnamon Cappuccino Pound Cake, 203–205
- Coconut Pound Cake, 203–205
- Lemon Blueberry Pound Cake, 203–205
- Lemon Poppy Seed Pound Cake, 203–205
- Pound Cake, 203–205

cake pans/tins, 15

capers
- Hawaiian Pizza Your Way, 139–141

caramel chips
- All-In Oat Cookies, 186–188
- Caramel Best Ever Banana Bread, 200–202

caraway seeds
- Honey-Roasted Carrots, 115–117

carrots
- Carrot and Apple Salad, 106
- Chicken Noodle Soup with Easy Bread Rolls, 150–152
- Chicken Pot Pie, 175–177
- Honey-Roasted Carrots, 115–117
- Spaghetti Bolognese, 166–168
- Spring Roll Salad, 112–114

celery
- Chicken Pot Pie, 175–177
- Spaghetti Bolognese, 166–168

celery seeds
- Honey-Roasted Carrots, 115–117

cheddar cheese
- Cheese and Herb Scones, 71
- Cheese Waffles, 84
- Chili Con Carne, 158–160
- Loaded Nachos, 146
- Mac & Cheese, 161–163
- Sweet or Savory Bread Pudding, 90–93

cheese. see also Asiago cheese; cheddar cheese; feta cheese; mozzarella cheese; Parmesan cheese
- Best Burgers, 130
- Caesar Salad, 108
- Chili Con Carne, 158–160
- Easy Peasy Taco Tuesday, 134
- Loaded Nachos, 146
- Mac & Cheese, 161–163
- Mediterranean Pizza Your Way, 139–141
- Omelets, 88
- Pizza Your Way, 139–141
- Puff Pastries, 62–64
- Sweet or Savory Bread Pudding, 90–93, 93

cherries
- All-In Oat Cookies, 186–188
- Dried Fruit Scones, 71
- Fruit Pie, 206–209
- Puff Pastries, 62–64

cherry juice
- The Juicy Popsicle, 216

chicken
- Best Burgers, 130
- Chicken Noodle Soup with Easy Bread Rolls, 150–152
- Chicken Pot Pie, 175–177
- Coconut Shake 'N' Bake, 124–126
- Creamy Pesto Pasta, 164
- Crispy Sesame Chicken, 136–138
- Easy Peasy Taco Tuesday, 134
- how to roast, 45–47
- Loaded Nachos, 146
- Roast Chicken, 45–47
- Sheet Pan Dinner, 181–183
- Shepherd's Pie AKA Pâté Chinois, 178–180
- Spring Roll Salad, 112–114
- Sweet or Savory Bread Pudding, 93

chicken stock
- Chicken Noodle Soup with Easy Bread Rolls, 150–152

chickpeas
    Falafel Veggie Burgers, 127–129
Chili Con Carne, 158–160
chili flakes
    Avocado Toast, 74
chipotle pepper spice
    Chili Con Carne, 158–160
chives
    Deviled Eggs, 122
chocolate. see also chocolate chips; cocoa powder
    Chocolate Milkshake, 214
    Fudge, 218
    Fudgesicle Popsicle, 216
    Neopolitan Milkshake, 214
chocolate chips
    All-In Oat Cookies, 186–188
    Chocolate Best Ever Banana Bread, 200–202
    Chocolate Pound Cake, 203–205
    Chocolate Scones, 71
    Double Chocolate Best Ever Banana Bread, 200–202
    Double Chocolate Muffins, 67
    Double Chocolate Pancakes, 78
    Granola Bars, 60
    Magnificent Muffins, 65–67, 67
    Pancakes, 76–78
cilantro
    Cilantro Lime Salad Dressing, 50
    Falafel Veggie Burgers, 127–129
    Guacamole, 104
    Herby Green Goddess Salad Dressing, 50
    Spring Roll Salad, 112–114
cinnamon
    All-In Oat Cookies, 186–188
    Apple Cinnamon Scones, 71
    Best Ever Banana Bread, 200–202
    Blueberry Spice Smoothie, 58
    Cinnamon Cappuccino Pound Cake, 203–205
    Dried Fruit Scones, 71
    French Toast, 79–81
    Fruit Pie, 206–209
    Gingerbread Cookies, 192–194
    Homemade Hot Chocolate Mix, 223
    Peach Muffins, 67
    Pineapple Cream Cheese Dip with Fruit Skewers, 98–101
    Raspberry Muffins, 67
    Stuffed French Toast, 81
    Sweet or Savory Bread Pudding, 93
cleaning up, 13
cloves
    Gingerbread Cookies, 192–194
cocoa powder
    Brownies, 198
    Chili Con Carne, 158–160
    Chocolate Peanut Butter Cup Smoothie, 56
    Chocolate Pound Cake, 203–205
    Chocolate Waffles, 84
    Double Chocolate Best Ever Banana Bread, 200–202
    Double Chocolate Muffins, 67
    Double Chocolate Pancakes, 78
    Homemade Hot Chocolate Mix, 223
coconut. see also coconut amino; coconut flakes; coconut milk
    Coconut Pound Cake, 203–205
    Coconut Shake 'N' Bake, 124–126
    Tropical Best Ever Banana Bread, 200–202
coconut amino
    BBQ sauce, 174
    Peanut or Sunflower Butter Dressing, 114
    Sticky Teriyaki Baked Salmon, 132
    Teriyaki Sheet Pan Dinner, 181–183
    Toasted Sesame Salad Dressing, 50
coconut flakes
    All-In Oat Cookies, 186–188
coconut milk
    Aloha Iced Tea, 96
    Pumpkin Spice Smoothie, 58
    Sweet Potato Thai Curry, 154
colander, 15
condensed milk
    Fudge, 218
    One-Pot Pumpkin Pie, 210
containers, storage, 17
cookie sheet, 14, 20
cookies
    All-In Oat Cookies, 186–188
    Gingerbread Cookies, 192–194
    Super Snappy Sugar Cookies, 189–191
cooling racks, 15
corn
    Chicken Noodle Soup with Easy Bread Rolls, 150–152
    Chicken Pot Pie, 175–177
    Chili Con Carne, 158–160
    Shepherd's Pie AKA Pâté Chinois, 178–180
    Sweet or Savory Bread Pudding, 93
    Sweet Potato & Corn Pie, 175–177
cranberries
    All-In Oat Cookies, 186–188
    Cranberry Orange Scones, 71
cream. see also cream cheese; sour cream; whipping cream
    Creamy Pesto Pasta, 164
cream cheese
    Omelets, 88
    Pineapple Cream Cheese Dip with Fruit Skewers, 98–101
    Puff Pastries, 62–64
    Sweet or Savory Bread Pudding, 93
creamed corn
    Shepherd's Pie AKA Pâté Chinois, 178–180
creaming technique, 20
cucumber
    Spring Roll Salad, 112–114
cumin
    BBQ sauce, 174
    Falafel Veggie Burgers, 127–129
    Guacamole, 104
    Pajama Pants Pulled Pork, 170–174
    Sticky Soda Pop Ribs, 142–143
cupcake pans, 15
cupcakes
    Birthday Cake, 220–222
currants
    Dried Fruit Scones, 71
curry
    Coconut Shake 'N' Bake, 124–126
    Sweet Potato Thai Curry, 154
cutting boards, 15

INDEX 231

D

dairy substitutes, 26
dicing, 21
Dijon mustard
    Balsamic Salad Dressing, 50
    BBQ sauce, 174
    Caesar Salad, 108
    Cilantro Lime Salad Dressing, 50
    Crispy Sesame Chicken, 136–138
    Deviled Eggs, 122
    Herby Green Goddess Salad Dressing, 50
    Honey Mustard Sheet Pan Dinner, 181–183
    Lemon Poppy Seed Salad Dressing, 48
    Sticky Soda Pop Ribs, 142–143
    Sweet or Savory Bread Pudding, 90–93
    Toasted Sesame Salad Dressing, 50
    Very Berry Salad Dressing, 48
dill
    Herby Green Goddess Salad Dressing, 50
dips
    Guacamole, 104
    Pineapple Cream Cheese Dip with Fruit Skewers, 98–101
    Veggie Dip, 102
divided, meaning, 22
Doughnuts, 195–197
Dr. Pepper
    Sticky Soda Pop Ribs, 142–143
dressing
    Balsamic Salad Dressing, 50
    Caesar Salad, 108
    Cilantro Lime Salad Dressing, 50
    Herby Green Goddess Salad Dressing, 50
    how to make, 48–50
    Lemon Poppy Seed Salad Dressing, 48
    Nuoc Cham Dressing, 114
    Peanut or Sunflower Butter Dressing, 114
    Toasted Sesame Salad Dressing, 50
    Very Berry Salad Dressing, 48

dried fruits
    Granola Bars, 60
drinks. *see also* smoothies
    Aloha Iced Tea, 96
    Berry Iced Tea, 96
    Chocolate Milkshake, 214
    Homemade Hot Chocolate Mix, 223
    Iced Tea, 96
    Milkshakes, 214
    Mint Iced Tea, 96
    Neopolitan Milkshake, 214
    PB&J Milkshake, 214
    Peach Iced Tea, 96
    Peach Melba Milkshake, 214
    Strawberry Shortcake Milkshake, 214
Dutch oven, 16

E

egg substitutes, 27
eggs
    All-In Oat Cookies, 186–188
    Avocado Toast, 74
    Coconut Shake 'N' Bake, 124–126
    Crispy Sesame Chicken, 136–138
    Deviled Eggs, 122
    French Toast, 79–81
    hard-boiled, 30–31
    how to cook, 30–33
    Omelets, 88
    scrambled, 31
    soft-boiled, 31
    Stuffed French Toast, 81
    sunny side up, 33
    Sweet or Savory Bread Pudding, 90–93
    Waffles, 82–84
espresso powder
    Cinnamon Cappuccino Pound Cake, 203–205

F

Falafel Veggie Burgers, 127–129
feta cheese
    Creamy Pesto Pasta, 164
    Mediterranean Pizza Your Way, 139–141

fish sauce
    Caesar Salad, 108
    Nuoc Cham Dressing, 114
    Peanut or Sunflower Butter Dressing, 114
    Sweet Potato Thai Curry, 154
foil, aluminum, 14, 20
folding technique, 21
food processor, 17
freezer ingredients, 24
French toast
    French Toast, 79–81
    Stuffed French Toast, 81
fridge ingredients, 24
frosting
    Birthday Cake, 220–222
frying pans, 17
Fudge, 218
fusilli pasta
    Creamy Pesto Pasta, 164

G

g, meaning, 22
garbanzo beans
    Falafel Veggie Burgers, 127–129
garlic. *see also* garlic powder
    Caesar Salad, 108
    Chicken Pot Pie, 175–177
    Falafel Veggie Burgers, 127–129
    Guacamole, 104
    Herby Green Goddess Salad Dressing, 50
    Peanut or Sunflower Butter Dressing, 114
    Roast Chicken, 45–47
    Spaghetti Bolognese, 166–168
    Sweet or Savory Bread Pudding, 90–93
garlic powder
    Caesar Salad, 108
    Chili Con Carne, 158–160
    Pajama Pants Pulled Pork, 170–174
    Pineapple Cream Cheese Dip with Fruit Skewers, 98–101
    Potato Salad, 110
    Shepherd's Pie AKA Pâté Chinois, 178–180
    Slow Cooker Baked Beans, 156

Sticky Soda Pop Ribs, 142-143
Veggie Dip, 102
garlic press, 16
ginger
 Blueberry Muffins, 67
 Gingerbread Cookies, 192-194
 Peach Muffins, 67
 Sticky Soda Pop Ribs, 142-143
 Sweet or Savory Bread Pudding, 93
 Teriyaki Sheet Pan Dinner, 181-183
glaze
 Scones, 68
gluten substitutes, 25
goat cheese
 Sweet or Savory Bread Pudding, 93
granola
 Granola Bars, 60
 Yogurt Parfait, 86
grapes
 Pineapple Cream Cheese Dip with Fruit Skewers, 98-101
 The Fruit Stand Popsicle, 216
graters, 14, 21
grating, 20, 21
Greek yogurt
 Cilantro Lime Salad Dressing, 50
 Herby Green Goddess Salad Dressing, 50
 Lemon Poppy Seed Salad Dressing, 48
green onions
 Easy Peasy Taco Tuesday, 134
 Potato Salad, 110
green peppers
 All-Dressed Pizza Your Way, 139-141
greens, salad
 BBQ Pork Buns, 174
 Spring Roll Salad, 112-114
griddle, 16

H

ham
 Avocado Toast, 74
 Hawaiian Pizza Your Way, 139-141
 Omelets, 88
 Puff Pastries, 62-64
 Sweet or Savory Bread Pudding, 93

hand mixer, 16
hand washing, 13
hard-boiled eggs, 30-31
herbs
 Omelets, 88
 Sweet or Savory Bread Pudding, 93
honey
 Aloha Iced Tea, 96
 Berry Iced Tea, 96
 Cilantro Lime Salad Dressing, 50
 Crispy Sesame Chicken, 136-138
 Granola Bars, 60
 Herby Green Goddess Salad Dressing, 50
 Honey Mustard Sheet Pan Dinner, 181-183
 Honey-Roasted Carrots, 115-117
 Iced Tea, 96
 Lemon Poppy Seed Salad Dressing, 48
 Sheet Pan Dinner, 181-183
 Stuffed French Toast, 81
 Sweet & Spicy Sheet Pan Dinner, 181-183

I

ice-cream scoop, 17
iced tea
 Aloha Iced Tea, 96
 Berry Iced Tea, 96
 Half 'n' Half Popsicle, 216
 Iced Tea, 96
 Mint Iced Tea, 96
icing bag, 17
icing sugar
 Birthday Cake, 220-222
 Brownies, 198
 Doughnuts, 195-197
 French Toast, 79-81
 Gingerbread Cookies, 192-194
 Homemade Hot Chocolate Mix, 223
 Pineapple Cream Cheese Dip with Fruit Skewers, 98-101
 Pound Cake, 203-205
 Puff Pastries, 62-64
 Royal Icing, 192-194
 Scones, 68

Super Snappy Sugar Cookies, 189-191
Icing, Royal, 192-194
icons, meaning, 12
infusing, 20
ingredients
 freezer, 24
 fridge, 24
 pantry, 23-24

J

jalapeños
 Deviled Eggs, 122
 Easy Peasy Taco Tuesday, 134
Jam, Quick, 72

K

ketchup
 BBQ sauce, 174
 Chicken Noodle Soup with Easy Bread Rolls, 150-152
 Slow Cooker Baked Beans, 156
 Sticky Soda Pop Ribs, 142-143
kg, meaning, 22
kidney beans
 Chili Con Carne, 158-160
 Loaded Nachos, 146
 Slow Cooker Baked Beans, 156
kitchen practices, 13
kitchen tools, 14-19
kiwi
 Pineapple Cream Cheese Dip with Fruit Skewers, 98-101
knives, 17

L

L, meaning, 22
lamb
 Best Burgers, 130
lasagna
 Spaghetti Bolognese, 166-168
lb, meaning, 22
lemon juice
 Avocado Toast, 74
 BBQ sauce, 174
 Caesar Salad, 108
 Falafel Veggie Burgers, 127-129

INDEX 233

lemon juice continued...
    Fruit Pie, 206–209
    Lemon Blueberry Pound Cake, 203–205
    Lemon Poppy Seed Muffins, 67
    Lemon Poppy Seed Pound Cake, 203–205
    Lemon Poppy Seed Scones, 71
    Lemon Ricotta Pancakes, 78
    Sheet Pan Dinner, 181–183
    Sticky Teriyaki Baked Salmon, 132
lemon zest
    Fruit Pie, 206–209
    Lemon Poppy Seed Muffins, 67
    Lemon Poppy Seed Scones, 71
    Lemon Ricotta Pancakes, 78
lemonade
    The Half 'n' Half Popsicle, 216
lemons. *see also* lemon juice; lemon zest
    Lemon Poppy Seed Salad Dressing, 48
    Roast Chicken, 45–47
    Sheet Pan Dinner, 181–183
lettuce
    Best Burgers, 130
    Caesar Salad, 108
    Easy Peasy Taco Tuesday, 134
lime juice
    Avocado Toast, 74
    Fruit Sorbet, 212
    Guacamole, 104
    Nuoc Cham Dressing, 114
    Peanut or Sunflower Butter Dressing, 114
Lime Salad Dressing, Cilantro, 50
lining pans, 20

M

M&Ms
    All-In Oat Cookies, 186–188
macadamia nuts
    Tropical Best Ever Banana Bread, 200–202
macaroni
    Chicken Noodle Soup with Easy Bread Rolls, 150–152
    Mac & Cheese, 161–163
mallet, 16

mango
    Fruit Sorbet, 212
    Mango Madness Smoothie, 56
    Super Green Smoothie, 58
maple syrup
    Apple Cinnamon Scones, 71
    BBQ sauce, 174
    Dried Fruit Scones, 71
    French Toast, 79–81
    Peanut or Sunflower Butter Dressing, 114
    Pumpkin Spice Scones, 71
    Sticky Teriyaki Baked Salmon, 132
    Stuffed French Toast, 81
    Toasted Sesame Salad Dressing, 50
    Very Berry Salad Dressing, 48
masher, 19
matchstick technique, 21
mayonnaise
    Caesar Salad, 108
    Deviled Eggs, 122
    Veggie Dip, 102
measuring cups, 16
measuring spoons, 16
meat thermometer, 17
melon
    Pineapple Cream Cheese Dip with Fruit Skewers, 98–101
milkshakes
    Chocolate Milkshake, 214
    Neopolitan Milkshake, 214
    PB&J Milkshake, 214
    Peach Melba Milkshake, 214
    Strawberry Shortcake Milkshake, 214
mincing, 21
mint
    Mint Iced Tea, 96
    Spring Roll Salad, 112–114
mise en place, 13
mixer, 16, 19, 21
mixing bowls, 14, 17, 19
mL, meaning, 22
molasses
    Gingerbread Cookies, 192–194
    Slow Cooker Baked Beans, 156
Monterey Jack cheese
    Loaded Nachos, 146

mozzarella cheese
    Loaded Nachos, 146
    Mac & Cheese, 161–163
    Spaghetti Bolognese, 166–168
muesli
    Yogurt Parfait, 86
muffin pans, 15
muffins
    Blueberry Muffins, 67
    Double Chocolate Muffins, 67
    Lemon Poppy Seed Muffins, 67
    Magnificent Muffins, 65–67
    Peach Muffins, 67
    Raspberry Muffins, 67
mushrooms
    All-Dressed Pizza Your Way, 139–141
mustard
    Balsamic Salad Dressing, 50
    Caesar Salad, 108
    Cilantro Lime Salad Dressing, 50
    Crispy Sesame Chicken, 136–138
    Deviled Eggs, 122
    Herby Green Goddess Salad Dressing, 50
    Honey Mustard Sheet Pan Dinner, 181–183
    Lemon Poppy Seed Salad Dressing, 48
    Slow Cooker Baked Beans, 156
    Sticky Soda Pop Ribs, 142–143
    Sweet or Savory Bread Pudding, 90–93
    Toasted Sesame Salad Dressing, 50
    Very Berry Salad Dressing, 48

N

Nachos, Loaded, 146
navy beans
    Slow Cooker Baked Beans, 156
nonreactive, meaning, 22
noodles
    Spring Roll Salad, 112–114
nori
    Deviled Eggs, 122
nutmeg
    Doughnuts, 195–197

nutritional yeast
  Caesar Salad, 108
nuts
  All-In Oat Cookies, 186–188
  French Toast, 79–81
  Granola Bars, 60
  Nutty Best Ever Banana Bread, 200–202
  Spring Roll Salad, 112–114
  substitutes, 26
  Tropical Best Ever Banana Bread, 200–202

O

oat milk
  Creamy Pesto Pasta, 164
oats
  All-In Oat Cookies, 186–188
  Granola Bars, 60
  Magnificent Muffins, 65–67
olives
  Easy Peasy Taco Tuesday, 134
  Hawaiian Pizza Your Way, 139–141
  Loaded Nachos, 146
  Mediterranean Pizza Your Way, 139–141
  Sweet or Savory Bread Pudding, 93
onion powder
  Mac & Cheese, 161–163
  Pajama Pants Pulled Pork, 170–174
  Pineapple Cream Cheese Dip with Fruit Skewers, 98–101
  Potato Salad, 110
  Shepherd's Pie AKA Pâté Chinois, 178–180
  Slow Cooker Baked Beans, 156
  Sticky Soda Pop Ribs, 142–143
onions. *see also* onion powder
  All-Dressed Pizza Your Way, 139–141
  Chicken Pot Pie, 175–177
  Chili Con Carne, 158–160
  Deviled Eggs, 122
  Falafel Veggie Burgers, 127–129
  Guacamole, 104
  Omelets, 88
  Potato Salad, 110
  Spaghetti Bolognese, 166–168
  Sweet or Savory Bread Pudding, 93
  Sweet Potato Thai Curry, 154
orange juice
  Cranberry Orange Scones, 71
  Creamsicle Popsicle, 216
  Fresh Berry Scones, 71
  Fruit Stand Popsicle, 216
  Juicy Popsicle, 216
  Mango Madness Smoothie, 56
  Mixed Berry Smoothie, 56
  Peanut or Sunflower Butter Dressing, 114
  Super Green Smoothie, 58
orange zest
  Cranberry Orange Scones, 71
oregano
  Cheese and Herb Scones, 71
  Mac & Cheese, 161–163
  Shepherd's Pie AKA Pâté Chinois, 178–180
  Spaghetti Bolognese, 166–168
oven mitts, 16
oven safety, 13
over easy eggs, 33
oz, meaning, 22

P

pancakes
  Double Chocolate Pancakes, 78
  Lemon Ricotta Pancakes, 78
  Pancakes, 76–78
  Pumpkin Spice Pancakes, 78
panko crumbs
  Mac & Cheese, 161–163
pans, 17, 19
pantry
  freezer ingredients, 24
  fridge ingredients, 24
  ingredients, 23–24
paper towels, 17
paprika
  Deviled Eggs, 122
  Mac & Cheese, 161–163
  Shepherd's Pie AKA Pâté Chinois, 178–180
  Veggie Dip, 102
parchment paper, 15, 18, 20
Parfait, Yogurt, 86
Parmesan cheese
  Caesar Salad, 108
  Creamy Pesto Pasta, 164
  Mac & Cheese, 161–163
  Spaghetti Bolognese, 166–168
  Sweet or Savory Bread Pudding, 93
parsley
  Carrot and Apple Salad, 106
  Falafel Veggie Burgers, 127–129
  Herby Green Goddess Salad Dressing, 50
  Honey-Roasted Carrots, 115–117
pasta
  Chicken Noodle Soup with Easy Bread Rolls, 150–152
  Creamy Pesto Pasta, 164
  how to cook, 39
  Mac & Cheese, 161–163
  Spaghetti Bolognese, 166–168
pastry
  Fruit Pie, 206–209
  Puff Pastries, 62–64
pastry brush, 18
peaches
  French Toast, 79–81
  Fruit Pie, 206–209
  Peach Iced Tea, 96
  Peach Melba Milkshake, 214
  Peach Muffins, 67
  Yogurt Parfait, 86
peanut butter
  Chocolate Peanut Butter Cup Smoothie, 56
  Peanut or Sunflower Butter Dressing, 114
peanut substitutes, 26
peanuts
  Spring Roll Salad, 112–114
pears
  Fruit Pie, 206–209
  Sweet or Savory Bread Pudding, 93
peas
  Chicken Noodle Soup with Easy Bread Rolls, 150–152
  Chicken Pot Pie, 175–177
peas, sugar
  Spring Roll Salad, 112–114
pecans
  Nutty Best Ever Banana Bread, 200–202
peeler, 18

penne pasta
    Creamy Pesto Pasta, 164
pepperoni
    All-Dressed Pizza Your Way, 139–141
    Pizza Your Way, 139–141
peppers. see also jalapeños
    All-Dressed Pizza Your Way, 139–141
    Loaded Nachos, 146
    Sheet Pan Dinner, 181–183
    Spring Roll Salad, 112–114
    Sweet or Savory Bread Pudding, 93
pickles
    Best Burgers, 130
    Deviled Eggs, 122
pies
    Chicken Pot Pie, 175–177
    Fruit Pie, 206–209
    One-Pot Pumpkin Pie, 210
    Pulled Pork & Apple Pie, 175–177
    Shepherd's Pie AKA Pâté Chinois, 178–180
    Sweet Potato & Corn Pie, 175–177
pineapples
    Aloha Iced Tea, 96
    Hawaiian Pizza Your Way, 139–141
    Pineapple Cream Cheese Dip with Fruit Skewers, 98–101
pinto beans
    Loaded Nachos, 146
    Slow Cooker Baked Beans, 156
pizza
    All-Dressed Pizza Your Way, 139–141
    Hawaiian Pizza Your Way, 139–141
    Mediterranean Pizza Your Way, 139–141
    Pizza Your Way, 139–141
pizza cutter, 18
poppy seeds
    Easy Bread Rolls, 150–152
    Lemon Poppy Seed Muffins, 67
    Lemon Poppy Seed Pound Cake, 203–205
    Lemon Poppy Seed Salad Dressing, 48
    Lemon Poppy Seed Scones, 71

popsicles
    Creamsicle Popsicle, 216
    Fruit Stand Popsicle, 216
    Fudgesicle Popsicle, 216
    Half 'n' Half Popsicle, 216
    Juicy, 216
    Yogurt Popsicle, 216
pork
    Coconut Shake 'N' Bake, 124–126
    Loaded Nachos, 146
    Pajama Pants Pulled Pork, 170–174
    Pulled Pork & Apple Pie, 175–177
    Shepherd's Pie AKA Pâté Chinois, 178–180
    Spaghetti Bolognese, 166–168
    Sticky Soda Pop Ribs, 142–143
    Sweet or Savory Bread Pudding, 93
potato masher, 19
potato ricer, 19
potatoes
    Chicken Noodle Soup with Easy Bread Rolls, 150–152
    how to mash, 36–38
    Potato Salad, 110
    Sheet Pan Dinner, 181–183
    Shepherd's Pie AKA Pâté Chinois, 178–180
pots, 19
puff pastry
    Chicken Pot Pie, 175–177
pumpkin. see also pumpkin seeds; pumpkin spice
    One-Pot Pumpkin Pie, 210
    Pumpkin Spice Pancakes, 78
    Pumpkin Spice Scones, 71
    Pumpkin Spice Smoothie, 58
pumpkin seeds
    All-In Oat Cookies, 186–188
    Granola Bars, 60
pumpkin spice
    One-Pot Pumpkin Pie, 210
    Pumpkin Spice Pancakes, 78
    Pumpkin Spice Scones, 71
    Pumpkin Spice Smoothie, 58

Q
quinoa
    Carrot and Apple Salad, 106

R
raisins
    All-In Oat Cookies, 186–188
    Dried Fruit Scones, 71
rasp, 19, 21
raspberries
    Berry Iced Tea, 96
    Fresh Berry Scones, 71
    Fruit Sorbet, 212
    Fruit Stand Popsicle, 216
    Mango Madness Smoothie, 56
    Mixed Berry Smoothie, 56
    Peach Melba Milkshake, 214
    Raspberry Muffins, 67
    Sweet or Savory Bread Pudding, 93
    Very Berry Salad Dressing, 48
    Yogurt Parfait, 86
red peppers
    Sheet Pan Dinner, 181–183
    Sweet or Savory Bread Pudding, 93
red wine vinegar
    Very Berry Salad Dressing, 48
rhubarb
    Fruit Pie, 206–209
    Puff Pastries, 62–64
    Sweet or Savory Bread Pudding, 93
Ribs, Sticky Soda Pop, 142–143
rice
    Carrot and Apple Salad, 106
    how to cook, 42–44
rice cooker, 18
ricer, 19
ricotta
    Lemon Ricotta Pancakes, 78
    Spaghetti Bolognese, 166–168
rigatoni pasta
    Creamy Pesto Pasta, 164
rolling pin, 18
Rolls, Easy Bread, 150–152
romaine lettuce
    Caesar Salad, 108

rosemary
    Cheese and Herb Scones, 71
    Sheet Pan Dinner, 181–183
roux, meaning, 22
rum flavoring
    Sweet or Savory Bread Pudding, 93

S

sage
    Chicken Pot Pie, 175–177
    Roast Chicken, 45–47
salads
    Caesar Salad, 108
    Carrot and Apple Salad, 106
    Potato Salad, 110
    Spring Roll Salad, 112–114
salami
    All-Dressed Pizza Your Way, 139–141
salmon. see also smoked salmon
    Sticky Teriyaki Baked Salmon, 132
sambal oelek chili sauce
    Nuoc Cham Dressing, 114
sauce
    BBQ sauce, 174
sausages
    Sheet Pan Dinner, 181–183
Savory Bread Pudding, Sweet or, 93
scones
    Apple Cinnamon Scones, 71
    Cheese and Herb Scones, 71
    Chocolate Scones, 71
    Cranberry Orange Scones, 71
    Dried Fruit Scones, 71
    Fresh Berry Scones, 71
    Lemon Poppy Seed Scones, 71
    Pumpkin Spice Scones, 71
    Scones, 68
scoring, 21
scrambled eggs, 31
seafood
    Coconut Shake 'N' Bake, 124–126
    Spring Roll Salad, 112–114
searing, 21
sesame oil. see also sesame seeds
    Honey-Roasted Carrots, 115–117
    Nuoc Cham Dressing, 114
    Peanut or Sunflower Butter Dressing, 114
    Sesame-Roasted Broccoli, 118

Sticky Teriyaki Baked Salmon, 132
Toasted Sesame Salad Dressing, 50
sesame seeds. see also sesame oil
    Avocado Toast, 74
    Crispy Sesame Chicken, 136–138
    Deviled Eggs, 122
    Easy Bread Rolls, 150–152
    Falafel Veggie Burgers, 127–129
    Sesame-Roasted Broccoli, 118
setting technique, 21
shredding, 20
shrimp
    Coconut Shake 'N' Bake, 124–126
    Spring Roll Salad, 112–114
sieve, 15
silicone mats, 18
simmering, 20
Skewers, Pineapple Cream Cheese Dip with Fruit, 98–101
slow cooker, 18, 21
smoked salmon
    Avocado Toast, 74
    Omelets, 88
smoothies
    Blueberry Spice Smoothie, 58
    Chocolate Peanut Butter Cup Smoothie, 56
    Mango Madness Smoothie, 56
    Mixed Berry Smoothie, 56
    Pumpkin Spice Smoothie, 58
    Super Green Smoothie, 58
soft peaks, meaning, 22
soft-boiled eggs, 31
Sorbet, Fruit, 212
Soup with Easy Bread Rolls, Chicken Noodle, 150–152
sour cream
    Potato Salad, 110
    Pound Cake, 203–205
    Veggie Dip, 102
soy sauce
    Sticky Teriyaki Baked Salmon, 132
soy substitutes, 27
Spaghetti Bolognese, 166–168
spatula, 19
spinach
    Creamy Pesto Pasta, 164
    Mediterranean Pizza Your Way, 139–141
    Omelets, 88

Super Green Smoothie, 58
Sweet or Savory Bread Pudding, 93
Sweet Potato Thai Curry, 154
spirulina powder
    Super Green Smoothie, 58
spoons, 19
sprinkles
    Birthday Cake, 220–222
    Doughnuts, 195–197
    Fudgesicle Popsicle, 216
    Gingerbread Cookies, 192–194
sriracha
    Honey-Roasted Carrots, 115–117
    Peanut or Sunflower Butter Dressing, 114
    Pineapple Cream Cheese Dip with Fruit Skewers, 98–101
    Sweet & Spicy Sheet Pan Dinner, 181–183
stew
    Chili Con Carne, 158–160
stock
    Chicken Noodle Soup with Easy Bread Rolls, 150–152
    Chicken Pot Pie, 175–177
    Creamy Pesto Pasta, 164
    Mac & Cheese, 161–163
    Sweet Potato Thai Curry, 154
stock pot, 18
storage containers, 17
strainer, 15
strawberries
    Berry Iced Tea, 96
    Fruit Pie, 206–209
    Mixed Berry Smoothie, 56
    Neopolitan Milkshake, 214
    Pancakes, 76–78
    Pineapple Cream Cheese Dip with Fruit Skewers, 98–101
    Puff Pastries, 62–64
    Sweet or Savory Bread Pudding, 93
    Very Berry Salad Dressing, 48
    Yogurt Parfait, 86
sugar peas
    Spring Roll Salad, 112–114
sunflower butter
    Peanut or Sunflower Butter Dressing, 114

INDEX 237

sunflower seeds
    All-In Oat Cookies, 186–188
    Granola Bars, 60
sunny side up eggs, 33
Sweet or Savory Bread Pudding, 93
sweet potatoes
    Sweet Potato & Corn Pie, 175–177
    Sweet Potato Thai Curry, 154

T

taco seasoning
    Avocado Toast, 74
    Chili Con Carne, 158–160
    Guacamole, 104
tacos
    Easy Peasy Taco Tuesday, 134
tamari amino
    Peanut or Sunflower Butter Dressing, 114
    Sticky Teriyaki Baked Salmon, 132
    Teriyaki Sheet Pan Dinner, 181–183
    Toasted Sesame Salad Dressing, 50
Tbsp, meaning, 22
tea
    Aloha Iced Tea, 96
    Berry Iced Tea, 96
    Iced Tea, 96
    Mint Iced Tea, 96
    Peach Iced Tea, 96
tea towels, 17
techniques, 20–21
Teriyaki Sheet Pan Dinner, 181–183
thermometer, meat, 17
thyme
    Cheese and Herb Scones, 71
    Chicken Pot Pie, 175–177
    Herby Green Goddess Salad Dressing, 50
    Honey Mustard Sheet Pan Dinner, 181–183
    Pajama Pants Pulled Pork, 170–174
    Spaghetti Bolognese, 166–168
timers, 13, 18
to taste, meaning, 22
tobiko
    Deviled Eggs, 122
tofu
    Coconut Shake 'N' Bake, 124–126

Spring Roll Salad, 112–114
tomatoes
    Avocado Toast, 74
    Best Burgers, 130
    Chili Con Carne, 158–160
    Creamy Pesto Pasta, 164
    Guacamole, 104
    Loaded Nachos, 146
    Mediterranean Pizza Your Way, 139–141
    Omelets, 88
    Spaghetti Bolognese, 166–168
    Sweet or Savory Bread Pudding, 93
    Sweet Potato Thai Curry, 154
tongs, 18
tools, kitchen, 14–19
tortilla chips
    Chili Con Carne, 158–160
    Loaded Nachos, 146
towels, 17
tree nut substitutes, 26
tsp, meaning, 22
turkey
    Best Burgers, 130
    Shepherd's Pie AKA Pâté Chinois, 178–180

V

vanilla
    Best Ever Banana Bread, 200–202
    Birthday Cake, 220–222
    Brownies, 198
    Chocolate Scones, 71
    Doughnuts, 195–197
    French Toast, 79–81
    Fruit Pie, 206–209
    Gingerbread Cookies, 192–194
    Granola Bars, 60
    Mixed Berry Smoothie, 56
    Pineapple Cream Cheese Dip with Fruit Skewers, 98–101
    Pound Cake, 203–205
    Puff Pastries, 62–64
    Scones, 68
vegetable peeler, 18
veggie ground
    Chili Con Carne, 158–160
vermicelli noodles
    Spring Roll Salad, 112–114

vinegar. see apple cider vinegar; red balsamic vinegar; red wine vinegar

W

waffle iron, 19
waffles
    Cheese Waffles, 84
    Chocolate Waffles, 84
    Rainbow Waffles, 84
    Waffles, 82–84
whipping cream
    Birthday Cake, 220–222
    Doughnuts, 195–197
    Scones, 68
    Shepherd's Pie AKA Pâté Chinois, 178–180
whisk, 19, 22
whisking, 21, 22
wooden spoons, 19
Worcestershire sauce
    BBQ sauce, 174
    Caesar Salad, 108
    Chicken Noodle Soup with Easy Bread Rolls, 150–152
    Crispy Sesame Chicken, 136–138
    Pajama Pants Pulled Pork, 170–174
    Slow Cooker Baked Beans, 156

Y

yogurt
    BBQ Pork Buns, 174
    Blueberry Spice Smoothie, 58
    Chocolate Peanut Butter Cup Smoothie, 56
    Cilantro Lime Salad Dressing, 50
    Creamsicle Popsicle, 216
    Herby Green Goddess Salad Dressing, 50
    Lemon Poppy Seed Salad Dressing, 48
    Mango Madness Smoothie, 56
    Mixed Berry Smoothie, 56
    Potato Salad, 110
    Pumpkin Spice Smoothie, 58
    Super Green Smoothie, 58
    Yogurt Parfait, 86
    Yogurt Popsicle, 216

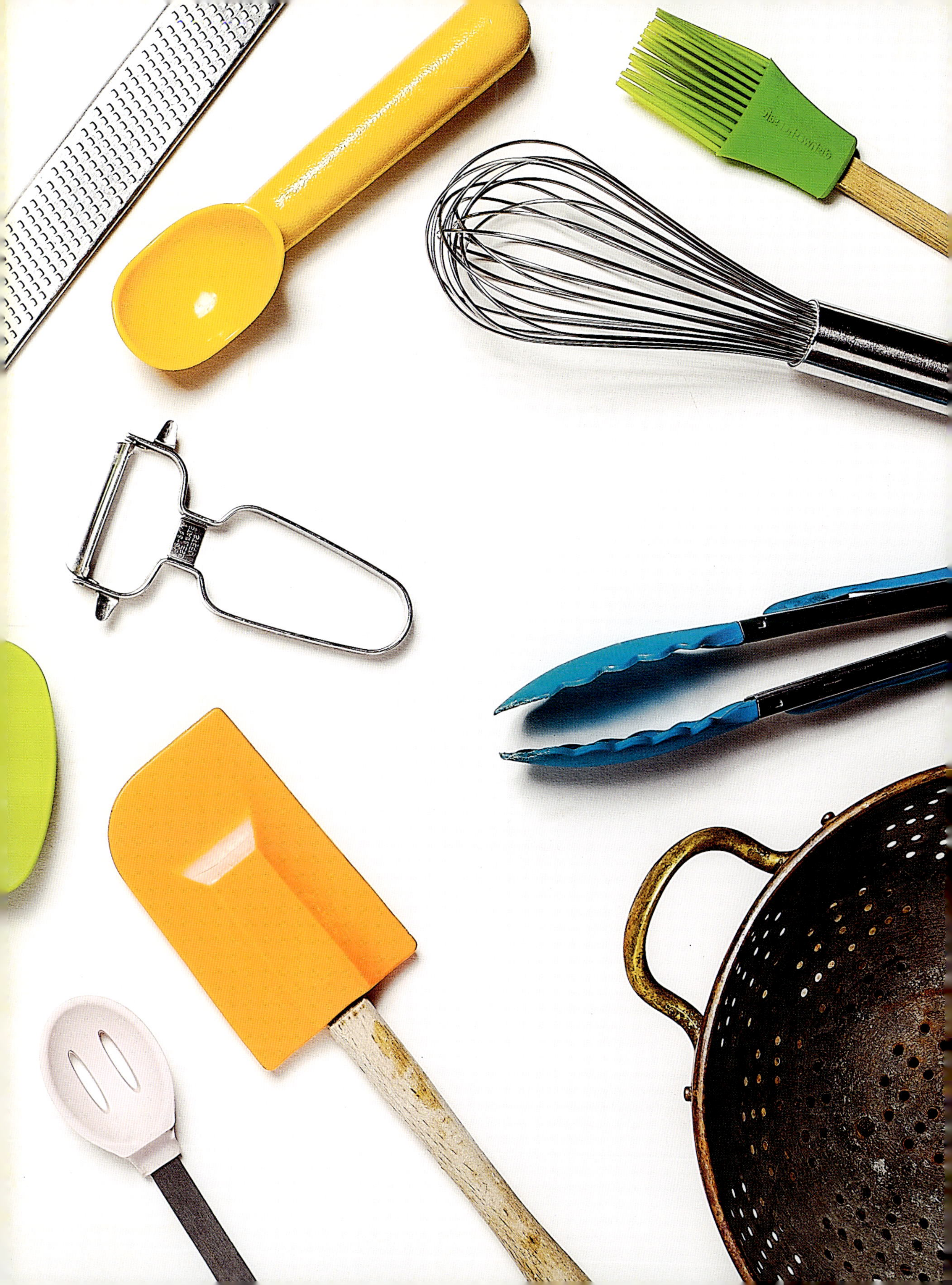

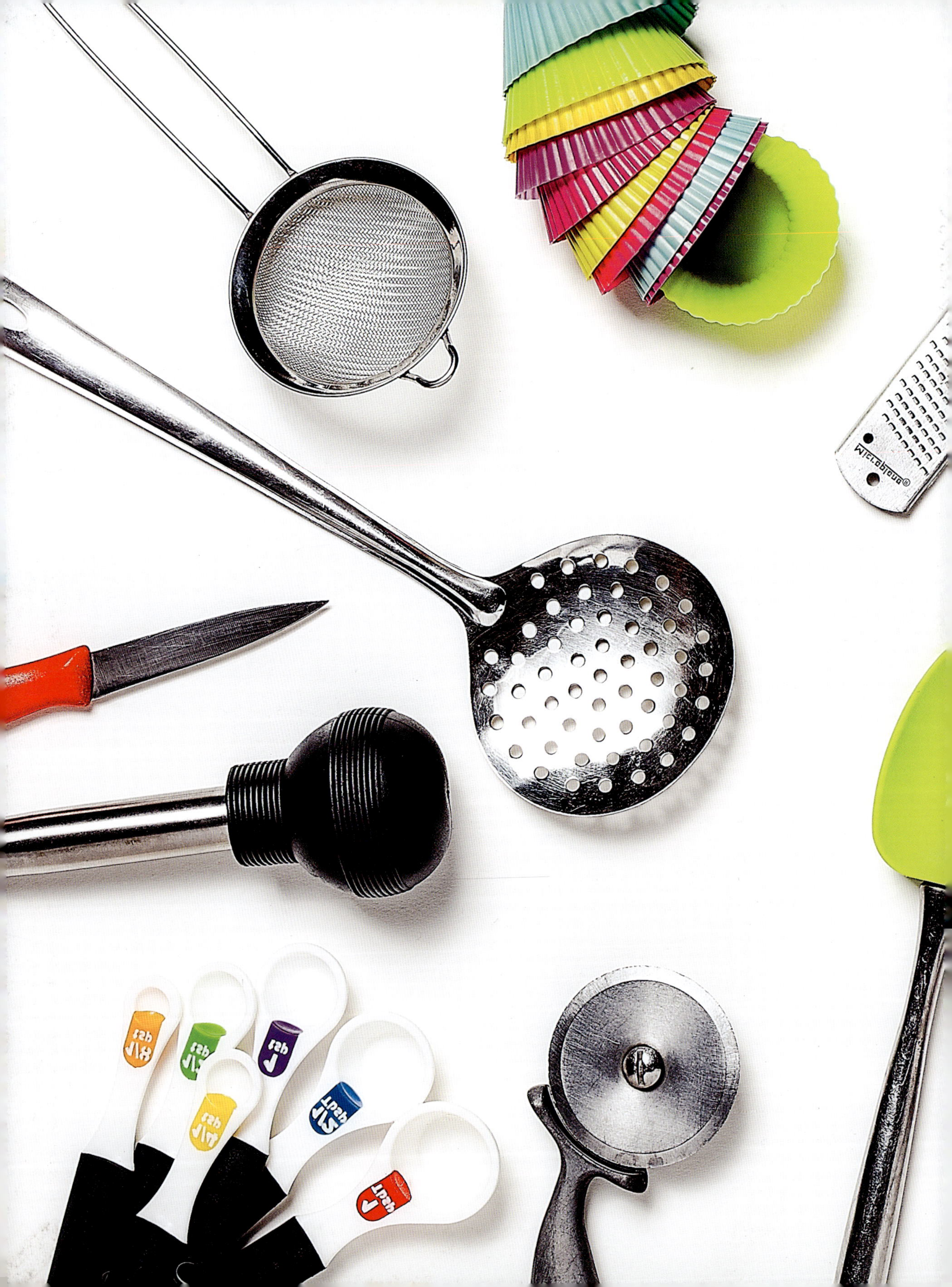
Microplane®